GOAT POOP
Reflections from the Last Section

GOAT POOP
Reflections from the Last Section

Steve - I hope you enjoy this collection of stories and lessons learned during my chaotic journey through life.

Fred Lowrey

W. Freed Lowrey

Acclaim Press
MORLEY, MISSOURI

More Praise for

Goat Poop

"Willis Freed Lowrey is a humorist, along the lines of Garrison Keillor and Patrick F. McManus, even sharing their displeasures. Keillor once opined, "Cats are intended to teach us that not everything in Nature has a purpose." Freed attests to that assessment. McManus could not have described so succinctly the heretical betrayal of acceptable reactions to losing the BIG ONE, as Freed hears from his wife, 'oh, it's off now'.

"I stick with this comparison as I follow Freed's creation of his continuing setting, where every post (to include West Point) becomes his version of Lake Wobegon. Freed's unnamed cast aids and abets the misfortune that always falls short of discouraging the pride and purpose of this unapologetic patriot. As Keillor might have said, "It's a shallow life that doesn't give a person a few scars."

"The balance of misfortune and scars versus pride and purpose is revealed in the final chapters of the collection where in-depth historical tributes contrast with the observed present day. Pride and purpose by a landslide.

"This collection will be enjoyed by audiences with no connection to the Army or West Point. Humorists touch our joys and frustrations no matter if you've never been to Lake Wobegon."

—*Major General Mark Hamilton (Retired)*
President Emeritus, University of Alaska

"In the annals of West Point, few people know its history, lore, and foibles better than Freed Lowrey, West Point Class of 1967. To start reading *Goat Poop* is to begin a mostly mirthful journey laughing at a unique form of humor best taken in small doses so it lasts longer, the mirth seasoned with deeply moving essays honoring Veteran's Day and Soldiers. Freed's ability to write well and bring to life subjects unknown to a reader, immersing them in all things patriotic, West Point, and Army is unmatched. From a military family and with a 23-year Army career that included two tours in Vietnam leading American Soldiers in combat, Freed lives and breathes West Point. So, if you're looking for a treat, consider treating yourself to *Goat Poop*."

—*Richard Barlow Adams, West Point Class of 1967,*
author of "The Parting: A Story of West Point on the Eve of the Civil War" and
"Eben Kruge: How 'A Christmas Carol' Came to be Written"

"To read Freed Lowrey's *Goat Poop* is, at times, to read a work from the pen of Dave Barry…IF that famous American humorist had endured four years at West Point and a 23-year Army career. Lowrey's *Goat Poop* is a uniquely hilarious account of life as a West Point cadet and service in Army green. But it is also a work that poignantly captures the author's admiration and love for the American Solider. It should be in the library of every military veteran, for in its pages, they will re-experience the spectrum of military comradery…from side-splitting laughter to the memory of deep friendships formed in harrowing situations. It is the perfect gift for all who have served…and their spouses. 5-Stars!"

—*Mike Mullane, USMA '67, NASA Astronaut, author of "Riding Rockets, The outrageous tales of a space shuttle astronaut"*

"A fascinating series of essays capturing the essence of Freed's experiences at West Point and in Army life. Written from his heart and soul, his storytelling is unbranded, refreshing, and enticing, landing the hook to read on to the end. His choice of words is often hilarious, 'literary stool specimens', as well as inspirational. A must read for graduates of West Point and those serving or who have served in the military."

—*Richard W. Enners, author of "Heart of Gray"*

P.O. Box 238
Morley, MO 63767
(573) 472-9800
www.acclaimpress.com

Editor: Randy Baumgardner
Book & Cover Design: Rodney Atchley

Copyright © 2021, W. Freed Lowrey
All Rights Reserved.

No part of this book shall be reproduced or transmitted in any form or by any means, electronic or mechanical, including photocopying, recording or by an information or retrieval system, except in the case of brief quotations embodied in articles and reviews, without the prior written consent of the publisher. The scanning, uploading, and distribution of this book via the Internet or via any other means without permission of the publisher is illegal and punishable by law.

Requests to publish work from this book should be sent to:
wfl1967@optonline.net

ISBN: 978-1-956027-17-4 | 1-956027-17-3
Library of Congress Control Number: 2021952088

First Printing 2022
Printed in the United States of America
10 9 8 7 6 5 4 3 2 1

This publication was produced using available information.
The publisher regrets it cannot assume responsibility for errors or omissions.

Contents

Preface 13
Essay 1: What's in a Name?...*January 1993* 21
Essay 2: The Joy of a PCS Move...*March 1993* 24
Essay 3: Rules...*May 1993* 30
Essay 4: The Manly Pursuit of Fish...*July 1993* 34
Essay 5: Pets Rule Our Lives...*September 1993* 40
Essay 6: The Ghosts of Christmas Past...*November 1993* 46
Essay 7: School Science Fairs...*January 1994* 52
Essay 8: Entertaining, Army Style...*March 1994* 58
Essay 9: The Curse of Secretaries...*May 1994* 65
Essay 10: Yard Sales...*July 1994* 71
Essay 11: A Dream Answered—
   How I gained Admission to West Point...*September 1994* 77
Essay 12: My German Adventure, Part 1...*January 1995* 84
Essay 13: Life in Government Quarters...*March 1995* 91
Essay 14: The English Language, as Spoken in the Army...
   November 1995 97
Essay 15: Bundle up—It's Wintertime...*January 1996* 102
Essay 16: Military Awards and Decorations...*July 1996* 107
Essay 17: Teaching High School JROTC...*September 1996* 114
Essay 18: Sixty-Seven Absolutely Essential Words...*November 1996* 120
Essay 19: Army Efficiency Reports...*March 1997* .127
Essay 20: My German Adventure, Part 2—
   A Trip to Grafenwöhr...*May 1997* 135
Essay 21: The Sixth Convalescent Center, Vietnam...*September 1997* 142
Essay 22: Bachelorhood, the Second Time Around...*November 1997* 149
Essay 23: The Sanctity of Names...*May 1998* 156
Essay 24: Trying to Beat the System as a Cadet,
   and the Slugs that Resulted...*September 1998* 163
Essay 25: The Joy of Cars...*March 1999* 170
Essay 26: The Recipe for a Perfect Mint Julep...*March 1937* 179
Essay 27: Thoughts on Veterans Day, 2017...*November 2017* 182
Essay 28: Thoughts on Veterans Day, 2020...
   Three American Heroes...*November 2020* 186
Essay 29: Thoughts on Memorial Day, 2021—
   Honoring a Fine Regiment and its Soldiers...*May 2021* 203
Essay 30: My Retirement from Active Duty Speech...*July 1990* 207
Glossary 211
About the Author 222

Dedicated to my wife, Vicki

Goat: *noun* 1. a stinky and exceptionally stubborn animal of foul disposition. 2. the mascot of the United States Naval Academy (aka Canoe U.). 3. in West Point cadet parlance, a cadet who ranks at the bottom of a class academically; the class academic dunce (frequently destined to become a Great Military Leader).

Poop: *noun* in military usage, information, usually vital information, the basis of critically important decisions.

Preface

I have had three careers.

First, I graduated from West Point, more properly known as the United States Military Academy, in the class of 1967. I was commissioned a second lieutenant of Infantry and spent the next 23-plus years on active duty, serving in assignments around the USA and the world, including two tours leading American Soldiers in combat in Vietnam. It was a lot of fun and was my life's dream job. I retired from active duty as a lieutenant colonel in the summer of 1990.

My next career—to use that term very loosely—kept me in my Army uniform, which was great. I spent seven years teaching ROTC at the high school level in Hampton, Virginia. Let's just say it was very interesting and leave it at that.

My last career was back at West Point—a return to the Womb—where I spent 18 years working for the West Point Association of Graduates (AOG), the Academy's alumni organization. That was also a lot of fun, but all good things come to an end, and I finally retired for good and hung up my military suit of lights on 31 December 2014. I have adapted well to retired life; apparently, not having anything I must do to stay productive and alive every day comes naturally to me.

During my active-duty career one of my assignments found me back at West Point, from 1978–1981, on the staff of the Commandant of Cadets. While stationed at West Point, I got "classmated" (i.e., shafted) by a couple of classmates at a picnic one lovely spring day in 1979, when they suggested I should assume the duties of class scribe, writing the class notes for the AOG's then-premier publication *Assembly* magazine. This magazine was published from four to six times a year and contained articles about West Point, cadets, military history, and important news from the Superintendent of the Military Academy, the Commandant of Cadets, the Dean of the Academic Board and the President of the West Point AOG, as well as obituaries of deceased West Point graduates. The meat of the magazine, however—well over

50% of each issue—were the "Class Notes," reports from each graduated class with living members on what they were up to and how they were making the world a better place. These class notes were written and submitted by the class scribes of each class.

Little did I know what an adventure that would turn into. Most importantly, it gave me the opportunity to get to know so many classmates whom I didn't know well as cadets, and probably never would have gotten close to. I learned there are some really interesting people in my class and telling their stories—even if I had to make those stories up in order to get them to participate—was a source of great entertainment. Indeed, I enjoyed it so much that my notes frequently far exceeded the editor's word and column length limitations, resulting in frequent admonitions from him to cut my input and just focus on the facts.

That caused me a problem. Just focusing on the facts resulted in stultifyingly boring articles, and I hate boring, so I tended to ignore the editor's rants as much as possible. Fortunately, after a couple of years I had a fan base that extended well beyond my class—I was frequently told by grads and wives of grads from other classes that they read my class notes before reading those of their own class. The editor knew this, so despite his pique, he cut me some slack.

This happy arrangement came to an end in the 1990s. No longer subsidized by the AOG's operating endowment, *Assembly* had to be completely self-sustaining, supporting itself by subscriptions and advertising. Unfortunately, this coincided with a serious decline in subscription sales, in large part because the younger graduating classes could not be bothered with reading anything hard-copy. If something couldn't be read online, it probably wasn't worth reading.

Faced with a serious decline in revenue, the editor (a delightful chap from the class of 1962, whom I really liked and had served on active duty with in Alaska) was forced to impose some draconian measures to reduce costs—primarily by drastically reducing the size of the magazine. One of his most dramatic actions was the imposition of very strict limitations on the number of words (not many) and photos each class scribe could submit, and those numbers were guaranteed to reduce the "Class Notes" to a bare recitation of "The Facts, Just the Facts, and Nothing but the Facts." Boring swill.

In the fall of 1992, faced with still declining subscriptions and revenue, the editor decided he needed to do something to spice up *As-*

sembly, hopefully to make it more appealing to the younger classes. At this point this normally sober-headed and clear-thinking professional went temporarily insane and asked me to write a feature column for each issue. He didn't care what it was about, he just wanted it to be "humorous." Oh, and "keep it short."

Thus was born "Goat Poop, Reflections from the Last Section." I submitted my first essay for publication in the January 1993 issue, and for the next six years managed to outwit the *Assembly* editor and censors and get twenty-four essays published. The subjects range from my kid's school science fair projects to my then-wife's love of yard sales; from the joys of a military household move (PCS) to fishing. And, naturally enough, since my target audience was West Point graduates, in particular, and Army folks, in general, a number of the essays deal with Army life and some of my experiences. They are filled with cadet slang and Army jargon that they would have no trouble understanding. However, I hope that this collection will have a greater appeal beyond the Army family, and I hope to sell many, many copies and be enriched enough to survive my remaining years in style. Knowing that much of the slang and jargon will read like ancient Hittite script and early Runes to civilians, I have thoughtfully included a brief glossary of sorts at the end of this tome.

Only one of my submitted essays failed the editor's taste test and was not published. He just couldn't bring himself to expose the tender sensibilities of West Point graduates to such crude and lewd language and innuendo. Ironically, the subject of that essay was about language—specifically the importance of words and vocabulary. It is, of course, included in this anthology. It's the essay that was submitted for the November 1996 issue of *Assembly*. You can be the judge of its acceptability in polite circles.

I need to point out that what you're getting here are the original essays as they were submitted by me—not the final, made-it-into-print versions. Mine and the editor's views of good taste varied rather dramatically. And keep in mind his original mantra: "Keep them short." Much of what you'll be reading here ended up on his cutting room floor. He was also a firm believer in the mantra, "Brevity is the soul of wit." Obviously, I'm too much of a blow-hard to subscribe to that theory.

Another fact needs pointing out. As you will see, in many of the essays my wife plays a significant role. Well, after you read the essays, many, if not most of you, probably won't be surprised to learn that ultimately that marriage crashed and burned and ended rather poorly. The good news is that I eventually remarried to the great love of my life, the only person on the planet capable of taming the raging beast in my soul and making me love her all the more for it. Life is very, very good. She has even turned me into a die-hard cat lover (read the essay for September 1993).

The March 1999 article was the last "Goat Poop" essay I submitted for publication in *Assembly*. Alas, my day job with the AOG had become too pervasive and demanding and interfered with my personal time, especially since, as class scribe, I was still churning out class notes for every issue. I had to make a choice: continue to crank out these literary stool specimens or go fishing. It should surprise no one which decision I made.

As I said, there are twenty-five "Goat Poop" essays published here, but I also decided to add a few more for good measure. One, my active-duty retirement speech, did appear in the September 1990 issue of *Assembly* (I included it in my class notes for that issue). It got good reviews from a lot of folks, and I've always believed it did a good job of expressing my love for soldiering and Soldiers. The others are more recent articles I've written and posted on Facebook in honor of Veteran's Day and Memorial Day.

Alas, despite the good editor's best efforts, *Assembly* magazine eventually gave up the ghost and ceased publication in 2011. It was replaced with a much slicker magazine, *West Point*, designed in part to appeal more to younger graduates and to focus more on stories of West Point and the achievements of cadets, rather than Old Grads. It is an outstanding publication. However, it does not contain obituaries—they were migrated to a separate, annual publication called *TAPS*. It also does not contain class notes—they were migrated to online publication only. I knew beyond any shadow of a doubt that my classmates, fast approaching true Old Fart status, were not going to go online to read their class notes. Many of them were not capable of getting online.

Knowing as far back as the mid-1990s that this bleak future was coming, and in revolt against the increasing oppression of free speech by the editor, with the full support of the class officers of the class of '67, I launched a class newsletter in 1996 called *The Pooper Scooper, the Latest Scoop on the Hottest Poop for the Class of 1967*, which would contain all the news about the class fit to print, and a lot that wasn't. Most importantly, I would be the sole arbiter of what would and would not appear in that literary hairball. It took a couple years to get it up-to-speed, but it is now alive and well—it has been published and distributed fifty-seven times as of June 2021. It is provided at no cost to over 600 members of the extended class of 1967 family, is written and printed in full color four times a year, and averages from fifty to sixty pages per issue, typically with over 200 photos.

I hope you all enjoy this trip through the collywobbles of my mind.
Go Army—Beat Navy!

—Freed Lowrey,
USMA '67

GOAT POOP
Reflections from the Last Section

1. What's in a Name?
January 1993

In my capacity as a class scribe, I've gotten used to receiving letters from the editor of this august publication, invariably taking me to task for being late with my material and for being too long winded. In fact, this has become fairly routine, so I wasn't surprised to find yet another letter from the AOG in my mailbox a few months back, after I had once again pushed the deadline to new limits. There was the usual diatribe about being on time, eliminating unnecessary verbiage, and so on, but then the editor took a new twist which, I must admit, finally got my attention. It seems that there has been a demand for some humor in *Assembly,* and the editor of this rag thinks that I should be the one to put it there. The reasons for this are not entirely clear to me; after all, I have never thought of myself as being humorous, and I know for a fact that others share that view, not the least of whom is my wife. She has accused me of being boring far more often than she has said I was funny, or even fun for that matter. Any humor that has crept in to my class notes certainly isn't my doing—I simply report on the comings and goings of my classmates. If their foibles and follies give others the giggles, that's certainly not my doing. Be that as it may, a challenge has been issued, and since I like challenges, I decided to see what I could make of this one. Actually, I suspect our fair editor has an ulterior motive: somehow, by my doing this, he thinks I will be forced to write shorter class notes, which is all he really wants anyway. Having taken up the gauntlet, I was immediately faced with my first problem: what do we name this column? The editor said something about "Pyrene II," but I've got to be honest with you: he may be the editor, but he doesn't pay me enough to write an article with that moniker. You all remember "Pyrene," don't you? A regular feature in *Pointer* magazine back in the day. I've always had some nagging problems with "Pyrene." For openers, the guy never wrote in complete sentences. I shed too much blood at the hands of the English Department to fall into that trap. And then there was the logo—a cat who looked like he had just spent

12 hours trying to understand what the hell a nested variable was, even though Colonel Nichols, the professor and head of the Department of Mathematics and author of the math textbooks cadets used in my day, had promised that it was intuitively obvious to any casual observer. We have three cats in our house, and I know that I don't want to be associated with that species in any way what-so-ever. Have you ever seen what they use their tongues for? And then, of course, there's the name itself. Just what the devil is a pyrene? Sounds like a Marine with pyorrhea. My curiosity getting the better of me, I blew the dust off my son's dictionary and looked to see if there really is such a word. Would you believe it; "pyrene: the stone of certain fruits." That did it. I'm supposed to write a regular column about peach pits? Not this guy. Besides, I really have a problem with things named *Something II*, as in *Rambo II* or *Child's Play II*. Let's face it: "Pyrene II" sounds a lot like a sequel, and sequels seldom play as well as the original. So, I say to myself, ok, just what do we call this thing?

At this point my wife decides to jump into the act with both feet. "I think you should call it 'Freed's Follies,'" she says. That makes perfect sense coming from my wife, who after all, thinks most of what I do is sheer folly, but I'm hesitant to publicly sign on to that theory. Besides, if her theory is correct, "Freed's Follies" would be redundant, and anyway, it's not a column about me. No, we'll have to do better than that. After all, we are talking about the alumni magazine of the United States Military Academy, and there are certain standards of dignity and decorum that must be maintained in such a lofty publication. There are Old Grads who read this thing, and they have a tendency to write letters to the editor. I do not want that on my conscience.

Finally, I decided it would be a good idea if I talked to the editor to get some idea of just what he might be expecting. After all, that could have considerable influence on a name. Besides, I was planning a camping trip to West Point with my sons, and it certainly wouldn't hurt to drop in for a little visit, offer my mea culpas for my transgressions as a class scribe, and get the straight poop right from the source.

I gotta be honest: it wasn't exactly what I expected. Unfortunately, the editor was in exceptionally foul humor that day. What I got was, "I don't care what you write, as long as it's humorous, in good taste, and, most importantly, gets here by the deadline." But he did give me one hint that has proven very valuable in the search for a name: he told me that he intends to make this column the last section in the magazine before the class notes. Now we're getting somewhere—if there's anything I can deal with, it's being in the last section.

How incredibly appropriate. If I was going to write a column for *Assembly*, then where else should it logically appear but in the last section? I felt like I had come home. All those years, in all those courses, in the last section. Always finding my grades posted in the last frame of the sally port. Plebe Math. Yearling Math. Nuke. Thermo. Physics. Chemistry. Solids, Fluids, and the mother of them all, Juice. The memories come flooding back, of my hircine companions, with their glazed eyes and trembling hands, trying to write something, anything, that the P wouldn't slug them for during daily writs. Some of them, alas, didn't make it, and they ended up sent to pasture, where all the great goats dwell. Suddenly, it all seemed so obvious. What kind of information would you expect to find in the last section? Goat poop, of course. So there it is. We'll call this thing "Goat Poop: Reflections from the Last Section," and I dedicate it to all those folks with whom I shared life in the intellectual basement of Bartlett and Thayer Halls.

There's only one small problem: the editor really likes the name "Pyrene II." I wonder what's going to appear at the top of this page if it ever gets into print.

Until next time, then, when we'll investigate how the right-hand rule changed my life forever. Keep in step, and ***BEAT NAVY!***

2. The Joy of a PCS Move
March 1993

It is the Christmas season as I write this, which means I have been put to work getting the house decorated for the holidays. This has caused me to spend many hours in fruitless searches for stuff that we only look for once a year. I've noticed that this process gets more and more difficult each year, but it wasn't until today that I finally realized what the problem was. After wading through three closets full of crap that I hadn't seen or used in years, and trying for an hour to open a drawer permanently wedged shut by God only knows what, it finally came to me: we've got far too much junk. And this set me to thinking: the reason we've got too much junk is because we've been in this same house for eight years. I have come to realize that one of the best things that happens to us while we're on active duty is that time-honored agony the Army puts us through every few years, or sometimes every few months, called PCS. We are forced by artificial and immutable restrictions called weight allowances to purge ourselves of all the junk that accumulates in our lives. No longer faced with the specter of waving goodbye to all our worldly possessions as they disappear around the bend in a moving van the Army has contracted for from the lowest bidder, we have allowed ourselves to be taken over by junk.

As I sipped a beer and contemplated this problem, something else suddenly occurred to me: of all the trials and tribulations we would be faced with in our Army careers, perhaps none would be as traumatic, as gut-wrenching, as marriage-straining, as the agony of a PCS move with Mom and the kids, not even combat. It's probably no mere coincidence that PCS sounds a lot like PMS. After all, I've managed to suppress most of the bad memories from two tours in Vietnam, but the horrors of many a PCS are still vivid in my mind's eye. And yet, it occurs to me that nothing in my training at West Point prepared me for this most insidious of all Army operations. In retrospect, I now realize what a grave deficiency that is in the education of our cadets. There is so much they need to be told, for a PCS move will require them to overcome countless obstacles and move many mountains. It will test their patience, their negotiating skills, their devotion to duty, and their ethics, and that's all before they actually get in the car and go anywhere. There's so much more to a PCS than just getting from point A to point B; indeed, the agony starts long before that nightmare. Today's lesson, then, shall be a primer on surviving a PCS. Pop a beer and remember past times with me.

For openers, there are the countless bureaucrats who believe their *raison d'être* is to make your life miserable, to be encountered and overcome. The first of these you'll usually deal with will be your assignment officer, for, unless you are a complete automaton and perfectly willing to allow the system to do to you what it wants, then most PCSs start well in advance of the actual move, when you begin the process of trying to influence just where it is you'll be going. *Trying* is the operative word here. We all know that dealing with a branch assignment officer is a lot like playing Russian roulette with five rounds in the cylinder. After all, bringing attention to *your* file may be the last thing in life you really need to do. This is especially true if you're a junior officer and haven't yet learned the proper mix of obsequiousness, devotion to duty, and righteous indignation when dealing with these guys, and the assignment weeny has got a particularly odious billet to fill, branch immaterial, right now. After all, you've got to remember—they've already got theirs; they've been told they're the best and the brightest, and one slip of the tongue, and you're likely to be on your way to an assignment as the PX officer in Thule, Greenland.

Lesson #1: Never, *never* let assignment officers know that you're smarter than they are.

After you've worn out a few pairs of knee pads, cashed in all your outstanding chits, and finally called that general officer you used to work for to beg his help, you may luck out and at least get a posting that your spouse will agree to accompany you to. Now the real fun begins: you've got to move.

Many things must occur before that day the moving van drives away with what few possessions you've still got left after the packers took their share. First, there's the negotiating with the local transportation officer, who will tell you that there is only one day in the next four months that they can get you moved. You are assured that the packers—some of the most fascinating people you will ever meet—will arrive at 0800 on one day, and the truck will take it all away bright and early the next. I must admit that this actually did happen to us once. We were coming back from Germany, and Germans, as we all know, are very ordered people. Eight a.m. means eight a.m.. The fact that we had been at a farewell party until four a.m. did not matter to the squad of folks that attacked our quarters at the stroke of the hour and, literally before my wife and I could stumble out of bed and shake the cobwebs from our very obtunded minds, had the truck half packed, including the clothes we were planning on wearing and the cat's food, still in its dish. But this sort of efficiency is an aberration; more often than not, the packers will arrive in time to eat lunch before starting work, having just been hired off the street that morning—remember, you're entrusting your family heirlooms to these people—and the truck, which will invariably wait for the rain to start before showing up, will not be big enough for all your stuff. This introduces you to a nifty concept called split shipments, which is another way of saying goodbye to grandmother's armoire, all your tools, and your favorite fly rods.

Lesson #2: Watch like a hawk, never go to the bathroom while they're there, and learn how to file a claim.

OK, you're all packed up and your stuff is gone to God knows where. If you've been living on post, you now get to experience what may be the greatest indignity of your career: clearing quarters. This means you must overcome the hurdle of The Inspector. You know the type: a little overweight, greasy hair, polyester pants. I vividly remember our first such experience. We were at Fort Bragg, and I was going to Vietnam. I was a young lieutenant, and lieutenants in 1968 didn't make a whole lot of money, so we gave no thought to hiring a cleaning team (we were too young and naive to know about the long-standing relationship between cleaning teams and housing inspectors). Besides, I was less than a year out of West Point; if there was anything I remembered from that experience, it was how to prepare a room for inspection. A surgeon would have been proud to have operated in our kitchen when we finished cleaning that place. But alas, the inspector failed us after a cursory glance. Didn't edge the sidewalk or trim the hedges, it seems. Well, I do catch on quickly. In a jiffy, I cut every hedge in sight to the roots, below ground level. They were now trimmed. I borrowed my neighbor's spade and excavated a one-foot-deep moat around every sidewalk for 100 meters in every direction. Having satisfied that requirement, I stuffed my wife in the car, and we drove away. After all, what were they going to do—send me to Vietnam? *Not* send me to Vietnam?

Through the years we had many more fun encounters with housing inspectors. Being cheap, and obstinate to boot, I was loath to spend good money on something I could do better myself, like clean a house, but it only took two failures for me to finally break the code.

Lesson #3: Pay for a cleaning team. Your wife's attitude is worth it. And when you move into a new set of quarters that has been given a Family Housing Stamp of Approval, don't be surprised by the half-eaten bologna sandwich that has been painted into the window sill.

OK, you've finally crammed the family and the cats and dogs into the car and headed down the road toward the future. These trips, unlike vacations, will provide fodder for nightmares well into your old age. It's even better if you're going overseas because not only do you get to ship your stuff, but you also get to ship your car. As I popped another longneck, the memories came flooding out of the footlocker I keep in the attic of my mind. I remember with stark clarity the day I went to the port in Germany to pick up our car, or what was left of it. While I was there I got to witness firsthand the German version of combat off-loading a ship. From a height of about fifty feet, someone's nice new Jaguar was launched from a poorly rigged sling onto the pier below, coming to rest in a pile of twisted metal and plastic. The German stevedores, of course, were nonplussed. After all, if it had been a German-made car, it would have survived the fall with hardly a scratch. Foolish American. And you wonder why your rates with USAA have gone up so much.

One of my most vivid memories was our move to Alaska in '81. It was summertime, and we were taking a circuitous route in order to visit all the parents before going to the far frozen north. It was 105 degrees outside, and 20 degrees hotter than that inside the car because the air conditioner, knowing it was going to Alaska and wouldn't be needed anymore, had decided to quit working. In the back seat, wallowing in pools of sweat, were my wife and baby. Up front seated next to me, buried under a mound of toys, books, cookie crumbs and a spilled chocolate milk shake, was my three-year-old son. We were in Louisiana, crossing the Atchafalaya basin on a 22-mile-long bridge, with no exits on any horizon. Suddenly an urgent voice next to me announces,

"I have to go poop!" If you've had any experience with three-year-old kids, you know that by the time they see fit to make the announcement, it's already too late. It took two Alaskan winters before the smell finally left the car.

Lesson #4: You drive, but fly the family. Everyone will be the better for it.

Once you arrive at the other end, there is still one huge hurdle to be overcome; you must now find a place to live. Basically, you are faced with three choices: government quarters and the prospect of dealing with The Inspector yet again; buying a home; or finding a place to rent that will accept your kids and your animals. This process has probably put a greater strain on our marriage over the years than any other single issue.

One of my more vivid memories was the move to Fort Ord, California, back in 1975. We didn't have any kids yet, so we had purchased a small motor home and camped our way leisurely across country. Upon arriving at Fort Ord, we discovered there were no quarters to be had on post, and finding a place to live on the Monterey Peninsula within a captain's meager means became a huge challenge. Fortunately, we did have the motor home, and it became our house for sixty-five days. As all of my cow year mechanics and fluids P's will attest to, I am not gifted in that way, and it never dawned on me that toilets in motor homes don't work like toilets in regular homes. If you don't keep a steady stream of water flowing, the solid stuff you put into the toilet doesn't go anywhere, and before long you end up with a tall pile of solidified, smelly stuff coming out of the seat. There's only one way to get rid of it, and unfortunately, my arm was too big to reach into the hole. But my wife's was just the right size. Remarkably, this woman remained married to me.

The process of finding a place to live at the other end of a PCS has probably reached the pinnacle of perfection at West Point, where the annual quarters drawing surpasses any event I can think of in terms of high drama, shattered dreams, and broken lives. The hopes and aspirations of countless wives have been dashed in the pitiless arena of South Auditorium, as some pusillanimous sycophant who graduated two files above their husband took the one and only set of quarters they could be happy in. All during your matriculation at West Point you are told that your graduation order of merit would be important to you some day. It is here, in this gladiator's pit, that the real meaning of that promise comes home to you. Since the great crapshoot of cadet branch selection was turned over to the computer several years ago, no event in the Hudson Valley comes close to the annual quarters drawing at West Point in terms of spectator excitement.

Lesson #5: Send your wife ahead three months before the move, and tell her to buy a house and be happy with whatever she chooses.

The Army has a quaint custom; it frequently gives medals to departing folks at the end of their tour somewhere. A sort of "thanks for a job well done" type of affair. I don't mean to diminish the value of these things, but I think the current system is all wrong. The award should be given when you arrive at the other end, and it should be given for having made it there. The degree of the award should be based on a formula that takes into account distance traveled, number of children accompanying, ages of the children, mental state of spouse at the beginning and end of the trip, time of year, and so on, and so on. For example, a basic PCS from, say, West Point to Fort Bragg in springtime, with a wife and one teenage child in a new car, might be worth an Achievement Medal. On the other hand, a trip from Alaska to Virginia, with a wife and three kids under the age of six in an eight-year-old Toyota with no air-conditioning in the middle of the summer, should be grounds for a Distinguished Service Medal and early retirement.

Until next time, then, when we'll look at the first law of thermodynamics, which says that, left to themselves, things go to hell in a handbasket, keep in step, and **_BEAT NAVY!_**

3. Rules
May 1993

I was having a little discussion the other day with my teenage son—you know, one of those periodic, angst-infested, father-son talks that are frequently necessary with adolescents—about rules and how nice it would be if he would ever choose to follow any of them. Those parents among you can probably picture with stark clarity in your mind's eye the kind of discussion I'm describing here. Like many teenage boys, my oldest son is an anarchist and does not believe in rules, or laws, or any form of structure what-so-ever. I find this somewhat unnerving, as I am, and always have been, very comfortable with rules. They provide nice, neat boundaries for the playing field of life. They give me a sense of direction and order (this, despite the fact that I'm not German). If nothing else, they provide me with a sense of what's expected, or not expected, of me. I like that.

The more I thought about it, the more intrigued I became with the idea of just how big a role rules play in our lives. And the longer I dwelt on the subject, the more impressed I became with the realization that virtually every aspect of our lives, from the most trivial to the most extreme, is governed, controlled, ordained—however you want to say it—by some kind of rule or law; and in those very few instances where there isn't a rule or law directing traffic, there's at least a theorem waiting to be proved to be a law. Hell, life isn't a matter of wanting to play by the rules or not. Virtually everything that happens to us during our journey down the rocky road happens because it's ***got to happen:*** there's some kind of rule that demands it. I'm talking about **EVERYTHING**, from the way electricity works (there's a rule that says it has something to do with your right hand), to what our bodies do to the junk we put in them, to the way the sun comes up in the morning. In most cases, we don't have any control. This kind of reasoning drives anarchists crazy, but that's life. It's a rule.

I decided that this was a subject worthy of some study, so sit back, pop a cold one, and come with me as we look at some of the Rules of Life. None of what follows is original material—after all, I didn't make up any of life's rules, and you've undoubtedly heard most of these before—but every now and then, as I reminded my son, it doesn't hurt to a have an occasional review to keep you from going too far "D" on life's semester writs.

At West Point we are inundated with the countless laws of physical science—the right-hand rule of juice, which, as I recall, says something to the effect that right-handed people will never, ever, pass a juice writ, which helps explain why I spent all of cow year in the last section gasping for air, being told by the Galloping Greek I was dangerous because I was a speckoid. This leads to the second law of electricity, which says that cadets banished to the last section will be further punished by having a P who knows juice better than any one else on the planet, for only someone who understands something absolutely can explain it so no one else can possibly understand it. Of course there are lots more rules and laws dealing with the black magic that is electricity, and I wasted countless hours as a cadet trying to remember them and understand how they apply to me. Much the same can be said for economics, thermodynamics, mechanics of solids, mechanics of fluids, nuclear physics, calculus and all the other mind-numbing, consciousness-degrading subjects that some bright person decided I needed to understand in order to get through life and be a good infantry officer. The years have taught me that there really isn't any good reason for me to dwell on this stuff; after all, I can't control it, I can't understand it, and if I break one of the rules of thermodynamics or economics or electricity, the penalties are probably so heinous I don't really want to know about them. So instead of wasting time on the rules that don't really matter in our lives, let's focus on the ones that actually make a difference. Of course, there are far too many rules and laws to even attempt to address them all, or to even scratch the surface, really, so I'll limit this discourse to those that are really, really important in our day-to-day lives.

Without a doubt, the Mother of all Rules, the one absolutely immutable fact of life from which all other rules and laws draw sustenance, is Murphy's Law. It is as familiar to all of you as is your name and doesn't need to be repeated here. It controls our lives every moment of every day. Anyone foolish enough to question the validity of Murphy's Law need only spend a day in my home. In fact, as a result of my own personal experience in life, I have developed a corollary to Murphy's Law, which says quite simply, "Murphy is an optimist."

Military life is chock full of rules that cover every aspect of soldiering. One of my longtime favorites is the Excuse Rule, which says, "The maximum effective range of an excuse is zero meters." That's profound stuff. Another very useful rule is attributed to an Air Force general, who is credited with the dictum that, in terms of career advancement, it is far more important to receive a medal for doing nothing than to have done something worthy and not received a medal. Along the same lines is the law that says, "An ounce of image is worth a pound of performance." For those contemplating service on a general staff, there is a lengthy list of valuable rules that deal with your relationship with the chief of staff. I won't list them all here, only the most important ones:

Rule #1: The chief is right.

Rule #2: In the impossible hypothesis that a subordinate may be right, rule #1 becomes immediately operative.

Rule #3: Whoever may enter the chief's office with an idea of his own must leave the office with his chief's ideas.

Rule #4: The chief is always chief, even in bathing togs.

Of course, no aspect of soldiering is more serious than combat, so naturally there are many, many laws that address the subject. Several years ago I came across a list of the thirty-five most important laws of the battlefield. I don't know who came up with these, but they were obviously born of experience and common sense. Some of the better ones:

Never share a foxhole with someone braver than you.
When in doubt, empty the magazine.
Never forget your weapon was made by the lowest bidder.
Tracers work BOTH ways.
Friendly fire isn't.
Incoming fire has the right of way.
The only thing more accurate than incoming enemy fire is incoming friendly fire.
No plan survives the first contact intact.
Radios will fail as soon as you need fire support.
If you are short of everything but enemy, you are in combat.

We could spend a lot more time on the do's and don'ts of military life, but the editor is really stingy with space, and there are other aspects of life that have rules worth reviewing. Probably nothing in our day-to-day life receives more attention or concern than our eating habits, so let's look at some of the more pertinent dietary regulations.

> If no one sees you eat it, it has no calories.
> If you drink light beer with chips and dip, they cancel each other out.
> Cookie pieces contain no calories. Breakage causes calorie leakage.
> Food eaten at movies, sports events, and the like have no calories because they are simply part of the entertainment experience and not consumed as fuel.
> Food and drink used for medicinal purposes, like brandy, toast, cheesecake, and so on have no calories.

We could run with this category all day, but you're probably more familiar with diet rules than I since I long ago put these into the same category as electricity—I can't control it, so why sweat it. Let's look at another part of life that frequently causes us problems—parenting. These rules come courtesy of my wife, who probably knows and lives by more rules than any other person alive (and, unfortunately, expects the same of me).

> When mothers are cold, children must be cold.
> (Think about it—how often have you told your kid to put on a coat, even if was 75 degrees outside?)
> If a mother's hungry, so are her children.
> A child's behavior reflects directly on his or her parents; on Dad, if it's a boy, and on Mom if it's a girl.
> At some point, a parent will look down and see his or her parent's arm coming out of his or her sleeve.

We could go on and on—I said at the beginning, no part of our life escapes the constraints imposed by some kind of rules—but I've already exceeded the 100 words the editor gives me, and he has a long list of rules of how to deal with people like me. Until next time, then, I'll leave you with one last rule, provided by my son: *All rules were made to be broken!*

Keep in step, and **BEAT NAVY!**

4. The Manly Pursuit of Fish
July 1993

It is spring. I know it is spring because all the signs are there: the dandelions and skunkweed that pass for grass in my yard are in riotous profusion; my three sons have already mentally gone on summer vacation, despite the fact there are two months of school remaining; and my wife has started her annual bathing suit try-on trauma (this is one of the more unpleasant rites of spring in my house). Even stronger indications are the strange things that I notice as I walk through my garage. The lawn mower seems to be grinning at me with that mocking smile that says, "Pretty soon, I'll own all your Saturdays"; the paint that my wife bought me for Father's Day last year so I could touch up all the trim on the house, but never quite got around to using, has mysteriously reappeared on my workbench; and instead of tripping over the hockey sticks my kids leave at the bottom of the stairs, I now trip over the baseball bats that replaced them. But by far and away, the surest sign that spring is here is the strange twitch I seem to get in my right arm each time I pass the cabinet where all my fly rods are stored. I actually thought I heard one calling to me the other day. And just this morning as we were getting in the car to go to church, I distinctly heard the piercing, high-pitched whine of line being stripped from a reel and felt my whole body vibrating with the tension that comes from trying to keep your line tight and your rod tip up when you've got the grandfather of all trout running on a #18 hook and a three-pound-test leader, and he's breaking for the fast water. Yes, by God, it's spring, which means it's *fishing* season once again.

There are few activities in life that are nobler than fishing. There are many people who aspire to this calling, but few really make the grade. Most folks who pick up rod and reel and head for the water think that fishing is nothing more than a hobby; their ignorance (or perhaps it's just naivete) deprives them of the uplifting spiritual encounter that fishing provides. Indeed, fishing, that is, *real, honest-to-goodness fishing*, is a sacred thing; it is an ennobling and enriching endeavor. Alas, what most people do under the guise of fishing is just a hobby. It's not really fishing at all; it's something far less. What's the difference? you ask. Well that, my friends, is the subject of our hircine homily for today, so pop a cold one, put your feet up, and come along as we navigate fast waters and deep, still pools in search of truth.

First of all, if you really want to be counted among the ranks of true fishermen, you've got to develop the right attitude toward what you're doing. In order to do that, you must understand the true nature of the enterprise. Those of you who cling to the notion that fishing is just a hobby or a pleasant diversion from the stress and strain of work-a-day life, can never fully appreciate nor partake of the soul cleansing experience that comes from taking up rod and reel and venturing forth in hopes of landing The Big One. It's a lot like going to church, but not paying attention or knowing what's going on. God doesn't give you full credit, so you don't get all the bennies.

Fishing is the same way; in fact, one of the things I've learned over the years in church—I always pay attention in church because my wife sees to it—is that fishing is actually an extension of the religious experience. Think about it: how many of the events in the Bible involve fishing? How many of the disciples were fishermen? What was the main course at the Sermon on the Mount? Why, fishing is practically sacramental, so in order to really get the most from it, you've got to treat it that way. With humility. With piety. With reverence.

OK, now that you understand just what fishing is, let's look at how to get the most out of it. To begin with, you must understand that the fish are much smarter than you. God made them that way in order to challenge you and to help you realize just how insignificant you really are. If you don't catch any, it's OK; you probably weren't supposed to. If, on the other hand, you do land a few, you've got to realize that it was most likely by design, and that your efforts really had little to do with it. And on those rare occasions you actually hook a wall-hanger and get it on the shore, before you start snapping photos to send to all your friends, you would do well to remember the sacred nature of what you have accomplished, and treat the event with the reverence it deserves. After all, such an accomplishment is a sure sign that you have somehow earned His favor. Failure to offer appropriate thanks and oblations or, even worse, sending a photo of you grinning stupidly with your prize to your class scribe for publication will undoubtedly cause you to suffer years of snagged lines, dull hooks, and fishless days.

Since fishing is a logical extension of religion, a fishing trip should be treated the same as a trip to church or perhaps even a pilgrimage to some holy shrine (after all, what shrine could be holier than a good fishing hole?). If your boss is properly enlightened, he should never complain when you say you're going fishing for the day—to do so would be to deny you spiritual enrichment. Of course, if he's not enlightened it's up to you to get him that way, and there's probably no better way to do that than with a rod and reel. Once the poor sinner has tasted of the heady wine that flows from a babbling brook and a leaping fish on the end of a reed-thin rod and gossamer line, he will come to know the truth and will never again voice complaint; indeed, your new challenge may be to keep him from always tagging along.

Another vitally important fact to keep in mind is that fishing is not work and must never be treated as such. Indeed, if we are enjoined from working on the Sabbath, then it would be sacrilege to work at fishing. When we turn it into work, we miss the whole purpose of the experience; our physical and spiritual juices cannot be replenished by work. No, fishing is the antithesis of work—that's one reason why it is so enriching. It's like going to confession. We do it to get rid of a burden, not to hoist a new one. There's more than a little truth to the proverb—or perhaps it's a psalm—that says, "A bad day fishing is better than a thousand good days working." I have a classmate and very dear friend who loves to fish and likes to think of himself as a true fisherman, but since he's never broken this code, he's little better than a heretic. A damned lucky heretic, to be sure, but a heretic nonetheless. He's a general officer, and like most GOs on the fast track, never lets himself slow down. A fishing trip with him is a lot like a night patrol in Ranger School. The only thing you're sure of when it's all over is that, somehow, you survived. Every now and then, my friends, you need to just sit down and smell the campfire. When fishing becomes work, it is the devil's doing; it's time to bring the boat back to shore and pop a cold one.

Finally, and perhaps most importantly, there is this immutable fact: women and fishing do not mix. If you really wish to savor the spiritually healing balm of a true fishing experience, leave the ladies at home. Please understand—in no way am I casting aspersions on the fairer sex. Indeed, they have few more ardent admirers than I, but the simple truth is that there is something about the feminine psyche that prevents them from fully understanding or partaking of the spiritual powers of angling. Quite frankly, they demean the solemnity of the occasion. I have learned this the hard way many times when, in misguided attempts to expand my wife's spiritual horizons, I have allowed her to accompany me in my search for True Serenity.

Nothing shatters the tranquility of a good day fishing quicker than the squeal of a woman faced with the prospect of having to bait a hook. There is nothing more annoying than being constantly asked to untangle a line, get a lure out of a tree, unsnag a hook embedded forever in some submerged obstacle, or detach a skewered fish that somehow blundered into the path of an errant hook. There are few experiences more terrifying than being in the impact zone of a woman trying to cast something with a hook attached to it. If a woman is along, it will always be too hot or too cold, there will be too much rain or too many bugs. But this is not the worst of it. No, the real problem is in their lack of appreciation for the true nature of the challenge.

I vividly remember a fishing trip my wife and I took with some friends many years ago to that holiest of southern bass fishing holes, Lake Jackson, Florida. This is no ordinary lake; there are largemouth bass in this lake that are the stuff of legends. Bubba calls this body of water his home, and I had a vision in a dream that Bubba was going to be mine. Alas, my wife insisted on coming along. Being young and naive at the time, I figured it couldn't hurt. I outfitted her with a rod as thick as a tree trunk, and a reel loaded with 30-pound-test line; attached to this was a bobber the size of a softball, suspended above a hook on which was impaled a minnow large enough to fillet. I figured it would keep her occupied and out of trouble—out of my way—and I would be left to pursue Bubba in peace. We started early in the day, and by mid-afternoon, after having beaten the waters to a froth in every likely looking spot on the lake, I had reached the conclusion that Bubba was not yet ready to be mine. For whatever reason, I was not up to the challenge. Suddenly from the back of the boat, where she's been idly sunbathing all day, I hear my wife's voice calmly announce "I'VE got one." Not "I've **GOT** one," mind you, with the emphasis on the verb, but **"I'VE** got one," as in, gee, this is easy—what are you doing wrong? Upon closer inspection I notice that my wife's rod is literally bent double, and the softball-sized bobber is far beneath the murky surface. Her reel was spinning at warp speed as line was being stripped off by something so big I could only tremble in anticipation. After a few seconds I regained my senses and, calmly as I could, said to my wife, "Set the hook! Set the @*^!@*% hook!" I KNEW what was on the other end of that line.

Suddenly, as quickly as it had all begun, it was over. The reel stopped spinning, the rod straightened out, and that huge bobber came flying back to the surface. My wife, in one of the few understated moments of her life, calmly said, "Its off, now," and began putting more suntan lotion on her shoulders, as though the whole episode were nothing more than a rude interruption of her reverie in the sun.

There have been other such episodes, from the banks of the best salmon streams in Alaska to the pure, crystalline trout waters of the High Sierra and the muddy, sluggish rivers of the deep south. No matter what the setting, no matter how grand the cathedral, a day spent fishing with a woman is a day in purgatory. Offer it up, and hopefully on your next trip to the famed Junction Pool, He will reward you with a trout worth taking a picture of and sending to your scribe.

Until next time, then, when we'll debunk the canard that classes after '67 had a plebe year, keep in step, and **BEAT NAVY!**

POSTSCRIPT: It is remarkable how we evolve as we age. My attitude about women and fishing is a case in point. Until I met my current wife, I believed with every fiber of my being that women and fishing should never, ever be combined. Well dear friends, I have evolved.

While I was courting Vicki, I was very anxious to demonstrate to her that I had some socially acceptable and refined qualities and talents, in the hopes she would find me worthy of her time and attention, not to mention her affections. For reasons that remain a mystery to me, I decided to expose her to the joys, challenges, and beauty of fly fishing. After all, what could be more uplifting and spiritually engaging than spending a day immersed in a beautiful mountain stream, surrounded by nature at its finest, being challenged on so many levels in pursuit of elusive and wily trout. It is calming while it is thrilling, it is relaxing while it is invigorating. It cleanses the mind and purifies the soul. I figured Vicki would be impressed.

4. The Manly Pursuit of Fish

I created a monster. Vicki fell in love with the sport and has fully embraced it. She cannot get enough of it. She loves being on the water, fly rod in hand, while a hefty trout hooked on gossamer line runs for the fast water. What's even better is she regularly out fishes me. A day spent fishing with Vicki is a day in paradise, and I cannot envision a better fishing partner—she makes it so much fun.

5. Pets Rule Our Lives
September 1993

It is a hot, muggy, spring day here in southeast Virginia, and I have just spent five hours laboring at one of my most hated chores: opening and cleaning the swimming pool. It was a particularly odious chore this year because the pool cover was worn out, and all the detritus from the surrounding trees, along with several thousand worms and frogs that the cover was supposed to keep out of the pool, managed to get into the pool and spend the winter, which was warmer than usual, fermenting into a grotesque 33,000-gallon bilious-green concoction. It reminded me very much of some of the sources of our drinking water in Vietnam or of some of the soup that the cadet mess used to serve us. What makes this chore even more distasteful is the fact that I didn't want a swimming pool in the first place because I knew that swimming pools were basically a pain in the butt, not to mention a massive drain on the wallet, and I also knew that when it came time to maintain said pool—which, it seems, is ALL the time, I would be the only one in the family with the requisite knowledge or expertise to perform that chore. I knew that would be the case because it seems that I am also the only one in the family with the right qualifications to clean the cat's litter box, and I didn't want cats, either. All of which brings us to the topic of this hircine homily, which is pets and the extraordinary ways they affect our lives. What does a swimming pool have to do with pets? you ask. Well, pop the top on a cold longneck, pull up a lounge chair, slap on some sun screen and come along for the ride through Father Freed's Fantasy Land, and ye shall be enlightened.

First of all, it must be recognized that some folks are pet people by nature, others aren't, and some are simply ambivalent. This is all OK. The problems with pets occur when pet people, who, like children (all kids are pet people), invariably think that ALL people are pet people, come into conflict with non-pet people (like some parents) or when one class of pet people, like dog lovers, come into conflict with another, lesser class of pet people, like cat lovers. This is as potent a formula for conflict as when two opposite personality types, such an ESTJ and ISFP in Meyers-Briggs Personality Profile language, decide to set up house and play life games together. For those of you who may not be familiar with the Meyers-Briggs system, ESTJ and ISFP is like pairing Hitler and St. Francis of Assisi, and by some Machiavellian twist of fate, it just happens to be the combination formed by my wife and me. Suffice it to say, there has never been a dull day in the Lowrey house. I won't tell you which of us is Hitler or St. Francis, but I will tell you that my wife is a pet person, and I am not. (Hitler had a pet dog.)

Before I raise the ire of the Sierra Club and the Lovers of the California Kit Fox and all the other folks on the lunatic fringe that think the Bill of Rights was actually written with animals in mind, let me assure you that I actually like animals. I think most of them are cute. I like to watch TV shows that show their mating rituals. I like to see them in zoos. I like to hunt them, and I especially like to eat them, or at least some of them. I just don't especially want them living in my house.

I haven't always been this way; I was actually a pet person once—after all, I did start life as a kid. I even had a dog for a while as a young boy, but for only a short period of time, and I must be completely honest: I never did form one of those deep, soul-sharing attachments, as between what's-his-name and Old Yeller, with this dog. He was more interested in chasing squirrels, and I was more interested in chasing fish, so when we moved to Germany and left him behind, I really wasn't particularly devastated. Nor, should I add, was my father, who had come to be on a first-name basis with the provost marshal and the dog cops at Fort Benning, Georgia, because of the many, many times my dog had been arrested for chasing mailmen, people on bikes, and MPs (who were frequently on the prowl on our street looking for reasons to arrest my dog or my older brother, who also did not like MPs). Now as I look back on it, I guess the fact that I spent most of my formative years without a pet in the house played a major role in shaping my philosophy that life without animals underfoot was actually OK.

I'm not real sure when I finally came to the conclusion that I didn't need a pet to be a whole person or why I ever reached that decision. Maybe it was because all my experiences with pets invariably ended prematurely and somewhat less than satisfactorily. In addition to my childhood dog, I experimented with a few pets while I was a cadet. In retrospect I realize that this was done not out of any need to bond with a furry security blanket, but rather as a way to fight THE SYSTEM, which is something I spent an inordinate amount of time as a cadet trying to do. At any rate, during the course of my four long years in the gray womb, I had several pets, including a couple of hamsters, Napoleon and Josephine. Alas, one of the hamsters met with an untimely demise when his parachute failed to open. The hamster's demise was particularly unfortunate, as it crashed and burned in Central Area from the roof of East Barracks (now known as Pershing Barracks), landing in a crumpled, pathetic heap at the feet of the officer in charge, who had decided at just that moment to come through the sally port. He was not amused. Not only was I slugged for harboring an illegal pet, but also, and far more harshly, for improperly packing a parachute, leading to the demise of said pet.

Oddly enough, I even continued to experiment with pets after I grew up and graduated. There was the pet black snake, Omar, that I had the summer that I was TDY at West Point, when my battalion from the 82nd Airborne Division was supporting cadet summer training at Camp Buckner. This was the summer after I had graduated. I was newly married and on orders for Vietnam, but my wife had decided to stay home in our lovely Wherry slum quarters at Fort Bragg, so I was batching it and was lonely and in need of companionship. Hence, the snake. The cadet barracks known as The Lost Fifties had been pressed into service as our BOQ. Each day I would tuck Omar into my fatigue shirt and take him to work with me, where he spent the day contentedly wrapped around my waist or slithering around my office looking for mice. Alas, one night I and my fellow lieutenants returned quite late from a lengthy search and destroy mission at the Fort Montgomery Bar & Grill. We were all in a rather obtunded state, and upon rising the next morning to go to work, I forgot to take Omar with me.

Well, the Housing Office at West Point had very generously provided us with maid service in the Lost Fifties, and unfortunately our maid, who did not speak English as a first, second, or third language, found the poor wretched creature in my underwear drawer. (I have never been given a satisfactory answer as to what she was doing looking in my underwear drawer.) Despite her problems with the language, she had no trouble communicating to the MPs (hundreds of whom descended upon my room, ready to sacrifice their all in her defense) that there was a vicious, vile poisonous carnivore on the loose and that she (and all the other maids) had no intention of returning to work until it had been properly dispatched.

The MPs huddled. Senior officers were called in, and a council of war was held in the 51st Division of Barracks. Heads were scratched. Options were discussed. Finally, Omar, being much smarter than the assembled forces, found an open door and left, only to be pursued and captured near the cadet gymnasium. I have always suspected that that episode was worth at least five decorations and two promotions for the MPs involved. Needless to say, I was the focal point of a great deal of vile invective from the Director of Housing and other Very Important People at West Point, of whom I came to learn, there are very many. Were it not for the fact that my departure to Vietnam was imminent, I'm sure they would have found some way to put me back on the area.

Despite all the bad experiences I had with pets, up to and including Omar, I really suspect that it was my wife that finally made me realize that animals and I were simply not meant to live together. You see, my wife is a more than just a pet person; she is a super cat person.

Like most male, studly, airborne - ranger infantry lieutenants in 1967, I considered cats to be little better than cheap dog food. Let's face it, men don't own cats. They own dogs. Rottweilers. Dobermans. Shepherds. They name their dogs nifty names like Frag or Claymore or Ripcord or Roadkill. They don't own cats. Of course, most men have never encountered a woman like my wife. Even at age nineteen—her age when we married—she was a rather formidable woman. She had grown up with cats and saw no reason why the simple fact that she had married me should change any of that. Even before the honeymoon was over, we were the proud owners of a registered Siamese kitten.

How many of you out there were aware that some Siamese cats have a desire to eat wool? And they do it rather well too. Within a few months, I had lost my two best sweaters, most of my winter socks, and one leg of the trousers of my best wool, green class A uniform. Partially in retaliation, I got a dog, a spritely collie named Sebastian, but he was no match for the Cat from Hell. Finally, one night while my wife was out with the girls, I let the cat out of the house, hoping it would run away. Alas, it had an acrimonious altercation with a very large dog and came home to die, which did not leave a favorable impression on my wife. I was, as they say, in very deep kimchi.

Goat Poop

Within a week, my wife had a new Siamese kitten. Within two weeks, all its hair had fallen out—seems the whole litter was infected with terminal ring worm, which as we all know, is highly contagious ... This kitten was replaced by yet another female Siamese, who can only be described as the meanest cat on Earth. This cat spent virtually all its adult life in heat—even after it was fixed. Have you ever made a real, real long car trip with a Siamese in heat? If you have, you needn't worry about going to hell. You've already been there. To make matters worse, within days after my departure for Vietnam, my wife gave my dog away and bred the damned cat. It produced a son, who was as stupid as its mother was mean and of course had to be kept because no one would buy it. And so it has gone through the years. We have had cats. Now we have three—one who is gay and can only survive on prescription cat food that costs more than chemotherapy; one who has a disease that periodically makes all its hair fall out; and a calico who, if it doesn't stop waking me up every morning at 3 a.m. with its gymnastics, will suffer the same fate as the first cat.

But what does all this have to do with the pool? you ask. Well, when we moved here a few years back, my wife, in one of her less lucid, but very determined, moments, announced at the dinner table one evening that she felt we needed a dog. This, of course, greatly raised her stock in the eyes of the kids, which I suspect was all she really wanted to do.

After choking on my meat, I asked, "Why the hell do we need a dog? We already have three little boys."

"That's exactly my point," she says. "Every little boy needs a dog."

After several hours of futile argument on my part, I knew it was a lost cause, and the next day we began the search for the family mutt. The search ended in the purchase of Dudley, a moderately expensive and, as it would turn out, extraordinarily stupid, golden retriever puppy. Within days, I began to get some idea of the scope of the impending disaster. Dudley came complete with a raging case of a disease called parvo, which in 99% of all dogs so inflicted is fatal. Alas, not so in Dudley. Our vet, who by some incredible twist of fate is named Dr. Freed (I'm not making this up), made a heroic and incredibly expensive medical breakthrough and salvaged the animal (after which Dr. Freed was able to add a new wing to his kennel club). As Dudley grew he became increasingly active and fleeting, which required our putting in a fence, to the tune of $750.00.

But Dudley's real claim to fame was his unparalleled capacity as a digger. Within a couple of months, my backyard, which had at one time been the Versailles Gardens of the neighborhood, looked like the Battle of the Somme had been fought there. Someone told me that the way to get a dog to stop digging is to sprinkle pepper on the ground where he likes to dig. I took that one step further and poured gallons of cayenne all over the yard. Dudley simply licked it up, which gave him a frightfully bad odor whenever he passed gas, which was frequently. Finally, much to my relief, he became too much even for my wife to deal with, and Dudley was sold to the lowest bidder. I was left with a backyard that was little more than an abandoned quarry. The only logical thing to do was fill it with cement and water, not to mention money. After all, we already had a fence.

Thus the pool, Dudley's legacy. And I'm still cleaning the damn cat's box too.

Until next time, when we'll take a voyage of adventure through all my kids' science fair projects, keep in step, and **BEAT NAVY!**

6. The Ghosts of Christmas Past
November 1993

If this issue of *Assembly* arrives on time, you should be reading it at the beginning of the Christmas season, a time of year when all sanity seems to fly out the window and go south. Actually, if where you live is anything like my neck of the woods, it's been the Christmas season for nearly three months, at least on our streets and in our stores. I swear the Christmas lights go up in the mall as early as September, and I have long since learned the futility of trying to buy summer clothing in August, even though I live in southern Virginia, and the temperatures don't get below 90 until mid-October. I can, however, outfit my entire family with gaily colored wool sweaters and buy plenty of Christmas wrapping paper for them as early as July. The fact that I won't be able to find any of those items in December, but will be able to buy a bathing suit, continues to vex me. Nevertheless, regardless of when the Christmas season starts in your neighborhood, by the time you've added this literary carrion to your bathroom library, it will be in full tilt, so it's a good time to contemplate the Christmas experience in our lives. Pour yourself a big tumbler of eggnog, pull up a chair by the gas-log fire, and come with me as we visit the ghosts of yuletides past.

Before we begin our journey, I must be completely honest: I am a hard-core, card-carrying grinch. I do not like Christmas time; in fact, it is quite possibly my least favorite three or four months of the year. It leaves me physically and emotionally, not to mention financially, impoverished, and with each passing year I find myself getting into a deeper funk with the approach of the season. This bothers me because I know what Christmas is really all about and what it really stands for, and that should give me a warm, fuzzy feeling inside. I even have three kids, at least one of whom can still be classified as a little boy, and we all know that little children are supposed to make Christmas a special time of joy and excitement. Alas, this is unfortunately not the case in my house. I'm not sure what it is exactly that has caused me to look upon this season of brotherly love with such angst and anxiety. In all likelihood it is a combination of factors, most of which are probably my own doing. I suspect, in the final analysis, what has actually happened is I have become a victim of my own intense desire to enjoy Christmas and, in my efforts to do so, have created a monster that gets more vicious each year.

It hasn't always been this way, of course. As a child I dearly loved Christmas, for the same reasons all kids love Christmas—lots of presents, lots of candy and cookies, and lots of attention. I was a very fortunate child. Santa was always good to me—too good—and I only had one sibling. He was (and still is) nine years older than me, which meant he was never a threat to MY stuff. (I have come to learn, as a father of three boys, that this is a very significant point.) Another reason I loved Christmas so much as a child was the fact that it was always a one-way flow of riches—my way. I was never burdened with hard decisions like what to get so-and-so. My mom always got something for Dad, and vice versa, and they would put my name on the cards. As for my older brother, well, hell, brothers never worry about giving each other presents at that age. Indeed, as a child Christmas really was a time of great joy in my life.

I continued to enjoy Christmas after I left home and went to West Point, though for decidedly different reasons. As a member of the class of 1967, I shared in the distinction of being in the last class to have to stay at West Point for plebe Christmas. While most folks found this to be a thoroughly distasteful experience, I reveled in it. For the first time I was able to walk around the Rock with my chin out and get a taste of the freedom that would come with being an upperclassman (freedom, of course, being a relative idea here). We could fall out in the mess hall and eat like pigs, or cows, as the case may be. My folks came up, brought lots of boodle—and there were no obnoxious yearlings around with whom I had to share it—and they also brought presents. There was some extracurricular activity going on in the company M-2 trunk rooms that made life all the more enjoyable. Yes, I really did enjoy plebe Christmas. It was kind of a double benny because not only did I have fun, but I also earned bragging rights by being able to claim I was a member of the last class to have to stay at West Point for plebe Christmas (and, therefore, the last class to have a plebe year), and we all know how important claims like this can be when grads get together to swap war stories.

My upperclassman Christmases were also enjoyable, due primarily to the fact that they afforded the opportunity to get away from West Point (back to the relative concept of freedom, here). At this point in my life presents and boodle had become secondary concerns, though Mom and Dad did make sure that I still got plenty of each. My firstie year Christmas was especially noteworthy, as I decided to get engaged.

Although I didn't realize it at the time, that was probably my last really happy Christmas. By the time the next one rolled around, I was a married man, and my cavalier approach to the season was about to be permanently dashed. It is safe to say that my first Christmas as a husband was an unmitigated disaster. For the first time in my life, I was faced with the responsibilities of (a) getting someone a Christmas present that really meant something to the recipient; and (b) selecting and decorating a Christmas tree.

To say that I failed miserably at each task would be an understatement of heroic proportions. The present—a Polaroid camera (I swear to this day she said she wanted one)—might not have been so bad had I remembered to wrap it appropriately, but handing it to her still swaddled in the brown PX bag with sales slip attached did kind of spoil the effect. This was made worse by the fact that the PX was closed on Christmas Day, and she had to wait until the following morning to rush down and exchange it for what she still swears she told me was the only thing in the whole world she wanted—electric hair curlers (remember folks, we're talking 1967 here—twenty-year-old girls had a different value system in those days).

What makes this picture even bleaker was the tree. Those of you who have put off shopping for the perfect tree until Christmas Eve can picture in your mind's eye the tortured vine that ended up in our Fort Bragg Wherry slum living room. After much effort I was finally able to make it stand almost straight, but this did require the only side with any branches on it to be facing the wall. In an ironic twist of fate, for reasons that remain a mystery to this good day, my bride insisted on decorating it entirely in blue—blue lights, blue balls, blue tinsel—although in retrospect, the color proved most appropriate. We still refer to it as "The Blue Christmas," for more reasons than one might at first imagine.

Well, while I may have more than my fair share of faults, I am a fast learner, and the lessons of this debacle were forever etched in my consciousness. I vowed never again to let my wife down at Christmas. The price for this folly was simply too steep.

Alas, the following Christmas was no better, as I found myself in a hospital in Vietnam. Actually, this wasn't all bad: it relieved me from the anxiety of (a) finding my wife the perfect present; and (b) having to worry about a damn tree. It also afforded me the opportunity to watch the Bob Hope show live, sitting on the beach at Cam Ranh Bay in the rain watching Ann Margaret and the other lovely, callipygian lasses accompanying Mr. Hope, while dreaming fondly of home and hearth.

The next Christmas gave me my first real opportunity to atone for the sins of that disastrous first experience. We were now in Germany, and I had the good sense to start asking my wife what she wanted for Christmas as early as June. She was very obliging, and it wasn't long before I had accumulated a want list of several pages. To be on the safe side, I chose the ten most desired, or most-frequently-mentioned items from the list, and got them all. I had them professionally wrapped. We shopped early for a tree and found a real beauty. This was going to be a Christmas to remember.

And it was too. Not so much for the presents or the tree or the several feet of snow, but for the fact that I was lucky enough to be the brigade staff duty officer on Christmas Day, and got to miss all the fun. My wife did bring me a turkey sandwich for dinner and thanked me for all the nice presents, but somehow it wasn't quite what I had in mind. Better luck next year.

That next year found me back in Vietnam. Not exactly the best circumstances to make merry. Add to this the fact that when we drove to San Antonio, where I was to leave my wife while I went back to the war, we encountered a freak, early, autumn snowstorm and were rear-ended by the biggest damn 18-wheeler known to man, resulting in the total and dramatic destruction of our car and all of our personal belongings—including all the Christmas presents she was going to open without me. Imagine, if you will, a grown man running around in a snowstorm wearing Bermuda shorts and a t-shirt, with a West Point bathrobe with tiger tail attached as an outer garment, trying to put out the fire engulfing his car by throwing handfuls of snow upon the flames. So much for the fourth Christmas.

After that second tour in Vietnam, we found ourselves at Fort Benning, Georgia, and an opportunity to really relax and enjoy the season seemed upon us. As the season approached, I made sure I covered all the bases with presents (by now, ten presents had become a tradition, and as we all know, tradition is something one doesn't mess with), and we sensibly decided to do the environmentally correct thing and buy an artificial tree. All seemed to be OK, until the week before Christmas, when my back decided to begin giving me a lifetime of trouble. I spent that season crawling around on my hands and knees. Ho, Ho, Ho.

And so it's gone through the years. The Christmas of 1978 was a watershed year, as that was the first Christmas we shared with children. I must admit, it really was fun. The excitement, the wonder of it all, the fact that as a baby our first son was too young to complain about not getting what he wanted. By now, though, it was getting harder and harder to satisfy the ten present requirement for my wife—a self-inflicted wound I will admit, but the memories of that first Christmas remain vivid—and the anxiety level began to creep up as I found it more and more difficult and expensive to outdo last year. By 1984 things were really out of hand. By then we had three boys, including the youngest, who for very good reasons had picked up the title of Dr. Doom, the Dark Lord of Destruction. That particular Christmas, his third, he developed an ingenious tactic. Eschewing the normal-child Christmas morning behavior of getting up before the dawn and rushing downstairs to see what wonders Santa had left, he opted to remain in his room until his brothers had opened all their gifts. Only then, when all their stuff was in plain sight and ripe for plucking, did he decide to make his appearance. He took one look at their stuff, one look at his, made a quick value judgment, and moved in for the kill. By the time the morning was over, we had experienced several hours of fights among the boys, and what little stuff remained unbroken was solidly in his possession, and his older brothers were reduced to tears. This pattern repeated itself the following year, at which point I learned a very valuable lesson: buy three of everything. Eliminate the competition. What's good for one is good for all. It also makes it easier to cannibalize for parts. This has worked pretty well for the past several years, but it has proven damned expensive.

Alas, I'm afraid this year that tactic will no longer work, as they are into clothes more than toys now, and they do not share the same tastes in fashion. Actually, that last statement is an oxymoron, as the term *taste* and what my kids choose to wear these days are mutually exclusive concepts. I'm finding it more and more difficult to find presents for my kids that they will enjoy and that I will not deem to be socially reprehensible. Add to this the pressure of the self-inflicted ten-present tradition, the never ending quest to have more spectacular outdoor lights than the neighbors, and the annual ritual of making sure everyone we got cards from last year is on this year's list, and it all makes the angst juices start boiling over by early November. By the time Christmas Eve rolls around, I just want to get it over with.

I know this is a terrible attitude, and I admit to feeling guilty about it. After all, as I said at the beginning, I know what Christmas is really all about, and for that reason alone the season should be nothing but joy and happiness. And I really do want it to be that way. Unfortunately, every Christmas Eve when we go to Mass to remember just what it's all about and to give thanks, all the seats are taken by the folks who only show up once a year.

Until next time, have a merry, blessed Christmas and a prosperous New Year. Keep in step, and **BEAT NAVY!**

7. School Science Fairs
January 1994

I was napping in my favorite chair the other evening when my middle son, the seventh-grader, woke me up. As I shook the cobwebs from my head, he held a piece of paper in front of my face and said, "My teacher says you have to sign this." Of all the things I hate to hear from my children, that simple statement is quite probably the worst, as it invariably means they've done something socially unacceptable at school. "What have you done now?" I bellowed, without looking at the offending paper he was waving at me.

"Nothing, Dad, nothing. This is about the science fair project."

With those words, a shooting pain coursed through my head. I felt my stomach beginning to churn, my hands became clammy, and little beads of sweat began to run down my face. God, I thought to myself, it can't be that time already; the school year's barely a month old. Tell me it's not true.

"What about the science fair project?" I asked.

"I've got to turn in my topic tomorrow, and you've got to sign this paper saying you know about it." I feel a scream welling up in my throat but managed to suppress it, or at least most of it. My worst fears were realized. At that point, I found myself wishing that the offending paper actually was a nasty note saying my son had done something hideous at school. I can deal with those far better than I can science fair projects, for the plain truth is I *hate* school science fairs with an intensity that is both unreasonable and unwavering.

I'm not sure why this is true. Well, that's not entirely accurate; there are lots of things that contribute to this paranoia of mine—I'm just not sure which is the one that finally put me over the edge, the one that elevated science fairs from the level of mild annoyance to major upheaval and trauma in my life. The fact that I have three sons, all of whom go to public school in a school system that loves science fairs—they start the kids out in the third grade and make them participate every year 'til they graduate—indicates that I'd better get a grip on the problem before I become a basket case. Either that, or move. Let's see, that's three kids, each of whom must do ten science fair projects, for a total of thirty. By the end of last year, we had completed thirteen. God, we're not even half done with this nightmare. Yeah, I guess it's a good time to pour a few fingers of Ireland's very finest and see if I can't figure out how to overcome my science fair phobia.

The problem probably has its roots in my own childhood science fair experiences. I don't remember having to do too many as a kid—certainly not as many as my kids do—but what memories I do have are invariably bad. This is true, in fact, not just in the case of science fairs, but for the entire range of scientific study and endeavor. The study and application of science, either formally or informally, is not something I enjoy or do well. Most scientific principles escape me, and I do not like dealing with things I can neither understand nor control.

I still cringe when I think of my eighth-grade science fair project. It was the mid-50s and we were living in Augsburg, Germany. For reasons that escape me, I decided it would be a neat idea to build a working rocket as a science project. After explaining the various principles of thrust, lift, aerodynamics, and the like, I would then demonstrate how it all worked by launching the rocket. Alas, no one bothered to tell me that gun powder was not a particularly good fuel source. The results, while very dramatic, were not what I had in mind. The launch pad explosion was horrific (I had packed in a *lot* of gunpowder), completely destroying the rocket and sending my eighth-grade classmates and teacher scurrying for cover. I can still hear Mr. Adams, my teacher, screaming. At that moment of my life I made a conscious decision to forever eschew all scientific study. There was no doubt that the humanities were my bag.

High school was tough because, of course, we had to take things like chemistry, physics, and biology. Actually, tenth-grade biology wasn't so bad because, by the luck of the draw, I got Lila Leveritt as my lab partner, and Lila was luscious. Unfortunately, that was during my extreme religious phase, when I was convinced I was called to be a priest, and I failed to capitalize on this opportunity. But Lila was very good at dissecting things, so I managed to survive biology with a fairly good grade.

This was not the case in chemistry or physics, however. Chemistry was particularly troublesome for me, despite the fact that some years before, my father, in one of those parental attempts to energize a child's creative juices in a positive manner, had given me a home chemistry set one Christmas. For a while I found it to be great fun. I quickly learned how to make stink bombs and dangerous acids and all the other noxious concoctions that any kid given a chemistry set learns to do. I never once concerned myself with learning any of the principles of chemistry, nor did I try to master any of the approved and recommended projects that were described in the set's instruction manual. I did, however, take my creations to school, with the resulting notes home to my father.

Unfortunately, my high school experience with chemistry wasn't any better. I vividly remember the day when an entire hallway of Fayetteville Senior High had to be evacuated when it was discovered that I had somehow managed to manufacture a highly toxic gas during a lab. It was all an accident, of course, but no one was willing to buy that line. However, the fact that a lot of kids got out of class early made me a very popular person, so it wasn't all bad.

Despite my obvious shortcomings in scientific endeavors, I managed to graduate with a high enough grade point average to gain an appointment to West Point. (How that was accomplished is a pretty good tale in itself, worthy of another "Goat Poop" column.) I did this despite the fact that my high school guidance counselor, when I told him I wanted to go to West Point, openly guffawed in my face and told me that I would be damn lucky to get into a decent trade school somewhere. I also did this in spite of the fact that West Point, in 1963, was quite probably the mother of all scientific schools. (This was before the curriculum had been softened to include Touchy Feely 101 and a host of other socially relevant fields of study.) I wanted to be an Army officer. It had not occurred to me that West Point felt the best way to achieve that goal was to cram my head full of useless scientific mumbo-jumbo.

The four years I spent at West Point can best be described as an academic Ironman Triathlon, and I was not in shape. Those of you from that era remember all too well, I'm sure, the curriculum required to become an infantry officer. In plebe year they started us out with ES & GS, better known as Squint & Print, which included little subcourses like astronomy and something to do with vectors and the introduction to computers. Remember the plebe year computer course?

Remember the damn computer? This was 1963, and computers were still a relatively new toy. The thing occupied the entire bottom floor of Thayer Hall. You had to use punch cards to make it work, for God's sake. Countless hours spent filling in little squares on stacks of cards only to have the machine eat them. That was the year the term "abort mode" became forever etched in my consciousness. And it was only plebe year; the best was yet to come.

Yearling year it was physics and chemistry. The closest I ever came to passing a lab in chemistry was when we beat Navy and the P gave us all two section tenths, which raised my grade to a 1.8. I once spent an entire organic chem lab analyzing a test tube full of distilled water because I got the tubes mixed up on the centrifuge. You would be amazed at what you can find in a test tube full of water if you put your mind to it.

Cow year was hideous beyond belief: Nuke, Thermo, Solids, Fluids, and of course, Juice. Nuke scared me—I have a natural aversion to things that make one glow in the dark—but Juice terrified me. It wasn't bad enough that the material was beyond comprehension and dangerous to play with, but the instructors in the last section were invariably humorless tyrants who felt they were being punished for having to deal with us less gifted folk. The only positive experience I ever had in Juice even ended on a sour note. My roommate, a corps squad athlete of some note, and I alternated in the ejection seat in our last section Juice class—he would occupy it one month, I would occupy the next. (We also tutored each other.) One day we arrived in class early and, in a flash of intellectual brilliance, decided to hook up a microphone to an oscilloscope and take bets from our classmates on who could generate the best wave pattern by farting into the microphone. I had won a handsome sum when the P stormed into the classroom. He was not amused, and my roommate and I were slugged for grossly facetious behavior in class. I never tried to be scientifically creative again.

Firstie year brought Ordnance and Civil Engineering and, with them, the dreaded Weapon System Design Study and the CE engineering project. The WSDS caused some especially bad moments, as we had to use an analog computer to help design an artillery piece, and I somehow managed to come up with a gun barrel several hundred feet long that increased in diameter as it went from the breech toward the muzzle. The CE design problem wasn't any better, and my grades on both projects left a lot to be desired. Fortunately, it was 1967, the Vietnam War was at full tilt, and the need for infantry lieutenants was growing rapidly. It was decided that despite my obvious scientific shortcomings, I could carry a rucksack and shoot an M16 rifle, so I graduated without ever knowing how to work the computer or design an electrical circuit, and I swore that I would never, ever try to learn how.

In the euphoria of the moment, it never dawned on me that one day I would have kids, and they would have science fair projects, and that it would fall on my shoulders to see to it that they got done.

As luck would have it, my children have inherited their father's distaste for things scientific. In fact, two of them have extended that attitude toward all academic endeavors, regardless of the field of study. Not a formula for success, I fear. Add to this potion my wife, one of life's most organized, anal-retentive, and structured human beings, and you have an extremely potent formula for stress and conflict. My wife is a list person. You may know the type: every day is carefully and precisely mapped out on a piece of paper. If, by some random happenstance, she does something during the day that isn't on her list, she must then put it on the list so it can be crossed off since it's been done. This wouldn't be so bad if she just made lists for herself, but she also feels compelled to make lists for the rest of us. Somehow, over the years, making sure the kids' science fair projects get done (and get good grades) has ended up on my list.

One of the biggest hurdles to be overcome is thinking up projects that are easy to do, require little work, can be done at the last possible minute (this is the part that drives my wife into a frenzy), can be intelligently explained by a disinterested child, and will result in passing grades. And, as I mentioned earlier, coming up with thirty of them that meet all of these parameters.

We partially solved that last problem a couple years ago. As each son moves on from elementary school to middle school, and from there to high school, they simply repeat the earlier ones. After all, it's a new school, and the truth is, there isn't a science fair project known that hasn't been done a zillion times. Even so, there is still pressure each year to come up with three different projects—projects which, ultimately, I can do, because, as we all know, it's usually the parent that ends up doing the damn thing since the kid doesn't really give a hoot.

Around here, as the science fair looms closer and closer, the pressure to complete the project (remember, it's been put on a list), or sometimes just to start the project, gets more and more intense. The concept of a slug-stopper is not lost on my kids.

To make matters worse, for some reason over the years, we seem to have become very fond of projects that involve growing things, which, of course, takes time. This is further complicated by the fact that we have a house full of cats, who by their nature are attracted to plants. There was one project we did a couple years ago that involved planting different types of seeds in different materials to see if they needed soil to grow. Alas, the answer must have been yes, as nothing grew. In a panic, we planted more seeds. These did manage to sprout, but the resulting growth was then eaten by the cats. With just a few days remaining, we planted a third batch of quick-growing seeds and crossed our fingers. By the day of the fair, several tender shoots could be seen rising from the shredded newspaper and kitty litter and other materials; maybe we could pull this thing off. But then the inevitable disaster struck: as my son was getting out of the car at school, he dumped the whole thing in the parking lot.

That episode pretty well sums up my experience with science and science fairs. That's why I get this nervous twitch and cold sweats every year about this time. However, my wife's list has already been made, so there's no escaping it this year. I might as well get to work now. I think this year I'll build a rocket. Maybe even design it on the computer. Mr. Adams would be proud.

Until next time, keep in step, eat your veggies, and **BEAT NAVY!**

8. Entertaining, Army Style
March 1994

It's Thanksgiving Day, and the house is filled with the aroma of roasting turkey, dressing, and pumpkin pie. We're still several hours away from the feast, but already my senses of taste and smell are in ecstasy overload. This is a scene repeated in countless thousands of homes across this great land today as Americans celebrate our most traditional holiday. What makes it so remarkable in our house is the fact that, unlike the rest of the civilized world, it marks a significant departure from our own tradition of celebrating special occasions. Basically, we don't usually make much of a fuss about special occasions. Or any other occasion, for that matter, except of course, when I host the Wednesday night poker group, but then we're talking *really special* occasion there, with beer served in real glass bottles. No, I'm afraid that entertaining on a grand style, or even a mediocre style, is something the Lowreys just don't do very often, whether it's for friends or just for family.

And that's too bad because it hasn't always been that way. After all, my wife and I are both Army brats and grew up in homes steeped in the traditions of the Old Army, and as anyone old enough can remember, those traditions included lots of entertaining, much of it quite formally. Even something as simple as Sunday lunch called for all kinds of special protocols and extreme formality. I still vividly remember the whole family coming to the table every Sunday afternoon, still in our best go-to-church clothes, with all the best china and crystal and silver, squirming in my chair for what seemed like hours as my father carved the roast or the bird or the pig, all the while waxing eloquent about whatever was on his mind. This of course took lots of time, as my father was a very precise carver and always seemed to have a lot on his mind. Hell, I was a grown man before I ever realized that in civilian homes, people actually got to eat their meat while it was still warm. Maybe this is what caused me to turn away from the genteel life as I got older.

8. Entertaining, Army Style

But not at first. Nope, as I said before, my wife and I were encumbered with an awful lot of tradition, and I was ready and eager to carry it into the future. Even though she was only nineteen when we married, my bride had been raised well—her father was the senior infantry colonel on active duty when we married—and between the two of us, we knew what was expected of professional Army officers and their wives, especially (by God) West Point graduates. We had our engraved calling cards and spent countless hours practicing the fine art of dropping them in the calling card tray without anyone noticing (remember that canard?). My wife had appropriate hats and gloves for every type of occasion and made sure she never missed a tea or coffee at the captain's or colonel's house; indeed, she frequently volunteered to host them at our quarters. In the evenings I would quiz her on different rank insignia, proper forms of address, and the chain of command. This last bit was somewhat harder than I thought it would be. It seems that when my wife was born, her father was already a lieutenant colonel—it was shortly after WWII, and people made rank quite young during the war—and so she had spent her whole life living as a colonel's daughter. She just kind of assumed that all officers lived that way. The shock of the reality of being a lieutenant's wife was kind of hard on her at first, but she got over it. Sort of. Of course, I've been paying for it ever since, but that's another story.

Our first Thanksgiving was a very memorable occasion, as it was her first opportunity to really show her stuff in the grand style to which we were both accustomed. I should point out that, while she was well schooled in the pomp, circumstance, and tradition of an Army officer's life, she was NOT so encumbered with a knowledge of cooking and, frankly, had no interest or desire to be. That's one reason this Thanksgiving dinner is so remarkable.

We were at Fort Benning, I had just finished Ranger School (and therefore had a generous appetite), and we were getting ready to head off to our first, real assignment at Fort Bragg in the 82nd Airborne Division, as soon as jump school was finished. We decided to invite several of my bachelor classmates over to share the holiday. Despite her ambivalence about cooking, my bride spared no effort: sweet potatoes, pumpkin pie, dressing, green beans almondine, and the biggest damn turkey I have ever seen. Of course, she had to spend several hours on the phone with her mom (her folks were stationed in Panama, which even today is an expensive, long distance call from Georgia) learning how to cook the bloody thing. We knew that there were supposed to be giblets (I have no idea what giblets are, and don't want to know) with that bird and spent more than a little time looking for them. Hell, the bird was big enough that I was able to stick my head inside with a flashlight; they were not there. It wasn't until a week later, when the turkey had been stripped to a mere carcass, that we found them, still in the plastic bag, somewhat melted. Now who would have ever thought that they would have been at THAT end of the bird? Nevertheless, our first significant entertaining experience was deemed a success, even without the giblets.

The next nine months were at Fort Bragg, North Carolina, home of the Airborne. It was 1968, the Vietnam War was the driving force in all our lives, and time for serious entertaining in the 82nd Airborne Division was pretty limited. While we didn't try anything on a grand scale, we did frequently have friends over for heated up C-rations and cold beer. While the bill-of-fare may have been somewhat limited, the accommodations were always immaculate: sterling silver, fine bone china, crystal, all laid out on our finest lace Army-Navy tablecloth that was covering the rickety, broken down card table that passed for a dining room table. Lieutenants in those days were dirt poor, and we certainly couldn't afford furniture, but man could we ever set a table. After all, ours had been an Army wedding—a big one—with a guest list that must have included most of the colonels and general officers around at the time. We got more silver and china and crystal—that's what people gave young lieutenants and their brides back in those days—than we knew what to do with. What we didn't get was anything that we did know how to use, like furniture or appliances or sheets or towels. We've still got all the silver and some of the china and crystal—what little that managed to survive fifteen moves and three trips to storage—and still don't know what to do with most of it. But, you know, serving C-ration ham and lima beans on fine bone china somehow made it palatable.

After a year in Vietnam, we ended up in Germany, where I was commanding a company in the airborne brigade. Being in command, I now had added responsibilities for entertaining, and, of course, these responsibilities ultimately impacted my wife. In addition to the usual teas and coffees and bridge parties, she was now the Old Man's wife and was expected to be a mentor for the wives of the young lieutenants under my charge, teaching them the finer points of Army life. The fact that by now she was a ripe old twenty-two herself, younger than several of the wives under her tutelage, never seemed to matter. Perhaps her crowning achievement was the night we were having a dinner party for several of the officers and their wives. Dessert was supposed to be brownies, but something went dreadfully wrong between the box and the table. It's amazing how much difference a little too much water will do to a recipe (3 cups as opposed to ¾ cup), and the resulting goop that came out of the oven was not quite like anything we had ever seen. Without even batting an eye, my wife simply poured the ooze into our best silver serving bowl, stuck in a bunch of forks, cut up some rolls, and announced that the chocolate fondue was ready. She still gets requests for the recipe.

While I attach great importance to custom and tradition, there was one old Army tradition that I would have loved to see go away back in those days, but it refused to die. I'm talking about the time-honored custom of dressing up in your dress blue uniform and paying a New Year's Day call on your CO. Hopefully, you hadn't gotten so hammered at the unit New Year's Eve bash that you had thrown up on your blues. You also hoped that your boss had been just as wrecked as you were so that he couldn't remember the things you had said or had done to his wife. At any rate, it was a good bet that the last thing anybody—including the unit commander or his wife—really wanted to do on New Year's day, after the customary New Year's Eve, was dress up in their military suit of lights and stand around making small talk, hoping that you could sneak your calling card into the old man's tray without anyone noticing.

It was at one such function in Germany where my wife suffered one of her greatest indignities. It was time for my unit officers to leave the brigade commander's house. Just as we got to the front door, a gaggle of officers from the next scheduled unit arrived. I managed to get out the door in time, but my wife was too long-winded in her goodbyes, and the next thing she knew, she had been shoved into the bathroom next to the front door, where she was forced to remain for the next fifteen minutes as the hostess effusively greeted all the newly arriving guests. We never went to another New Year's reception again, which is undoubtedly why I retired as a lieutenant colonel and was never draped with the mantel of probity reserved for full colonels.

After a second tour in Vietnam, we found ourselves at Fort Benning, Georgia. It was now 1971, and the Army was undergoing profound change, largely as a result of the upheaval caused by the war. Many time-honored traditions were disappearing as the Old Army began to give way to the pressures of the '60s generation. In retrospect, I have come to realize what a shame that was. Entertaining had become much less formal; parties seemed to take on a free-spirited, animalistic character.

I will never forget one such affair at our quarters, in the spring of 1974. It started out in the planning stage as just a quiet little affair—one of those "pay back" parties. You know the kind—you need to repay a couple of social obligations, so you invite the folks over for a few drinks and finger food. We had no sooner issued the invitations than people started showing up from everywhere, including my mother-in-law. What started out as a civilized affair for ten ended up as the party from hell for sixty. We had everything from priests to perverts crammed into our house, including a lot of people I have never seen before or since. I knew something was amiss when I arrived home the afternoon of the party from fishing (getting ready for parties is woman's work, right?) and found two strange children—I knew they weren't mine, as we didn't have any—taking the food that was cooking on the stove and throwing it around the room. In the living room I found their mother—another last minute, unannounced out-of-town arrival—my wife, and mother-in-law, all well-oiled with whiskey sours. It was obvious that we were as ready for the party as we were going to get.

Much of what happened that night is a blur, since by about 10 o'clock I had retreated to a corner of the dining room with my own bottle of Irish whiskey, but what I do remember is still vivid. There was the incident when I walked into one room just in time to hear one guest, a classmate, telling another guest (from a different class), "You know, I've hated your guts ever since we were cadets." And then there was the couple who decided to end their marriage, and destroy one of our tables in the process, at about the half-way point of the evening. I think that's when I decided to retreat. The really remarkable thing about the party was the aftermath: for weeks we got phone calls from people we didn't even know, raving about how it had been the greatest party they had ever been to and asking when were we going to do it again.

I think that's probably when we began to take a more laid-back attitude toward entertaining and special occasions. There have been two notable exceptions since then. The first was the occasion of my wife's thirtieth birthday. I have been led to believe that this is a significantly traumatic event in a woman's life and needs to be treated appropriately. In my wife's case it occurred while we were stationed at Fort Ord, California, and she was pregnant with our first child. I decided to mark the occasion with a formal, black tie reception, held at the Naval Post Graduate School Officers' Mess, complete with open bar, five gallons of champagne punch, lots of very good food, a throne for my wife, engraved invitations—in short, the whole nine yards. It was a grand affair, but I'm afraid by this time, Army people were really taking a jaundiced view toward formality. I had specified black tie, and that's what people wore: rugby shorts and black ties, bathing suits and black ties, jeans and black ties, sneakers and black ties, and an occasional mess jacket with black polka dot tie. Yes, the times were a-changing.

The next several years took us back to West Point for an assignment in the Tactical Department and to Alaska for my last assignment with troops before we ended up in our current digs. After my wife's thirtieth birthday party we pretty much gave up any pretense at formality. The closest we came to it at West Point was the night I invited the cadet Outdoor Sportsmen's Club over for sloppy joes and beer—I was their officer-in-charge—and our next door neighbor, who shall remain nameless because he is now a general officer and at the time was a company tactical officer, decided to put on a mask and run through our quarters flashing everyone. You could have heard a pin drop—the cadets even stopped eating which, as anyone who has ever entertained cadets knows, is no small feat. What I've never been able to figure out is how my wife instantly knew who the culprit was.

Our last grand affair was the summer of 1992, when we decided to celebrate our twenty-fifth wedding anniversary with a big, outdoor party round the swimming pool. It was a lovely evening—lots of good catered food and drink, sixty or seventy friends, a balmy June night—just what you hope for on one of these occasions. My mother-in-law was even there, almost fully recovered from the Fort Benning fiasco of twenty years earlier. Unfortunately, during the evening, a large gaggle of geese flew over, and they had obviously recently eaten something that did not agree with them. I will never know how one gets an entire gaggle of geese to drop their loads at the same time, but they did, right over our party. Do you have any idea how much of a mess ten or twenty pounds of goose guano makes when dropped from a considerable height? Fortunately, it all missed the food and beer, but a lot of people who hadn't planned on swimming that night ended up in the pool.

Well, dinner's almost ready, and I do not want to miss out on any of the goodies. I can only assume my wife had a temporary attack of insanity when she planned this meal, but I will take full advantage of it. I know that next month, when Christmas Day rolls around, we'll be back to our customary pizza, shrimp, and bloody marys.

Bon appétit, and ***BEAT NAVY!***

9. The Curse of Secretaries
May 1994

I was glancing at the calendar the other day when I noticed that National Secretaries Day is almost upon us. Well, that is certainly an event worth celebrating, and I intend to do so with gusto. I suspect that my celebration will be a little different from most, though, for I shall be celebrating the fact that I don't have a secretary.

Before I raise the ire and hackles of all you hardworking, underpaid, loyal, and faithful girl and guy Fridays out there, without whom I know your bosses would be so much bean dip in the quest for success, let me assure you that I do not have anything against secretaries as a group or as an occupation. Indeed, my own wife was once a secretary - an ***executive*** secretary, mind you. Nope, it's just that my own personal experiences with secretaries in the workplace have been almost universally bad. No, worse than bad. Incredibly, unbelievably bad. I can only conclude that at some early point in my life I did something that really upset the patron saint or the fairy godmother of secretaries, and I was cursed from that point on.

My troubles began as a cadet. Naturally, I didn't have a secretary as a cadet, but I wanted one. Not for shorthand, of course, but for recreation. Virtually all the secretaries working in and around USCC were lovely, nubile young things, most of whom were unattached and eager to change that status. That is, after all, why they were working in the U.S. Corps of Cadets, all of whom, in those days, were hot-blooded young men. During my yearling year I joined the cue of cadets trying to find favor with this collection of young, callipygian, love goddesses, focusing on one in particular in the commandant's office. Alas, and alack, she obviously had her sights set on something far higher than a mere yearling and put me in my lowly place in no uncertain terms. My lifetime of angst with secretaries had begun.

After that initial experience, and a second, equally dismal attempt to curry the favors of a secretary in the library during cow year, my close contact with the species ended for some time. By the time my firstie year rolled around, I was engaged and no longer needed the services of a secretary. After graduation and commissioning, I was assigned to rifle platoons and companies stateside and in Vietnam—certainly no need for clerical help in those circumstances. I did spend a year in Germany as a company commander, where the closest thing I had to a secretary was my company clerk, a Soldier from Brooklyn who had enlisted in the Army at the behest of a judge. Seems he had been given one of those classic choices, and I ended up as the surrogate warden. It quickly became evident he could neither type nor read, so I made him my driver. This may have been the smartest thing I ever did, as my jeep soon became the only company commander's jeep in the 1st Airborne Brigade that had a new heater, new tires, and a new top. At least I was able to determine where this Soldier's real talents lay. I also remember the brigade commander complaining about his missing heater, but I had been around long enough at that point to know not to ask questions, and besides, it was a particularly cold winter, and I enjoyed the comfort.

Speaking of the brigade commander, he of course, did have a secretary, and in the course of my duties I had frequent contacts with her, none of which, as I recall, was pleasant. She was German—very, *very* German—and nobody gained access to Herr Oberst, the colonel, without her approval, and she did not approve of many people. She was also, without a doubt, the greatest comma momma that has ever lived and scrutinized every piece of paper sent to the old man as though it was a letter bomb, ensuring grammatical perfection. The fact that English was not her native tongue didn't phase her one bit. It was during this assignment that I began to have an appreciation of just how big a role secretaries play in the great scheme of things, and I began to be somewhat awed by it all.

After another trip to the war, followed by the Infantry Officer Advanced Course, I found myself assigned to the staff and faculty of the Infantry School, buried in an office on the fifth floor of Building Four, better known as Infantry Hall. Here, the secretaries outnumber the troops by about three to one, and you would think that it would be easy to get your work done neatly and quickly. I quickly learned that in that environment only two classes of people had priority when it came to clerical support: young, unmarried captains; and old, crusty colonels and above. The rest of us were cast to the wolves. We were on our own.

I learned to type. I spent countless hours standing in line, behind legions of young women, at the copying machine. I even learned the intricacies of the Army's "functional filing system" (there's an oxymoron if ever there was one). And I dreamed of the day when I would be senior enough and important enough to warrant my very own secretary.

It was in my next assignment, then, that my real nightmares with secretaries began, for it was there, at Fort Ord, that my dream came true. I was assigned as one of the assistant G-3s of the 7th Infantry Division, and my duties included being the division school's officer. With that important office came a secretary, my very own executive assistant! Finally, I had made it to the big leagues.

We'll call her Louise. She was an elderly lady—about 60 as I recall—and had been a civil servant longer than I had been alive. She was long since divorced, and at the time I inherited her, she was having an affaire de coeur with another GS civilian there at Fort Ord. Alas, it seems the relationship went sour at about the time she began working for me, and Louise took it rather hard. She became obsessed with the idea that this rake was attempting to gain control of her mind by transmitting lewd and lascivious brain waves to her, waves which were apparently strong enough to capture her eyes and cause her to snap her head up at odd times throughout the day and follow his movements around the post. This was particularly unnerving as Louise and I shared a very small office, just large enough for our two desks to be wedged in, facing each other. It was the small room on the end of the second floor of one of those ubiquitous WWII "temporary" barracks you see on every Army post, the room off which you find the balcony and fire escape ladder.

As the days wore on, and the brain waves became increasingly debilitating for Louise, she tried a variety of tactics to overcome them. First, she strung a metal chain from the ceiling to a point about four inches above her head as she sat at her desk. After a week I couldn't stand the suspense any longer and asked her what it was for. Turned out to be her directional antennae, by means of which she had hoped to deflect the incoming brain waves in another direction. I was now really concerned, for I was clearly in the kill zone.

When the antennae didn't do the trick, she moved to the next phase, which was to swaddle her head with aluminum foil as a wave barrier. Imagine, if you will, trying to get work done for a very demanding boss, when sitting across the desk from you is an old lady with her head wrapped in foil, her eyes constantly darting about the room, capped off by an antenna on her head. Things were starting to get serious. I did prevail upon her to wear a wig, but the sight of all that aluminum hanging out around the edges made it even more bizarre.

Her next step really caused me some trouble. She decided that an effective means of dissipating the incoming waves would be to disrupt them by blowing a very loud whistle whenever the transmissions got strong. Suddenly she would jump out of her chair, usually striking her head on her antenna, run around to my side of the desk, throw open the door to the fire escape balcony—which was right next to my chair—step out on the balcony, and start blowing the loudest damn whistle you've ever heard. Traffic all over post would halt, thinking they were being stopped by some irate MP. I still remember with stark clarity the day I was giving a very important briefing—the G3 briefing room was adjacent to my office—to the division commander and the chief of staff, a West Point grad from the class of 1951, who has never been known for his sense of humor. Suddenly, the atmosphere was shattered by the high shrill of what sounded like an incoming 8-inch artillery round. When I explained to the somewhat nonplussed chief that it was just my secretary in the next office breaking up incoming hostile brain waves, I was skewered to the wall by a stare that still gives me night sweats. I was also told, in no uncertain terms, to fix the problem. This, I learned, was far easier said than done. Have you ever tried to have a civil servant—one who has been around for decades—removed from a job? It simply can't be done.

The last straw in this bizarre episode came about a week after the briefing incident, when I walked into my office to find Louise sitting at her desk, wig, aluminum foil, antenna, and whistle all in place, with a .38 caliber Smith & Wesson revolver sitting on the desk next to her coffee. "Louise," I said, "go home. Take some leave. Lots of leave. I'll call you when it's safe to come back." She was last seen driving down the Coast Road toward Big Sur with her windows rolled down, blowing that damn whistle for all it's worth. I swear to you, this is a true story. I have witnesses.

After Fort Ord, it was back to the Rock, where I was assigned to the Office of the Commandant of Cadets as the scheduling officer and chief of the Summer Training Programs Office—the guy responsible

9. The Curse of Secretaries

for determining which cadets went where and when for their summer assignments. Again, this lofty office brought with it a secretary, and again the gods did not look upon me with favor. This woman was very angry. Always. I never could tell if it was something I said or did, but it probably wouldn't have mattered. She was just one of those people who was always mad at life. She also could neither type as well as I, nor do shorthand. I suspect she also didn't do windows either, and I was sure as hell not about to ask her for a cup of coffee. On top of all this, she had a great deal of trouble with the concept of time, which meant her arrival and departure in the office was an iffy thing. Why, you ask, did I keep her around? Well, to be brutally frank, none of the qualities she lacked was nearly as important as the one she had—quite possibly the most important thing someone at West Point can have, particularly during the football season: she had a teenage daughter who did not date (for obvious reasons) and, because of that, was available to babysit. By this time there were two babies in the Lowrey house, and a guaranteed babysitter was worth any inconvenience, even if it meant an occasional chewing out by my boss for the quality of the typing on my staff papers. This service cost us dearly, however, as this child liked to eat. I have seen more food left on corps squad football tables in the mess hall than this babysitter would leave in our house after my wife and I would go out for a couple of hours of R & R.

After West Point it was back to troops, as I was assigned as an infantry battalion S3 in Alaska. Finally, a much needed break from the terrors of dealing with a secretary with constant PMS and soured love lives. It was great to be back in the trenches, where my every whim was responded to by a staff of highly trained and motivated NCOs who knew how to keep the boss happy and, most importantly, out of trouble. But all good things come to an end, and this reverie was no exception. Against all odds, I got promoted to lieutenant colonel and had to leave the battalion. Worse, it meant a new job on the staff and another secretary.

It seems that just before I arrived on the scene in my new job, the secretary moved on to bigger and better things, and my predecessor—an old friend of mine—wanted to make sure the position was filled before I came on board, so I could concentrate on learning the new job. That was quite considerate of him; unfortunately, he was also a bit rushed, as he was PCS-ing back to the Lower 48, and couldn't spend a whole lot of time interviewing candidates. He took the first one that applied. Her first day on the job was my first day on the job. It was interesting.

This was a lady, about 50-ish, divorced, who had never been a secretary in her life. She had come to Alaska to get away from something. She could cuss a blue streak and liked her beer cold and wet. What she couldn't do was type. She couldn't take dictation. It turned out she couldn't even answer the phones (to be fair, we worked in the Operations Center, and the phones were kind of complicated if you'd never been around one with more than ten buttons on it). I had countless phone calls from really angry people that got beamed out to who knows where by the push of a button. She also did not have a daughter who could babysit. In retrospect I have come to believe that she was sent to this planet as an ambassador or advance scout from La La Land, to kind of check things out. We worked in an office that was a vault and had a cipher lock. For one year, she had to be let in each and every day because she could not remember the cipher combination.

In the space of one month, she got lost three times on the drive from her home to work. This is made doubly remarkable by the fact that she always lived in the same place and only had to remember one main road, and in Anchorage, Alaska, one can either go towards water or mountains. You would think that after a fairly short period of time the route would have become familiar. Perhaps the most telling incident, though, was the morning she decided to stop for gas on the way to work. She dozed off for a moment in her car while the gas was being pumped and, upon awakening with a start, realized she was late. She roared out of the gas station still firmly attached to the pump by the hose. I was told by the station attendant several days later that he was really surprised the geyser of gasoline that resulted when the pump was wrenched from its moorings was so high.

And so it's gone through the years. For whatever reason, secretaries and I have not worked out well. I envy all of you out there who have managed to find that perfect combination of professional skill and decorum that makes a good secretary such a valuable treasure. I shall raise my glass in your honor on your special day. I'll even drink to Louise, wherever she is.

BEAT NAVY!

10. Yard Sales
July 1994

I suppose that I should have seen it coming since all the classic signs were there: my wife's increasingly strident carping about the amount of junk cluttering our house (all of it mine, of course), the number of drawers we couldn't pry open and the number of closets we were afraid to open, the increasing difficulty in navigating around the piles of stuff in the garage where once upon a time my car used to reside, but nonetheless, I was taken by surprise a couple of weeks ago when my wife made the announcement that we were going to have a yard sale. My reaction to that news was much the same as my reaction to my kids' science fair projects. I loathe them both intensely. However, I knew that my wife had made up her mind—indeed, she had already put "Yard Sale" on one of her lists, so there was no point in debating the issue. The only recourse for me was to become fully involved in the folly, not because I wanted to be part of it, but solely out of a sense of self-preservation. I knew from past, bitter experience that if I wasn't fully involved in the whole sordid affair, it would mostly be my stuff that ended up on the auction block, and I would never see any of the money either.

My wife has long had a fascination with yard sales—not going to them, fortunately, but having them, which can be just as bad, if not worse. Every few years she feels the need to purge our home of everything she considers to be extraneous, which in her case includes anything that hasn't been used or worn within the past month or which must be dusted. This has frequently given me some scary moments, as I often have the impression that I am the most extraneous item in the house. She is not an accumulator. Unlike a lot of folks, my wife attaches very little sentimental value to most things; stuff is valued for its utility, period. Anything that dust can settle on and serves no purpose other than to be looked at and admired is automatically yard sale fodder. I, on the other hand, am a great accumulator. I love stuff—at least stuff to which I can attach pleasant memories or fantasies—and my drawers and closets, not to mention my office walls and shelves, burst at the seams with various and sundry leftovers from my stumbling journey through life. There are favorite trout flies, the trappings of my military career, memorabilia from far flung travels, zillions of books and magazines, and all kinds of stuff that might be useful someday. I do not know when that someday might be, but when it arrives, I want to be ready for it.

And then, of course, there is the problem of my wardrobe. My level of physical activity not being what it used to be, I can no longer wear most of my clothes from a couple of years ago. They have shrunk. According to my wife's convoluted logic, that is reason to get rid of them. Why? I ask; after all, there's nothing wrong with them, and we all know that it's just a matter of time before I will lose all this temporary carry-on baggage around my middle and be able to wear them again. By then, 1-inch-wide neckties and polyester leisure suits will be back in style, and I'll be ahead of the power curve. Whenever my wife decides it's time to have a yard sale, my first defensive perimeter goes up around my clothes closet.

Yard sales don't just happen, of course; there is a huge amount of planning and preparation involved. I'm convinced this is the part my wife likes the best, for it offers her almost unlimited opportunities to make lists: lists for her, lists for me, lists for the kids—hell, she makes lists just to keep track of her lists. Picking a date, making the signs, putting the ad in the paper, finding enough tables to put all the crap on—I've been on joint readiness exercises that required less planning than a Lowrey yard sale.

There are four distinct phases to a yard sale.

Phase one, the identification and collection of the stuff to be sold, is by far and away the most traumatic and divisive part of the operation. This is where the battle lines over what's junk and what's not are drawn, and I am traditionally on the defensive in this phase. This year was no exception. My wife managed to get to my closet before I had the concertina and claymores in place and, before I knew it, had identified the majority of my wardrobe for elimination. I noticed that this year she took a slightly different tack: she first picked out all my clothes that she wanted—most of my sweaters and some of my shirts. Most of the rest was consigned to the auction block. I counterattacked; this time I decided that a compromise might work to my advantage. I would give her the sweaters and shirts she wanted—after all, I could always sneak into her closet later on and retrieve them—and agreed to sacrifice some of the remaining clothes to the sale. Maybe by doing this, I reasoned, the pressure to unload the rest of my treasures would be diminished. Foolish me.

A few minutes later she called me downstairs. "What do we need these for?" she asked, holding up several of my books.

I glanced at the titles: *The Officers Guide,* 1967 edition; *The Army Wife,* 1967 edition; and *Service Etiquette* (also the 1967 edition). "They're valuable historical references," I replied. "If they're so valuable, why don't you sell them?" she retorted.

"The boys might want them someday; besides, I don't think you'll find too much demand for books about etiquette or tradition these days. Those concepts seem to be out of vogue." "Well, what about those?" I followed her finger to the stack of *Assembly's* going back to 1967.

"More valuable historical material," I replied. "I may write a book about the achievements of my class someday." In the interest of good taste, I will not record her reply. I could tell she was just getting warmed up, and I was going to have to be extra vigilant, or a lot of my most valuable possessions were going to be lost forever.

The next day she turned up the heat considerably. I was in the garage taking an inventory of my tools and things when she showed up, reached into the closet where I keep my fishing rods, and pulled one out. "Why do you keep this old piece of junk?" she asked.

I looked up from what I was doing and immediately felt the blood go cold in my veins. The "piece of junk" she was holding so casually and irreverently was nothing less than my father's handmade, split-bamboo fly rod, purchased at Abercrombie & Fitch in New York City in 1949, which he had lovingly passed on to me many years ago. This magnificent piece of fishing artistry had provided countless hours of pleasure, and even a few successes, in the never ending quest for piscatorial perfection. I explained this to her as calmly as I could, as I gently removed the precious reed from her grasp and inspected it to make sure no harm had come to it.

"Well, you never fish with it anymore. What good is it now?" Of course I don't fish with it anymore; it's a sacred relic. Fishing with that rod would be like drinking beer out of the Holy Grail. It is for admiring and remembering good times past. It is not yard sale material.

As if the incident with the fly rod wasn't bad enough, the next day proved even worse. By now my wife was no longer just on the attack; she was on a crusade, and nothing was safe from her clutches. In her zeal, she inflicted upon me what may be the ultimate indignity. "Come here, please," she cooed innocently.

I knew I was being set up. When I arrived in the bedroom, she was standing there, her face an impassive mask, her jaw set in determination, holding up my two most valuable possessions. "These rags are hideous, and they smell bad. You should get rid of them."

In her left hand was my cadet B-robe, with tiger tail still attached after all these many years. In her right hand was my Navy B-robe, won as a result of our victory over Canoe U. in the Army - Navy game of 1964, quite possibly the greatest football game ever played. Every time I see that robe, my mind is filled with the image of Roger Staubach being buried under a pile of Army jerseys in his own end zone.

Something in my mind snaps. "That's it!" I bellowed, "This time you've gone too far. My god, woman, is nothing sacred anymore?" I snatched the robes from her grasp and stormed off, looking for something—anything—of hers to sell. For the next two days I was on a constant search and destroy mission, filling the garage with her stuff.

"Why is it," she snarled, "that you only want to sell my stuff?"

"Because," I replied, "All the *junk* in this house happens to be yours!" And so it went, day after day, right up to the moment of the sale, each of us more concerned with securing our own treasures from the other, rather than actually eliminating the real junk in our lives.

Phase two of a yard sale is pricing the stuff that has finally been culled out for sale. In some quarters, this is a real science and requires a lot of thought. We have our own system: my wife asks me what I think something is worth. If it's one of her things, she multiplies whatever I say by ten, and that's the price; if it's one of my things, she divides my estimate by ten. If it's mutually owned—like the few surviving wedding presents that we haven't used since the '60s, she figures the original price, factors in inflation and the labor costs involved in dusting, polishing or washing said item over the years, and comes up with a price. One very important aspect of pricing is determining whether or not things that are supposed to work, like motors and compressors, for example, actually do so. This is very important in deciding whether something will be sold as a functioning item (like an old sewing ma-

10. Yard Sales

chine or trolling motor) or as a charming and unique antique, a conversation piece, if you will. Alas, this year an inordinate number of items we thought would fit in the functional category (and bring a higher price) ended up as charming antiques. When things aren't plugged in for a few years, they tend to get surprised when you suddenly ask them to go to work, and the results are often less than satisfying.

The third phase is the actual sale itself. Some people, who I can only assume to be seriously sadomasochistic, make this a two-day affair. At least my wife is content to deal with this insanity for only one day. Anyone who has ever been through the yard sale experience knows the kind of idiocy I'm talking about.

First, there is the issue of what time it starts. It doesn't matter what time you advertise, there are always some cretins that are going to show up at the crack of dawn, or before. I remember one sale at Fort Benning where some fool was banging on my front door at 0530. At that hour of the day I didn't care how much money he wanted to spend, I wasn't in a selling mood. Despite the fact that I let him know in no uncertain terms what I thought of him, he still didn't leave, but simply sat out in his car waiting for me to start setting the junk out. All of this just to have first crack at empty mayonnaise jars and broken bicycles. You figure it out.

Another part of the circus is trying to keep your eyes on everything you've got spread out all over your yard to make sure it doesn't walk away (it may be junk, but it is MY junk) or get broken by someone's young child. Over the years I've learned one of the tricks employed by professional yard sale attendees is to show up with several young kids in tow, who they turn loose on your stuff, while they try to convince you to lower your prices on your already undervalued treasures. "But it's broken," they'll tell you, as they try to justify their insulting offer. The fact that it wasn't broken before they and their kids showed up usually doesn't dawn on you until after this conversation has been held three or four times. Kids and yard sales do not mix. I should point out that this includes your own kids, too, especially if any of the junk you're trying to unload is theirs. It's amazing how something that hasn't been touched, looked at, played with, or used for years, and is probably broken, suddenly becomes their most prized possession when a kid sees it for sale. Keep the kids away.

Dealing with the crowds can be a real hassle, especially when they start fighting among themselves over your busted junk and when they start asking to use the bathroom and the telephone. I managed to avoid most of that problem this year by scheduling the yard sale on a day when I knew I would be gone most of the morning at my son's soccer game (I had to be there—I'm the coach). Of course, I didn't bother to tell my wife about that until after the ad appeared in the newspaper. After all, this yard sale was her idea; she could deal with it. I did get up at 0600 to set it up for her and by 0700 was greeting the early shoppers—it was scheduled to start at 0900—but for the most part, she was going to have to handle this event by herself. I shall pay for that decision for a very long time.

When I returned home at noon, I was distressed to find that there was still a lot of junk in my yard (including some of my treasures that I thought I had managed to hide from my wife), and there were still throngs of shoppers lounging about. As soon as I got out of the car, my wife announced it was time for her nap, spun on her heels, and disappeared into the house without another word, leaving me at the mercy of the crazed crowd. At that point I decided it was time to announce the final going out of business blue-light-special sale: for the next thirty minutes, no reasonable offer would be refused. In some cases, the definition of "reasonable" became pretty flexible. By two o'clock, when I discovered I was out of beer, I knew it was time to shut things down. There was still a large lady and her three screeching kids haggling over a couple of items; I made her an offer she couldn't refuse, helped her load her treasures and her kids in the back of her pickup truck, and formally went out of business.

The fourth and final phase is recovery. This involves figuring out what to do with the junk that didn't sell (according to my wife, you bag it up and save it for the next one), counting the money, and arguing over what to do with it. This is always a very short argument in my house, as my wife has usually already determined what she intends to do with it well beforehand. The fact that most of the revenue was raised by selling my stuff never seems to matter; after all, she points out, if I hadn't collected so much junk, we wouldn't have had to have the yard sale in the first place. Hard to argue with that kind of logic.

At least it's over now, and I can actually walk through the garage in a straight line. My wife has already spent most of the money on stuff that we will undoubtedly end up selling at the next one. And so, the unbroken cycle of life goes on.

Until next time, stay in step, count your blessings, and **BEAT NAVY!**

11. A Dream Answered—
How I Gained Admission to West Point
September 1994

I was dozing off in front of the boob tube the other night, kind of half listening to the news, when an announcement caught my attention. It seems that the senior member of the U.S. House of Representatives has announced his retirement at the end of this term. Normally, that kind of news wouldn't be enough to drag me from my slumber—I think they should *all* announce their retirement—but the individual in question played a rather important role in my life many years ago, so I sat up and took notice. The Honorable Jamie L. Whitten, from the 2nd District of Mississippi, the gentleman who gave me my appointment to West Point, was finally hanging up his hat. As I sat and sipped on my longneck pondering that fact, the events of that fateful spring so long ago came flooding out of the footlocker full of memories I keep in the attic of my mind. For a seventeen-year-old kid full of dreams, it was a period of high drama; for a congressman full of promises, it was a time of great turmoil. It's a story worth telling.

First, we need to set the stage. My decision to go to West Point took everyone—everyone except for me—by surprise. Never mind that I was an Army brat whose father was a career infantryman and great Soldier. Even the fact that my older brother—we're nine years apart—had gone to West Point didn't prepare folks for the shock caused by my decision. I'm not real sure why this was the case; in fact, that's always been a bit of a mystery to me. As a young kid I had never made a big deal out of wanting to go to West Point, if I ever even mentioned it at all. To me, it was as natural as breathing: I had always just assumed that it was the natural order of things and not worth discussing. It was the only thing I had considered doing with my life, except for a very brief period—before hormones and testosterone kicked in—when I had considered the priesthood. Apparently, that was lost on the rest of my family. My brother was a jock, a stud, and an outgoing, hard-charging, hell-raising kind of dude, who played a mean game of football and was always looking for challenges or challengers to conquer. He was a

West Point natural (the fact that he was also extremely mathematically challenged didn't seem to matter much). I, on the other hand, collected stamps, played tackling dummy on the high school football team, and liked to stay home at nights and study Latin and read history books. I was also an introvert. The idea of my going to West Point just didn't seem to fit the image people had of me.

This point was brought home early in my senior year in high school, when I had to report to my guidance counselor for one of those mandatory "what do you want to do when you grow up" sessions. I will never forget the sneer on his lips nor his laugh when I told him of my intention to go to West Point. "Freed, get serious," he said, "you'll be damn lucky to get into a decent trade school somewhere." For me, that episode began a lifetime of contempt for most high school "guidance counselors," reinforced today by my own experiences of dealing with those of my son's. I don't know what my "counselor" did with the next thirty years of his life, but I'll be happy to compare my accomplishments to his any day of the week.

My folks recovered from the surprise quickly. It wasn't that they didn't think I could cut the West Point mustard so much as it was they had simply never thought I would want to, but then we all know that God gives us kids to keep our lives full of surprises and challenges.

Once I had made my intentions known, my father was galvanized into action. It was already late in the appointment-getting season, and I was behind the power curve. Things were further complicated by the fact that I was born in Arkansas but had never really lived there since my papa was a career Soldier. At the time of my quest for an appointment, we were at Fort Bragg, NC. (A lot of people erroneously believe that the kids of career officers have an easier job getting service academy appointments than most folks do; the opposite is true. Due to the mobility of Army folks and the political nature of appointments, our elected brethren seldom feel any obligation to vagabonds from out of district.)

Since I was born in Arkansas and living in North Carolina, we decided to try for an appointment from both states, and I duly penned letters to the senators from each, as well as the representative from the North Carolina district in which Fort Bragg was located and the one from my home district in Arkansas. It was the Arkansas congressman "Took" Gathings whom we had the highest expectations from: he was an old family friend, my father had supported him in his first successful run for congress back in 1938, and he had given my brother his appointment. Alas, we quickly heard from him that he had no vacancies for the West Point class of 1967; he did, however, have an appointment for Annapolis that he would be glad to give me. Never in my life had I been so insulted. The stigma of spending life as a graduate of Belly Button Academy was more than I could bear. I politely declined his offer and crossed my fingers that someone else would come to my rescue.

Surprisingly, within a couple of weeks, I had some success from two sources: both Senator Fulbright of Arkansas and Congressman Lennon of North Carolina offered me competitive nominations, allowing me to take the entrance exam in competition with a whole slew of other folks (this was back in the days before SATs ruled the day). I was euphoric; with two chances for success, my odds were looking good, indeed.

Alas, the Army quickly threw water on my premature celebration. A week before I was scheduled to take the entrance exam, I received a nasty letter from the Adjutant General saying that I could not take the exam for members of congress from two different states, as that constituted a conflict of residency, and I could only be a resident of one place at a time. This seemed rather petty to me, but he was adamant, and if I didn't choose one of the two nominations to give up, he'd cancel them both. This called for a family strategy session. We gathered round the dining room table and discussed my options. After much scratching of heads and analyzing various courses of action, I decided to give up the nomination from North Carolina. The reasons were pretty simple, really: I knew a couple of the other guys nominated from North Carolina, and I knew they were pretty smart fellas, as well as being Army brats like myself. I didn't know any of the Arkansas nominees, but then, what the hell, they were homebred Arkansas good-ole-boys. How could they possibly have an advantage over an urbane world traveler like me. I knew I was smart, and they were, after all, from Arkansas.

On 27 February, 1963, I reported to the test site at Fort Bragg, North Carolina, full of hope and expectations. There were about fifteen other candidates there, including a couple of friends, and we nervously cracked jokes and made mental notes of who we expected to see later that summer wearing cadet gray. There was no doubt in my mind that

I was going to be one of the chosen few. The exam was tougher than I thought it would be, but I felt like I did OK—the extra difficulty just reinforced my conviction that I had it made over those farm boys back in Arkansas.

So much for logic. A couple of weeks later I received the bad news that while I had indeed passed the exam and was fully qualified for admission to the United States Military Academy, someone else—someone in Arkansas—had scored higher than I had, and he had been given the appointment. Talk about depressed, about having one's over-inflated ego balloon burst. What a marvelous lesson in humility that was (although, I must admit, at the time I didn't look at it that way).

At that point I decided that the battle was lost, at least for that year, and began contemplating life as a party animal at Ole Miss. My father, though, had other ideas. The day after I got the bad news, he came into my bedroom and said, in his best father-son tone of voice, "Son, we're not licked yet. This letter you received says that you are fully qualified for admission to West Point this year. You simply don't have an appointment. You're going to have to find someone that will give you one."

"How do I do that, Papa?" I asked.

He handed me a Greyhound bus ticket. "Tomorrow morning, you're going to Washington, DC, and you're going to walk the Halls of Congress until you find someone who will give you this appointment. I know you can do it. I've already made arrangements for you to stay with friends." It took a couple of minutes for the impact of this news to sink in. My dad was sending me off to Washington, on my own, to shape my own destiny. I was seventeen years old and being given the opportunity for the adventure of a lifetime. I was going to have one hell of a good time. Who knows, I might even get an appointment too.

On 29 April, 1963, my dad put me on the bus in Fayetteville, NC, bound for DC. The ticket cost $16.30—I've still got the stub. He also gave me a list of names and biographical sketches of representatives and senators to study on the way north. The most important thing he gave me, though, was a list of "do's and don'ts" which I still treasure to this day: DON'T—chew gum, mumble, or look at the floor when talking to people. DO—speak clearly and concisely, smile, look at the person to whom I am talking, and <u>THANK EVERYBODY</u>. Pretty good advice for anyone, anytime, under any circumstances.

11. A Dream Answered—How I Gained Admission to West Point

I arrived in DC in mid-afternoon, found the family friend waiting for me at the bus terminal, and got settled in for my odyssey, which was to begin bright and early the next morning. I went over my plans, which were pretty simple: since there were only 100 senators, I'd start in the Senate Office Building and work my way from office to office. Walk in, introduce myself to whomever was there, tell them what I wanted, see if I could meet the senator, plead my case, and move on to the next one until I'd gotten them all, then repeat the process in the House Office Building. As a teenager naive in the ways of Congress, I figured they would all be hard at work in their offices, and I could probably see most, if not all of them, in three or four days.

By the end of the second day, my feet were sore and my morale was low. This was not as easy as I had thought it would be. I don't know where these people were, but most of them were not at work, and I was getting nowhere fast. I had managed to see a few senators and congressmen, about twenty altogether, with no success but lots of encouragement, at least from most of them.

One of my more memorable office calls was with the quixotic and outspoken congressman Adam Clayton Powell from Harlem in New York City, who just happened to be on one of his infrequent visits to DC from his hideaway in Bimini. The Honorable Mr. Powell was more than a little amused that an Anglo-Saxon child of the deep south would have the cheek to ask him for an appointment to the Military Academy and got a great laugh at my expense, as did the representative from Puerto Rico who asked me point blank "*Señor*, what in the world makes you think that I would give you anything since you are not from Puerto Rico?" Lots of answers ran through my mind, but even at the age of seventeen, I had the common sense to stifle them. I even remembered to thank him for his time.

On the third day, reinforcements arrived. My big brother, then a first lieutenant in the 82nd Airborne Division at Fort Bragg, showed up to give me encouragement and assistance. Renewed in spirit, I hit the Halls again, now with him at my side. We decided to pay a visit to Mississippi Senator Eastland. His administrative assistant foolishly ushered us in to the senator's office without checking with the old man first; he was sound asleep at his desk. The assistant cleared his throat and said, "Excuse me, Senator, but there are a couple of constituents who would like to talk to you." Without looking up or opening his eyes, the senator, still half asleep, mumbled, "Well, where are the sons of b----?" to which the assistant nervously replied, "They're right here, sir." The instantaneous transformation from sleep to full, effusive wakefulness was a thing to behold, but we left the senator's office empty-handed.

That afternoon we returned to the House side of the Hill, and sometime in mid-afternoon found ourselves standing outside the office of the Honorable Jamie L. Whitten, 2nd Congressional District of the State of Mississippi. For some reason which shall always be clouded in mystery, I had never asked Congressman Whitten for an appointment during my earlier search. The reason this is so mysterious is the fact that the Lowrey family—my dad and his kin since 1816—were from that part of Mississippi. Hell, my cousin B. G. Lowrey had been the congressman from the 2nd District in the 1920s. My grandfather had just been buried there the previous month. My brother was named after Confederate Brigadier General Mark P. Lowrey, our great-grandfather from Mississippi. The soil of the place ran in our veins. The fact I was born in Arkansas was because that's where my mother was from, and Dad had moved there to find work as a young man during the Great Depression and fallen in love, and we all know what havoc that can wreak.

Armed with this background, my brother and I confidently entered Congressman Whitten's office. Much to our surprise, he was there and willing to talk to us. Even more surprising was his stunning news that he did indeed have an appointment available for the West Point class of 1967. The bad news was, there were a couple of good old boys back home who had expressed interest in it, and as much as he'd like to help, considering my Mississippi pedigree, there really wasn't much he could do for me since I didn't live in Mississippi (and therefore, couldn't return the favor politically). After a pleasant chat about relatives and whatnot, my brother and I excused ourselves. Within five minutes we were on the phone to my father with the news: Jamie L. Whitten, from your home district in Mississippi, has an appointment, but he doesn't want to give it to me. Get *help*, now! The date was 3 May, 1963, a day I suspect Mr. Whitten has never forgotten.

Within five minutes of our phone call home to my father, the phone lines between North Carolina and Mississippi were burning up. There are **lots** of Lowreys in Mississippi, and they all vote, and they were all about to get in on the act. The phone calls were followed up with telegrams and letters. Within 24 hours, poor Congressman Whitten was being deluged by mail, phone calls, and telegrams from his constituents back home. I've got copies of most of them—they fill a three-inch loose leaf binder; the poor guy never had a fighting chance. There's even a letter from his old buddy and fellow congressman "Took" Gathings of Arkansas—the guy that tried to send me to Canoe U.—reminding Mr. Whitten of his obligations to friends and colleagues. My favorite letter is from Congressman Whitten's own brother, whom to this good day I've never laid eyes on, who strongly suggests that Jamie might not want to come home if he doesn't give "this fine son of Mississippi the appointment he so richly deserves." There's a similar letter from the congressman's own banker back home, as well as lots of other folks across the state. He stood his ground for as long as he could, but in the end, this "son of Mississippi," by way of Arkansas, got his appointment to the United States Military Academy. On 16 May, 1963, thirteen days after he accidentally spilled the beans to a couple of strangers that he had an appointment available, the Honorable Jamie L. Whitten of Mississippi gave Freed Lowrey the answer to his dream.

There are a couple of postscripts to this story. After Beast Barracks, I reported to my new cadet company, D2. On the first day of Reorganization Week, as I was rushing back into the 11th division of barracks from formation, I was stopped dead in my tracks by a very serious and stern cow. "Do you know who I am, Smack?" he asked. "No sir," I replied. "Mister, I am Jessie Whitten, Congressman Whitten's nephew, and I'm here to make sure you get the most you can out of this place. We want you to make Mississippi proud." It was to be a very long plebe year.

And finally, a note about the guy from Arkansas who beat me out for Senator Fulbright's appointment. His name was Allen Etheridge, and we became good friends as cadets. He was killed in action in Vietnam on 15 July, 1969. He made Arkansas and all the rest of us proud.

Until next time, stay in step, and never forget, if you want it bad enough and you're willing to work for it, it can be yours. **BEAT NAVY!**

12. My German Adventure, Part I
January 1995

I was scanning the local newspaper the other day when a photograph caught my eye. It was a photo of a line of parked cars—sixteen of them—at a car dealership in upstate New York, all squashed flatter than a cadet mess discus pancake. Seems they had been run over by an errant bulldozer. I was instantly overwhelmed, or least whelmed, by a case of *déjà vu*. I had seen this before; indeed, I had lived such an event.

Before I knew it, the floodgates holding back the bad memories in the cesspool of my mind burst, and I was awash in images from an assignment many years ago in Germany, back during the dark, dark days of Vietnam and the Cold War at its most frigid and the hollow, beleaguered Army of the late '60s. Pop the top on a longneck, sit back in your favorite BarcaLounger™, and come along for the ride as we revisit the Assignment from Hell.

It was the autumn of 1969, and I was a young captain fresh out of Vietnam, where I'd done my time as a rifle and reconnaissance platoon leader in the 173rd Airborne Brigade. Those of you who were around then know all too well that the Army of those days was not a particularly fun place. The war wouldn't go away, the country appeared to be falling apart at the seams, and the Army was fighting for its survival as an honorable institution. Nowhere was this more evident than in Germany, where I found myself assigned after my tour in Vietnam.

I didn't realize this at the time, of course. In fact, my bride and I were delighted at the prospect of going to Germany, where we had both lived and had tons of fun as kids. It would certainly be a nice change of pace from Vietnam. It offered the opportunity to drink infinite amounts of real beer, not the lukewarm Carling Black Label slop or Ba Muoi Ba from the rice paddies. We were filled with visions of ski trips and adventures in Paris and London and lots of unbridled debauchery. I was even excited about the assignment for professional reasons, for I was going to the 1st Airborne Brigade, in Mainz, which meant I would get to stay on jump status and keep sucking down an extra $110.00 a month airborne jump pay. Visions of a new Porsche danced in my head. I was the proverbial eager-beaver when I reported for duty to the brigade commander. I was delighted to learn that he was going to make me a company commander, though my joy was quickly tempered when I learned it was the Brigade Headquarters Company that was to become my fiefdom. But, what the hell, it was a command, it was an airborne unit, and he did promise me a rifle company somewhere down the road. I accepted the challenge, saluted smartly, and left his office to survey my new domain.

That was my last happy moment for a year. Very quickly, I began to realize that things in the 1st Airborne Brigade weren't the stuff professional dreams are made of, for lots of reasons. Even getting command of a rifle company after three months in headquarters purgatory didn't make things much better.

First of all, we were *airborne*. Those of you who share that tradition know that there is a certain mentality associated with airborne Soldiers and units. We don't put much stock in non- airborne types, or "legs," and don't have much interest in the way leg units do things. Non-airborne units are a lesser breed, not worthy of a paratrooper's attention. The problem was, we were in Europe, where the primary threat was the Russian Bear and his zillions of tanks massed along the border. Our airborne mission had nothing to do with the bigger picture. We were also expected to do our part in keeping the Red Hordes from overrunning Europe in the event Armageddon was initiated. To this end, we were equipped with armored personnel carriers. We were that strangest of all American hybrid military units; we were airborne/ *mechanized*, the only such unit in the entire United States Army.

To this day, I get cold shivers whenever I think about it. First, there wasn't a single Soldier in that brigade with any mechanized infantry experience; all the troops, NCOs and officers had spent their careers jumping out of airplanes. We didn't know (nor did we want to know) diddly-squat about tracked vehicles: how to maintain them, how to fight them, or in some cases, how to drive them. We didn't like being mechanized, as it got in the way of what we considered our only role: to jump out of airplanes, of course. Death from Above, and all of that rah-rah.

But the tracks couldn't be dropped. To make matters worse, all our senior leaders were legs: the division commander, the corps commander, the USAREUR commander. In fact several of them were the worst kind of legs; they were, if you can possibly imagine such foolishness, actually *anti-airborne*. They expected us to be as fully qualified in our mechanized infantry role as all the professional tread-head units blighting the German countryside. It was a situation guaranteed to make nobody happy.

This bad situation was made considerably worse by the fact that airborne-qualified track vehicle mechanics were unheard of in 1969. After all, why would an airborne unit need tank and armored personnel carrier fixers? As a result of this shortcoming, and the fact that we were at the bottom of the priority list for spare parts (the logic being that an airborne unit didn't need track parts), by the time I arrived on the scene, most of the vehicles in the brigade didn't work, and the few that did were held together by gum and bailing wire.

Case in point: on the way to the field one day, my command track (an M114, quite possibly the greatest white elephant the Army ever spent a trillion dollars on) decided it wasn't going to make the trip. Seems the transmission linkage fell apart. The closest thing we had to a repair part was the insert to an army-issue ball point pen, which my driver deftly used to connect the whole thing back together. When I left the unit months later, that was still the only thing holding it together. I vividly remember a parade we had for a visiting dignitary. It was decided that we would line up all the tracked vehicles on the parade ground, and then have the troops form up in front of them. The pass in review would be on foot since more than half of the vehicles had to be towed out to the parade ground. Someone started the rumor that the VIP, some 3-star general, wanted to see the tracks pass in review too. The brigade commander very nearly had a nervous breakdown, but, alas, it didn't come to pass. I've always harbored a secret wish that the rumor was true; maybe things would have gotten better if someone had known just how bad things really were.

Having to live with armored vehicles wasn't our only problem. The Army in Germany in 1969 was really an Army in name only. Units, especially ours, were pitifully under strength. My rifle company had an authorized strength of 168 troops and 6 officers. The largest number of folks I ever had on my morning report was 111. My average daily present-for-training strength, after accounting for all the sick, lame, lazy, AWOL and deserters (of which there were lots), and special duty types, was 40. Not much with which to stop the Warsaw Pact. Despite this, each rifle company was expected every year to have nine squads qualified on the Mechanized Infantry Squad Proficiency Test (MISPC). Every company was expected to pass its ATT (Annual Training Test) and ORTT (Operational Readiness Training Test). And every company had damn well better pass the annual IG and Command Maintenance Inspections.

Needless to say, this made for creative training and reporting. I regret to say that integrity had a rather muddy definition in those days. USAREUR demanded nine qualified squads in the MISPC. No problem. Find the one Armored Personnel Carrier (APC) in each company that could run the course nine times without breaking. Put all ten of your available riflemen in the back of it, and run them through the course nine times, each time with a different squad leader. That's the way we survived in the turbulent environment of those dark days.

Surviving the IG inspection also took some ingenuity; however, I did have one leg up. This was back in the days when every company had its own complete field mess. For some reason never clear to me (you learned never to ask too many questions) my company had a complete extra set: brand, spanking new and not on anybody's books. The battalion always managed to ensure that my mess section was the first inspected. As soon as the IG weenies were through marveling at how meticulously clean my cooks kept their equipment, I would invite them to my office for some good army java. No sooner were they out of sight than a squad of troops from the next company to be inspected would descend on my supply room, quickly scarf up my mess gear, and hie themselves off to their own barracks. And so it went, company by company. Whatever its failings may have been, the 2nd Battalion, 509th Parachute Infantry Regiment always got kudos for the best mess teams in the division.

Even the things we liked to do were fraught with great peril. Our greatest passion, jumping, was always an event to remember. Mainz is located in west-central Germany, in wine country, and our drop zones were invariably either a farmer's beet fields or potato fields, bordered by vineyards, where the vines were supported by tall concrete posts. By some freak of nature, that part of Germany is always windy—usually too windy to make a regulation jump (the book says you don't jump if the winds exceed 13 knots). But we managed. I vividly remember one jump—it wasn't much different than all the others, really—when the smoke marking the drop zone was blown away before it could be seen. During the jump I was blown away from the drop zone, across a very menacing vineyard to another beat field, and then dragged through 300 meters of the biggest damn sugar beets I'd ever seen before I could get out of my parachute. After dusting myself off, removing a large sugar beet from my trousers, and expending my entire repertoire of expletives (a lengthy list), I set off in search of the Drop Zone Safety Officer, who happened to be one of my own lieutenants. It was a difficult hike, as I had to walk into the wind, which must have been at least 25 knots. I found him huddled in the bottom of a ditch, holding the wind gage in one hand and shielding it from the wind with his other; that was the only way he could get the reading down to 13 knots. "Hi, sir! Enjoy the jump?" It's amazing what we would do for $110.00 a month in those days.

I remember another drop, this one in Norway, on a NATO exercise. An early winter blizzard was chasing us. We infantry troops jumped in OK, but the entire artillery battalion heavy drop was blown wide of the drop zone and landed in a huge fir forest. You haven't really lived until you've had to run through the woods dodging falling artillery pieces.

We had a lot of very quirky characters in the 1st Airborne Brigade back then, both officers and enlisted. This was also the time when drug abuse within the Army was at its worst, and we certainly had our share of problems. I remember Halloween night of 1969 with particular fondness. My wife and I were at the Halloween costume party at the officers' club—we had just been announced as the winners of the best costume contest—when I got word from the MPs that they suspected a drug party was going on in my company's barracks and were going to conduct a raid; would I mind accompanying them? Imagine the surprise on the troops' faces when The Old Man showed up in Halloween costume for an unannounced shakedown inspection. The haul was bountiful, and I suspect most of the miscreants involved never knew who the masked man was.

Just showing up for work could be treacherous. This was back in the days of cash paydays, when the company commander or one of his officers had to pick up cash—up to $50,000—from the division finance clerk and pay each Soldier as he came through the pay line, after which the first sergeant would usually collect most of it for contributions to various causes. This meant that the pay officer had to be armed and escorted.

One payday in particular remains indelibly imprinted in my mind. The 2nd Battalion Headquarters Company pay officer, whom we shall call Lieutenant Ripcord (since he's a USMA graduate and may know people who read this drivel), had finished his duties and was reporting to his company commander. Lieutenant Ripcord decided to clear his .45 pistol in the Old Man's office. It never occurred to him to remove the clip from the weapon. Standing in front of the CO's desk, he pulled back the slide, released it, and pulled the trigger. Boom! The round went through the desk and into the floor between his company commander's feet. This so surprised Lieutenant Ripcord that he spun around and squeezed off another shot, which went through the wall. At this point Ripcord, convinced that the pistol was cursed, threw the thing out into the hall, where upon landing, it discharged another round down the length of the hall, just as the battalion commander stuck his head out of his office to find out who was attacking. Subsequently, the bullet that went between the company commander's feet was dug out of the floor and was named the Lieutenant Ripcord Award, in honor of the hapless marksman. Each month, at the battalion officer's call at the club, it was presented to the officer who had committed the most grievous error of professional judgment during the month, and he was expected to have that bullet on his person 24 hours a day. I've often wondered what happened to that trophy. Perhaps it's on display in the regimental museum.

But what does any of this have to do with bulldozed cars in New York? you ask. Well, one night one of my Soldiers, who had significantly altered the chemical state of his brain with LSD, decided to take a little trip. He broke into the battalion motor park, confiscated the M578 tracked vehicle retriever—think of it as a fully tracked tow truck for tanks, if you will—drove it through the back wall of the caserne, and went on a tour of our neighboring village of Gonsenheim. This town had been settled by the Romans in 80 BC, and the streets had never been widened. Our young hero flattened twelve German cars, took out the corner of a thousand-year-old house, in which two families had tucked themselves in for the night, and drove to the Astoria club (better known by the troopers as the Hillbilly Bar), where he alighted from his chariot and went inside to get a six pack of Mainzer Bier for the next leg of his journey to—where else?—California.

And so it went, day after day, week after week. Finally, after ten months I couldn't take it any longer. I had to get back to a real army somewhere. One morning when I reported to work, I told my company clerk to type me up a request for an immediate transfer to Vietnam, which I then hand-carried as far up the chain of command as I possibly could. Two months later, almost exactly one year after my arrival in Germany, my wife and I boarded the Freedom Bird back to the world, and I was off to another tour in the war, this time as leg rifle company commander. I suspect that there was never a Soldier so happy to be going to combat as I was. After the demons I had spent the past year fighting, the NVA were a welcome relief.

A postscript. There's a lot of truth to the old adage about misery loving company. The peculiar stresses of that particular assignment caused all of the officers and wives in our unit to become very close, and even though the assignment lasted only a year, it produced more lifelong, close friends than every other assignment my wife and I shared over the next twenty-three years. So you see, you really can fall into a bucket of you-know-what and come up smelling like a rose.

Until next time, when we'll take a look at some of the incredible things kids can say with a straight face, keep in step, shine your brass, and **BEAT NAVY**.

13. Life in Government Quarters
March 1995

It is late at night, and the house is finally, mercifully quiet. The furniture is all back in place, the pictures are back on the wall, the pots and pans are back in the cupboards, and for the first time in three months, I can actually walk from room to room without tripping or climbing over something or having to take a detour outside and come in a different door. And I can finally find things when I need them, or at least those things that my kids don't find first. Have we moved? you ask. No, we've just endured a little home maintenance, one of the real joys of being a homeowner.

It all started out innocently enough. A few months back my ever-vigilant wife detected that we had a minor bit of water damage in the floor by the back door. This required replacing a small section of the flooring and the linoleum in the kitchen. By any measure, a small job requiring no more than two days. Even the insurance adjuster said so. A few hundred bucks, a day out of the kitchen, and everything will be as good as new.

Armed with the knowledge that I would be only slightly inconvenienced by this problem, and assured that my insurance company would pay the lion's share of the bill, I set out to get the job done so I could move on to more important things, like planning my next fishing trip. The first step, of course, was to find a contractor to do the job. This is where a lifetime in the Army began to take its toll. Being the well-trained and indoctrinated Soldier that I am, I set out to find the lowest bidder. That is, after all, the way the Army always does things. I forgot that the first of Murphy's Laws of Combat—Never forget that your rifle was made by the lowest bidder—was meant as a warning, not an approved solution, and that things like the Sgt. York anti-aircraft gun, the M-114 APC, and the Gama Goat were all made by the lowest bidder. Obviously, I slept through most of cow year economics classes, but that can be explained by the fact that Econ was always right after lunch, and we all know the short-term effects of chili con carne over rice and brownies combined with a metronome lecture on economic theory. Major Z-attack.

My search didn't take long, and I settled on a jovial chap named Melvin who talked a great line, promised the job would be done quickly, correctly, and most important of all, cheaply. That was three months and seven thousand eight hundred dollars ago. Perhaps you've seen the movie "The Money Pit," about the house that was in a perpetual state of remodeling/repair. That was small potatoes compared to what has gone on around here. I won't bore you with all the details because that's not what this little essay is all about, but suffice it to say that Melvin and his crew, Bing and Bong, who for a while became part of our extended family, were neither quick (physically or mentally) nor cheap, nor did they have the slightest idea of what they were doing. Because of their efforts, we now have new floors in two rooms, new walls in three rooms, new carpets in four rooms, new linoleum in three rooms, a new ceiling in the kitchen and family room, a permanent squeak in the kitchen floor that sounds like a Siamese cat in heat when you step on it, a flood under the back door (the original source of the problem) every time it rains, and a whole slew of new best friends: the wall guys, the floor guys, the carpet guys, the linoleum guys, the ceiling guys, the painters, the adjusters, and on and on, all of whom have keys to the house so they can come and go as they please (not as WE please mind you—we want this job to end some day). We also now have a running gun battle between the insurance company, the adjustor, Melvin, the new contractors (we fired Melvin after the kitchen flood, a long story), and a possible lawsuit. All because I slept through the cow Econ lecture on the perils of the lowest bid.

By now you're asking yourselves, Where the hell is he going with this little sob story? What's the teaching point here? Well, it's very simple, and it's aimed at all you young folks, and some of you old farts on active duty. You don't realize what a good deal living in government quarters is. I don't care what they say: home ownership is a pain in the ass. If said home has a pool, the pain is increased exponentially. Avoid this problem for as long as humanly possible. When your wife begins to whine about the cramped quarters with the weird size windows that require specially made curtains and puke green walls that clash with everything you own, just send her home to Momma for a while until she regains her composure. No matter how bad they are—and *believe*

13. Life in Government Quarters

me, I know how bad some of them can be (I did live in Corregidor Courts at Fort Bragg and Custer Terrace at Fort Benning and for three years in a New Brick palace at West Point, after all)—the inconveniences of these places is minor compared to the trauma of owning one.

What could make me speak such heresy? you ask. Simple: living in a set of government quarters is like having a rental car on TDY. If it breaks, it's not YOUR problem. When was the last time you worried about taking your rental car cross-country? You wouldn't do that to your car, would you? Well, when was the last time you worried about how many holes you had to put in the wall of your living room until you got that trophy trout hanging just right? Now if you own the house, your wife is going to raise hell, but if Uncle Sam owns the house, you just fill in all the extra holes with toothpaste and hope the inspector doesn't notice the different shade of green when you move. When the stove or the fridge or the furnace in your house breaks, it requires many hours of anguish, either looking for the lowest bidder to fix it or applying to the World Bank for a loan to replace it. If, on the other hand, it's the government's, you just pick up the phone and call your friendly post engineer and presto, a new widget or gadget or appliance is delivered to your front door with a smile.

Well, maybe not exactly presto. I remember when my wife and I were stationed in Germany back in 1969. We had been in our captain's chalet (green walls with mint toothpaste hole repairs, purple carpets, brown tweed furniture with lots of cigarette burns) about a month, when the oven stopped working. A call to the facilities engineer galvanized them into action. Within a couple of weeks, a squad a German engineers descended on our quarters, rousing my wife from her bed at the unheard of hour of noon, which for her at that young age—Before Kids—was the crack of dawn. After several hours of frenzied work and a great deal of frothy beer, they announced their verdict: the oven does not work, and will have to be replaced. It will be taken care of immediately. About a month later, another squad of sweating Germans, not engineers this time, arrived at the even more distasteful hour of 0800, carrying a brand-new range, which they plopped down in the middle of the kitchen floor and then left. My wife, still clearing the cobwebs from her brain, did manage to ask if they were going to hook it up or take the old one away. "*Nein, Nein, junge Frau*," she was told. "That is not our job. We only deliver." A couple weeks later a third squad—the oven hooker-uppers—showed up (they never call first). At least this time they came at a decent hour—1500—and my wife was hosting the ghetto bridge group. As they were leaving, my wife noticed that we still had two ovens in our kitchen, which was about the size of a linen closet. "Aren't you going to take the old range away?" she asked sweetly. "*Nein, nein, junge Frau*. Not our job. We only hook up new stoves." For the next three months, we had two stoves in our tiny kitchen, as we waited patiently for the squad of broken-stove-taker-away experts to arrive. Finally, one day while I was away at that garden spot of western Europe, Grafenwöhr, my wife called the facilities engineer. By now, she was in a real snit, which as any anyone who knows this angelic creature knows, is not a pleasant thing to experience. It did not help matters that the hapless engineer upon whom she vented her wrath was a mere lieutenant. For the only time in my career, being a captain on an Army installation paid off. By the time my wife had finished with the feckless fellow, he was convinced that if the old stove wasn't out of our quarters before her husband the captain got home from the field, he would be on his way to the Eastern Front, which in those days was in the far, *far* east, in a place called Vietnam. The very next day, an entire platoon of German engineers arrived to remove the offending appliance. They even checked the new one to make sure it was still working properly. Now I ask you: where can you possibly get that kind of service for free, except in government quarters?

One of my favorite government quarters stories has to do with a general officer I worked for at Fort Monroe. The GO quarters at Monroe are old—everything at Monroe is old—and huge, which was the style 150 years ago when they were built (probably as a lieutenant's quarters). Seems the good general was setting up an office on the top floor of his new digs and wanted to run some computer and phone cables up from the basement. Not being a patient fellow—certainly not patient enough for the post engineer to get around to the task (even Great Military Leaders are at the mercy of the post engineer)—he decided to take matters into his own hands. Not being able to find any drills in his tool kit, he used a field expedient—his service automatic. Just blew a hole through the floor where he wanted the cables to go. Now I ask you, would anyone do that to their own house? I don't care what the pundits say, you can't beat living in quarters. Do it for as long as you can, kids. You never know, you might even be able to tell your grandkids some day, "I used to live in Robert E. Lee's house!" Of course, they'll probably ask who the heck he was, but that's a topic for another soap box.

POSTSCRIPT. This little homily would be seriously deficient if I failed to add one brief story about my mother's experience living in government quarters. The primary target audience for this bit of history are the young officer's wives out there for whom military life is a new and bewildering experience. You need to be able to put things in proper perspective.

In 1940, my father was a 1st Lieutenant in the 153d Infantry Regiment, an Arkansas National Guard Regiment. Dad was the Executive Officer of B Company, and owned a small business in the Mississippi River town of Helena. As luck would have it, the 153d Infantry Regiment was one of first National Guard Regiments called into active Federal service prior to our entry into WWII and was deployed overseas, to Alaska in the spring of 1940. Their mission was to help the Corps of Engineers build and secure a string of airfields to support the movement of airplanes to Siberia in the Soviet Union, under provisions of the Lend-Lease Act. Since the regiment was allowed to take their dependents with them, this was my mother's first real exposure to military life. I need to mention here that mom was from a storied and very prominent family whose roots in Helena dated to the 1770s. She was the quintessential genteel Southern Belle, a lady of impeccable upbringing and culture. She was not a lady of the frontier.

Dad's company was assigned to the very remote fishing village of Yakutat, Alaska. Mom and my brother Mark, who was three years old, joined Dad by ship in Yakutat in late 1940, along with other wives and kids from the regiment. As an officer with a family, Dad was authorized a set of living quarters, and what grand accommodations they were: a ten-foot by ten-foot walled tent! In that space—the first set of government quarters my mother and Mark ever lived in—resided Mom and Dad, Mark, and my maternal grandmother (that would be Dad's mother-in-law!), whose husband had died years earlier and always lived with my parents. It should be pointed out that there was no bathroom, only an unheated outhouse, and there was no hot water. Remember, this was in Alaska, where the four seasons of the year are June, July, August and Winter.

The family quarters in Yakutat, Alaska.

The following spring of 1942, after the Japanese attack on Pearl Harbor, all the dependents were evacuated by ship, and Mom, Mark and Granny spent the war back in Helena.

Truth be told, my mother – who would become the greatest Army Wife any Soldier could hope to have – absolutely loved the experience and said many times the year she lived in that tent was among the happiest in her life. I could write an entire essay just based on her stories. Until next time, when we'll examine the mysteries of the universe as explained by a child, stay in step, keep the faith, and **BEAT NAVY**.

14. The English Language, as Spoken in the Army
November 1995

Like many folks who don't have enough money to fill their lives with real excitement and adventure, I must get most of my thrills vicariously, through reading. I read a lot, both for entertainment and enlightenment (although my wife would say that I have yet to gain any of the latter). Because of this, I have long been fascinated with language and how powerful and useful a tool it is. I am also fascinated by how many different ways it can be used and abused.

English is an incredibly rich and comprehensive tongue, far more expressive, I suspect, than most other languages on the planet. It is also a remarkably flexible language; there seems to be no end to the number of permutations, dialects, idioms, accents, and branches. Indeed, the scope of the language is so great that it is often possible to be listening to a conversation or reading something and not even know that it's in English. My teenage sons come immediately to mind, especially when they are communicating with other teenagers. They tell me they are speaking the Mother Tongue, but I'll be darned if I recognize it.

Another example of an unknown, and equally unintelligible form of the language, was developed by Colonel Nichols, head of the Math Department at USMA when I was imprisoned there. He insisted on writing his own textbooks. You knew you were in trouble just from the titles. Instead of calling his textbooks something catchy like "Math Book," or "Calculus for Idiots," he chose to call them "Standard Topic Memorandums," or "STM" for short, and there were thirty-something of them. (Before I became a West Point plebe, I didn't know there was enough BS about math in the world to fill ten books, much less over thirty. I still don't believe there really is.) Now I ask you: just what the hell does "STM" have to do with math? We, the hapless young victims of his obfuscation, simply called them "The Green Death," which was a far more accurate description of what they really were. I don't remember any of the math theory they contained, but I still vividly remember some of the more penetrating language that Colonel Nichols used to explain it, such as "This is a bridge to be crossed rapidly" (translation: 75% of your semester writs will be based on this mumbo-jumbo), and "It is intuitively obvious to the casual observer" ("it" being the previous thirty pages of ancient Egyptian hieroglyphics—the other 25% of your writs would come from this).

The past twenty or so years have been especially harmful to the language, or at least to the uniquely American version of it. This is a result of the 1960s touchy-feely make-everybody-feel-good-about-themselves imperative foisted upon us by the shrinks, the politically correct demands of the '80s and '90s, and perhaps most insidious of all, the women's movement. Janitors are now sanitation engineers, housewives are now domestic engineers, babysitters are child care managers, and God forbid that someone should be labeled stupid or dumb-as-a-rock, no matter how overwhelming the evidence may be. No, today they are intellectually challenged, or in keeping with the new philosophy that everyone is a victim, intellectually deprived. And when was the last time anyone was told to report to the **man** in the red sash. Nope, today it's the person in the red bustle. Pretty soon instead of going to the crapper, you'll have to excuse yourself to go to the body-waste management and treatment facility.

One of the best examples of the flexibility of the English language is how virtually any group of two or more people united in a common endeavor can develop their very own version of it. It's sort of their way of proclaiming to the rest of the world, "We have a special club, and you haven't been voted in. You are not privy to the language." Language, like knowledge, is power, and whoever can master the language of the organization is destined someday to run that organization. This is especially true in the various professions, from journalism to medicine and, especially, to the legal profession. We all know that there is no other group on Earth more capable of turning the blatantly obvious into the absolutely unfathomable quicker than lawyers. If you don't believe that, spend some time trying to understand the fine print on a credit card contract. (However, they are fast being replaced by the people who write instructions for how to use computers and software.)

Of course, the most extreme example of how the English language can be turned into something almost unrecognizable to the uninitiated, and even many of those privy to the dialect, is the military. Ameri-

14. The English Language, as Spoken in the Army

can military English is a mutation of the language that defies rational explanation. Nothing is as it seems. Hundreds of lines of meaningless verbiage are preferred where a simple one-syllable word would suffice. Words and phrases that we all thought we knew and understood absolutely take on entirely new meanings when used by the U.S. Army. Nowhere is this more true than on that most important of documents, the Officer Efficiency Report.

It hasn't always been that way. There was a time, not too terribly long ago, when you could tell it like it was. I remember one day about fifteen years ago when I was rooting through the footlockers in my father's attic and came across his Army records, including all of his OERs, ranging from about 1940 to the early '60s. This was fascinating stuff, indeed. My father is the most professional and solidly competent officer I have ever known and has the reputation to match this assessment. Based on my own experiences of reading and writing OERs in the inflation-plagued era of my career, I naturally expected his to portray nothing short of a God. Whoa, was I surprised. There really was a time in this man's Army when you could ascribe merely human qualities to an individual, and no one would be taken aback. If my father were on active duty today, as good as he was, and got the kind of OERs that people used to write, his career would have ended before it ever started.

Today, a statement on an OER such as "Knowledge of operations exceeds that of his peers" means "a little smarter than dumb-as-a-rock." "Possesses open-ended potential for future service" really means "give this turkey the next assignment as PX officer on Diego Garcia." And "performs this duty better than most officers" really means "there is nothing wrong with this officer that a large caliber, high velocity, soft-nosed bullet, fired from close range into a vital organ wouldn't fix."

As West Pointers we start learning the military way of writing and speaking from the very first day of Beast Barracks. By the time we've graduated, we have at least a working knowledge, if not total fluency, in two distinct forms of the language: military English and real English. As cadets we are completely immersed in this new language; it permeates our lives. We learn how to write the Army way (I got lots of practice here, mostly by writing H-reports trying to avoid huge slugs, always without success), and speak the Army way. Our vocabulary is expanded exponentially with the addition of those purest forms of the military tongue, jargon and acronyms. We learn that all really important sentences have at least one "i.e." in them, such as "For gross lack of judgment, i.e., failing to thus and such ..." I was always intrigued by the new spin the Army could put on certain words. For example, when some miscreant was slugged for some heinous breach of discipline, he was always "awarded" some number of demerits, punishment tours, and months of confinement. Despite the many times I was so honored, I never really came to think of my fate as an award, which I have always associated with winning.

Several years ago, I came across what may be the best example of what happens to our fair language when someone in the military decides to write it in their own terms. I present to you the military version of a famous fairy tale:

HOOD, RED, RIDING, LITTLE

Once upon a time there lived a WAC whose name was Hood, Red, Riding, Little. She was a girl, little, happy. Her duty uniform consisted of the following items:

1. Dress, cotton, shade AG76, FSN 097865432, 1 ea.

2. Cape, red, w/hood, FSN 34768964, 1ea.

Her MOS was 765B1, Handler, food.

One day Hood, Red, Riding, Little received a TWX from her Mother, Grand, Old, who lived off post in 1 ea. Cottage, brick, red, Capehart type, w/chimney, w/o TV. The TWX read as follows: SUBJECT: SITREP. Morning Report should read Duty to sick, confined to quarters, effective 0100 hrs. 22 Aug 95. LD: yes. ADDED: Request you check into separate rations.

Hood, Red, Riding, Little replied with the following 1st endorsement: Basic communication complied with. ETA your location 1600 hours. ADDED UNOFFICIAL: Please bake cookies, ginger, w/nuts, w/o icing.

Hood then signed out in the Orderly Room and departed on TDY carrying the following items:

1. Basket, wicker, picnic, w/o top, 1 ea.

2. Sandwiches, salami, w/pickles and onion, w/o mustard, 4 ea.

While en route she came to 1 ea. forest, thick, primeval. Suddenly, out of a thicket, briar, thick w/o berries, emerged 1 ea. Wolf, bad, big, brown, ugly, w/teeth, large. Wolf said "Halt, who goes there, and what are your last four?"

Hood answered, "Hood, Red, Riding, Little, 9508, and I'm looking for the quarters of my Mother, Grand, Old."

14. The English Language, as Spoken in the Army

"Advance to be recognized," replied the Wolf, bad, big. After determining that Hood, Red, Riding, Little was in proper uniform and had five sets of orders, he instructed: "To reach your objective, proceed down the MSR 1200 meters to Check Point Able. From there, proceed on an azimuth of five eight hundred mils approx. 1700 meters to bldg. T2300."

"How is it you are cognizant of the coordinates of my mother, grand's quarters?" inquired Hood.

"I've pulled guard duty in that AO," replied Wolf, as he hurried to catch the next shuttle bus to Granny's. Upon arrival, Wolf, Bad, Big proceeded to swallow Granny in 1 ea. swallow. Wolf then policed up the area to ensure that nothing of intelligence value was visible and jumped into a bunk, single, steel, donning granny's gown, night, wool, shade AG 988.

Hood entered, showing proper military courtesy. "Good evening, Mother, Grand," she said.

"The fool, stupid, little doesn't know that it is really me, the wolf, bad, big," chuckled the Wolf.

"What big EENT (Eyes, ears, nose, and throat) you have!" exclaimed Hood.

"All the better to maintain maximum efficiency at minimum cost and labor," replied Wolf, and subsequently swallowed Hood, Red, Riding, Little in 1 ea. swallow.

"At this point enter 1 ea. Chopper, Wood, handsome, ranger-qualified, w/axe, double-bladed, sharp. Quickly gathering and processing the EEI, Chopper dispatches Wolf w/1 ea. blow of his axe, sharp. He then takes Wolf to the First Aid station where the Battalion PA performs necessary surgical procedures to extract the Mother, Grand and Hood, Red from the abdominal cavity of aforementioned Wolf. Chopper is written up for ARCOM w/V device; PA is mentioned in dispatches and given a 10-point good spot report. With BAQ, BAS, and VHA, they all live happily ever after. End of statement."

If you are as concerned as I am about the state of the language today, I've got some good news for you: I teach high school now, and I see what today's generation is doing to it. Within just a few years, it will be as dead as Latin, and we can create a new one, pure and unsullied.

Until next time, keep in step, remember to wash behind your ears, and **BEAT NAVY!**

15. Bundle up—It's Wintertime
January 1996

As I left the house to go to work this morning, the unmistakable signs were there: my car and lawn blanketed under half an inch of frost, my breath floating away on the morning breeze in little gossamer clouds, and a gray, leaden sky hanging low in the heavens. Winter has arrived in my corner of southeastern Virginia. I shivered, I shuddered, I was depressed beyond words. The Prozac season has finally arrived, and it's a long time 'til spring and the return of joy. Oh, I know, I know—winter in southeastern Virginia is certainly no match, either in intensity or length, for much of the rest of the country, but it does take its toll on me nonetheless. It's not the cold that I mind—shoot, it really doesn't get very cold here, and I actually prefer cold weather to high heat and humidity. After all, I did thrive through three Alaskan winters. No, it's all the dismal memories that I associate with the season that gets me in my cups so badly.

As with most things in my life, I haven't always felt this way about winter. As a child it was my favorite season; I associated it with fun and frolic. As an Army brat I lived a good deal of my childhood in places where winter meant lots of snow and all the fun things a kid associates with the white stuff. Careening down breakneck hills on the sled or being towed behind the family car by Dad. Snow forts and snowball fights with the kids from the next street. Perhaps best of all, the steaming mugs of hot chocolate with those tiny, little marshmallows floating on top that my mom always had waiting for me whenever I could be coaxed back into the house to thaw my hands and feet by the roaring fire Dad always had built. And, of course, winter also meant Christmas and all the joy kids associate with that holiday, including the annual quest in the forest primeval with my dad to slay the perfect tree. No doubt about it: as a child, winter was a magical time of ice palaces and dancing fairies, of fun and fancy.

But I am no longer a child, and the bloom on the winter rose began to fade for me a long time ago. Plebe year at West Point, to be exact. In that one, trauma-filled, life-altering period of purgatory, winter went from being a time of great adventure and excitement to a seemingly endless dirge of doom and gloom. There is a reason it's called "Gloom Period," you know, and in that first of my winters at West Point, I was to discover why.

My first real indication that the times had changed was plebe Christmas. My class was honored by being given title to the bragging rights of being the last class to have to stay at West Point for plebe Christmas, and therefore, the last class to have a plebe year. What a good deal. When I think of all the mileage I've gotten out of that boast over the years and compare that to the thrill of spending Christmas morning in Grant Hall with several hundred other classmates and their families or Christmas dinner in the cozy confines of the cadet mess, I am left wanting. Quite honestly, it wouldn't have hurt my feelings one bit if the class of '66 had been given the bragging rights, and I could have gone home to family, friends, and Mom's pumpkin pie.

As if plebe Christmas wasn't bad enough, the following January brought two more winter tragedies. First, there was that semi-annual game of you-bet-your-buns we all played known as WGRs, or Written General Reviews. Going into my first plebe math WGRs about 100 tenths "D" and having to rely on my ability to decipher the hieroglyphics in ten volumes of Colonel Nichols's Green Death textbooks in order to survive didn't do much to dispel the gloom in my heart. To make matters worse, the Math Department wasn't content with just one writ. Oh no, it took nine of the bloody things to prove to us just how stupid and unenlightened we really were. You younger grads don't know how good you had it—ah, but there I go, falling back on my "last plebe year" boast again, searching for some measure of solace. Sorry.

Close on the heels of my first experience with WGRs was my first experience with walking the area under arctic conditions. Unfortunately, it was not my last. I personally know of no other experience more capable of wringing every last vestige of passion from even the most ardent winter aficionado than the agony of walking back and forth across Central Area for three hours on a January afternoon. The area—cleared of the previous night's snow fall by the ever-zealous BPs and clanking, hissing steam pipes—reverberated from the blasting of arctic air that rushed down from the North Pole, accelerating to warp speed as it is funneled through the Hudson Valley between Newburgh and West Point, careened across the Plain and slammed its way through the Nininger Sally Port, flash freezing everything in its path. As I recall from Yearling Physics or Cow Fluids or Thermodynamics, or one of those other courses deemed so vital to the education and cultivation of infantry officers, there's a principle named after some dude named Venturi that says something to the effect that a ten knot, 80-degree breeze in Newburgh will reach 100 knots and minus 50 degrees by the time it gets to the area squad in Central Area. You learn very quickly that the thirty pounds of wool in the long overcoat will stop a caliber .50 bullet but won't keep out the cold.

By the time I graduated, my childhood attitude toward winter had taken quite a beating, though I wasn't completely bowed. After all, I did enjoy a few heart-stopping afternoons crashing down Victor Constant ski slope. I must admit that my skiing skills never amounted to much—kind of like rolling a cannon ball off a cliff—and I wasn't really all that interested in the mechanics of the sport, beyond how to stay alive, anyway. No, I looked upon skiing as an opportunity to meet ski bunnies. Going down an ice-covered cliff on a pair of boards at twice the speed of scream was a necessary part of the ritual. I must be completely honest, though: the thrill was definitely in the chase, and not in the prize. My efforts remained remarkably unrewarded. It's interesting that I met my future wife about as far from ski slopes and cold weather as you can get: along the banks of the Panama Canal. There was probably a subliminal message there of sorts, especially in view of the fact that my wife is probably the most ardent non-winter person I have ever known. This became another vital factor in my transition from winter warrior to summer Soldier.

I remember once, after we had been married a couple of years, I decided to take my mate on a skiing holiday to a popular ski resort. Our friends were all very big on the sport, and my memories of my cadet experiences had faded enough to make me think we could have fun on the slopes. At the end of the first day, safely snuggled up to a roaring fire in the lodge, I figured that the one trip my wife had attempted down the Twinkie Hill had cost about $175.00. I realized that for the money I could have gotten a couple of really fine fly rods and a bottle of damn good Scotch. It was becoming increasingly obvious that in the Lowrey house, winter was a season to be endured, not enjoyed.

But I'm getting ahead of myself. I suspect that the fatal cracks in the walls of my childhood ice palace really occurred within six months of

15. Bundle up—It's Wintertime

my graduation. What little toleration I could still muster for winter weather after three winters of walking the area was dashed once and for all by Ranger School. I once heard one of my Vietnam buddies say that the most gut-wrenching sound in life was the thump of a mortar round leaving a tube at three in the morning, when you knew the closest friendlies were 10 kilometers away and didn't have mortars. Your life was about to get real exciting. Well, for me at least, that sound is music to my ears compared to the most dreaded experience in Ranger School. You're on patrol, it's the middle of the night, the temperature is hovering a hair above 10 degrees, and from somewhere up front, you hear the unmistakable sound of people wading through waste-deep ice water. I have had far more nightmares over the past twenty-eight years as a result of nine frigid weeks in Ranger School than I have from two tours as an infantryman in Vietnam. I actually associate Florida with freezing, not sunshine. Some scars never heal.

With the exception of a brief tour of duty in Germany, much of which was spent in the field in the winter, my wife and I managed to spend most of our first ten years in warm weather assignments, which suited us just fine. But in 1978 I came home to the Rock for a three-year stint in the Tactical Department. By then we had become the parents of a young son (a second was born at West Point, and our third was born in Alaska, would you believe, on a night cold enough to freeze your thoughts). When my firstborn was two years old, I decided that, despite the fact that I no longer enjoyed the season, he should be given the same opportunity to experience winter fun and frolic that I had as a child. With the first snowfall, I pulled the old Flexible Flyer sled out of mothballs—the same one I had used as kid—and we headed off for a suitable sledding hill. We mounted the sled and roared off the edge of the precipice, plummeting to the bottom at breakneck speed. When we finally stopped in a cloud of fine white powder, I was full of enthusiasm and excitement, just as I had been as a little boy. "Wow!" I exclaimed, "that was FUN! Do you want to go again?" His pale blue eyes looked up at me solemnly, and after a few moments of reflection, he answered, "Not!" And that was that. So much for reliving the thrills of my childhood through my own son. He was definitely his mother's boy and wanted nothing more to do with this winter stuff.

I have since learned that there is another far more serious reason for my not enjoying winter: the fishing stinks. For three or four months of the year you're left with nothing worthwhile to do on the weekends. Some people are really big on ice fishing, I know, but let's be honest: that's not really fishing. It's a meat hunt. I tried it a few times in Alaska, and I just couldn't get fired up about it. First, you've got to blast a hole through the ice. Then you just stand around shivering, hoping that the ice under your feet stays intact, waiting for some stupid fish to blunder into your hook, hanging in ambush under the ice. I did know a guy who used to drive his motor home out on the ice, drill his hole, drop in his line with a little flag on a stick to tell him if any fish came calling, then went inside to watch TV and drink Irish coffee. He even occasionally came home with fish, but that's not fishing. No, winter is definitely a wasted season.

As I was scraping the ice from my car windshield this morning, contemplating the arrival of the season, I heard the hiss of an electric motor starting up and the whir of a high-speed fan turning, and I suddenly realized what it was that I hated most about winter. For the past eleven years, I have lived in a house whose climate is controlled by a modern engineering marvel called a heat pump. I can't begin to tell you how much I hate heat pumps. I don't know who invented the damn things, but whoever it was must have been a genius at marketing because he was a miserable failure at thermal engineering. Don't get me wrong: heat pumps do pump heat. They are guaranteed to pump every last calorie of heat from your home and fill the house with frost. Despite this, every builder in this part of Virginia puts them in the homes they build. I'm convinced they are in collusion with the local power company, which delights in the six-figure electric bills I generate each month in my futile attempt to heat my castle to the levels my wife and children deem acceptable. I finally had to give my kids a choice: they could have money for college, or they could have a warm house in winter, but not both. They chose heat, which is too bad, because sending all three of them to Harvard would be a hell of a lot cheaper.

For now, all I can do is cast a longing glance at the cabinet where the fishing rods are stored and hope for an early spring. But of course, that just means yard work and pool work and my wife's honey-do list that she spends the whole winter writing. Geez, I wish I was a kid again.

Until next time, friends, when we'll explore the differences between bourbon, rye, sour mash, Irish and Scotch whiskey, keep the faith, and **BEAT NAVY!**

16. Military Awards and Decorations
July 1996

I was driving down the road in some pretty heavy traffic the other day—actually, the traffic was so heavy I wasn't driving at all, but just sitting still, which meant I was really, really bored—when the license plate of the car in front of me caught my eye. Virginia probably allows more different types of vanity and specialty plates than all of the other states in the union combined. Just about any organization with more than two or three people in it can get the state to authorize a special plate design, from schools to veterans' groups to the various and sundry different environmental groups running around. Sometimes it can be a lot of fun to try to figure out some of the not-too-subtle messages contained on them—especially when the car is being driven by some nubile, young, callipygian lass. Unfortunately, this particular car wasn't so blessed; the driver was some crusty old fart about my age and girth. His license plate had a picture of a Purple Heart on it, and the letters "NAM X5," which led me to the conclusion he had been wounded five times in Vietnam. Bad break. Within five minutes, I saw another license plate showing a Bronze Star medal and some cryptic message. This, of course, got me to thinking—a condition my wife has always found deeply disturbing, but I do it occasionally none-the-less, especially when there's nothing else to do. This time the focus of my mental gymnastics was awards—military awards in particular—and how I felt about them.

I don't have anything against awards, per se—medals, ribbons, and the like—in fact, I'm a great supporter of them in principle. They serve a legitimate purpose, when administered properly. They boost morale, they recognize accomplishments above the level deemed ordinary, and they make the uniform look better, at least to a certain extent. I've got a couple of them, and I've been known to wear them on special occasions. Personally, I'm not the kind of guy that feels the need to display them on my license plate, but what the hey—different strokes for different folks.

While I was sitting there in my car wondering about the guy and his five Purple Hearts, I came to realize that, while I generally support the concept of military awards and decorations, I'm not always sure that we—that is, the U.S. Army—have quite gotten the formula right for these things. There are a number of reasons why I feel this way.

First, I'm concerned that we give them out too freely, and that the criteria for receiving some of these baubles is, well, not exactly demanding and is sometimes downright capricious. Quite frankly, if the theory is that they are given to people to recognize accomplishments that exceed the ordinary level of achievement, then I'm afraid that sometimes our definition of *ordinary* gets pretty darn low. Hell, today, by the time Soldiers finish basic training and AIT, they come home with their chest covered with ribbons. We have a worldwide reputation for being rather liberal with our decorations. When I was stationed at West Point back in the late 1970s, one of my jobs was to run the foreign academy exchange program. One summer, we hosted a contingent of cadets from the Royal Military College of Australia. Their trip from Down Under to West Point was via space-available travel on several different RAAF transport planes, took a couple of days, and they had to land in several foreign countries before finally reaching the Sacred Soil. I remember one of the Aussies remarking, "If I was in the American Army, I'd have gotten three medals just for getting here." It wasn't said entirely in jest.

Even some of our more important medals can sometimes be given for rather dubious reasons. The Purple Heart comes to mind. You know, when you think about it, the Purple Heart may be the only medal you can get for being in precisely the wrong place at precisely the wrong time. There's absolutely no skill involved in earning a Purple Heart. Interestingly enough, the back of the medal is inscribed, "For Merit," but that's a throwback to the Revolutionary War, when the original award actually was given for merit, not for wounds. Like the guy with the license plate, I've got a few of those from my fun-filled days in Vietnam. I could have one more but chose not to accept it. I really didn't think the deed deserved such recognition. You be the judge.

One day my rifle platoon was chosen to be the first lift of a battalion combat assault into a landing zone (LZ) deep in bad guy land. I was told to expect a hot LZ—words always guaranteed to tighten the sphincter muscles of even the most hardened of hearts. Fortunately, the only reception committee waiting for us was a gaggle of water buffalo, who were more than a little agitated by all the artillery and aircraft fire that had preceded our arrival in their dining room. For those of you who have never had the pleasure of dealing with a highly PO'd water buffalo, I can only tell you that a hot LZ would have been more fun. In fact, my very first fire-fight in that ill-conceived war was with a herd of water buffalo. I've always felt that I actually did deserve a combat decoration for that affair—but that's another story.

Anyway, once my platoon had cleared the LZ of hostile buffalo and secured it for the next lift of troops, I suddenly had to answer a very urgent call of nature. I'm not sure if it was because I had put too much tabasco and onions on the chili LRPP I'd had for breakfast or if it was a delayed reaction to the excitement of the morning's events, but whatever the reason, I had a very pressing problem. After telling my platoon sergeant what the situation was and pointing out to him where I intended to do my business—something you always made sure to do in Indian country—I moved to a quiet part of the LZ, which was covered in chest-high elephant grass, dropped my drawers, and assumed the squatting position—for about one nanosecond. As luck would have it, I chose for my field latrine the one spot on the entire LZ where there was a very sharp punji stick, probably left over from the French Indo-China War, still poised to strike, and strike it did, right in my sphincter. My platoon sergeant later told me that I was damn lucky the entire platoon didn't gun me down when I launched vertically about ten feet out of the elephant grass, howling like a banshee, momentarily convinced as they were that NVA sappers had managed to infiltrate our meager perimeter. But the real indignity came after the medic had swabbed and bandaged my swollen butt: he wrote me up for a Purple Heart. When I asked him what he was doing, he replied "What the hell, lieutenant, that was a damned hostile punji stick, and it was put there by the bad guys. You've been wounded in action." Only when I threatened to wound him in the same type of action did he tear up the wound tag. I saw little Military Merit associated with that scar.

On the other hand, I've known a few guys that were more than willing to accept awards under rather dubious circumstances. After all, it is a well-known military axiom, voiced in public by a general officer, that in terms of career advancement, it is far more important to receive a medal for doing nothing than to have done something worthy and not received a medal.

Case in point, again from those dark days of Vietnam. I remember when some rear echelon major from the USARV Public Affairs Office was sent to our battalion fire support base to talk to the troops about The War and get some pithy quotes for the folks back home. He wasn't real happy to be there, as the local NVA had been flexing their muscles a lot and things were a little tense for all of us. As luck would have it, after he arrived, the weather got kind of bad, and his helicopter couldn't come get him for a couple of days. He had the foresight to bring a bottle of Scotch with him; however, he was loath to share it. By the second night, he was no longer concerned about where he was; he wasn't concerned about anything. He was, however, out of Scotch. Sometime during the night, some bored NVA mortar squad decided to send a few greeting cards into our perimeter. When the first round hit outside the wire, the good major was jerked into fitful semi-consciousness. When the second round landed, he was galvanized into action. Dashing from his tent for the nearest bunker, the poor man tripped over a tent rope, sending him sprawling, badly scraping a great deal of his skin and rendering him, once again, unconscious. After the fireworks display was over, he was found, carried to the aid station, cleaned up, bandaged, and written up for a Purple Heart. After all, the theory went, had it not been for the mortar attack—clearly a hostile act—he would not have been rushing to the bunker, would not have tripped, and would not have been injured. Thus, his "wounds" were the direct result of hostile fire, and he was duly awarded the medal, and I'm here to tell you, no one has ever worn it more proudly. The fact that he would have tripped over the same rope, with the same result, on the way to the latrine and that no mortar round ever landed within 100 meters of him made no difference. He could now go back to his air-conditioned office at Long Binh a certified, decorated veteran of the field.

I mentioned the sometimes-capricious way we pass out our baubles. I guess the examples of this that disturb me the most are in the awarding of our most precious award, the Medal of Honor. While I do not know of any recipient who didn't richly deserve his medal, I am aware of several folks who didn't get it who should have. In particular, I've always been disturbed by a couple of cases from Vietnam. A number of Soldiers and Marines in that war, as in previous wars, were justly awarded the Medal of Honor posthumously for throwing themselves on enemy hand grenades that had landed amongst a group of Soldiers, invariably resulting in the death of the person doing so. I can't imagine a more selfless act of courage. I know of at least two incidents from Vietnam where Soldiers performed this act—unhesitatingly throwing themselves on enemy grenades to protect their comrades—but the grenades didn't explode, and the brave men who were so willing to sacrifice themselves survived unhurt. In these incidents, the heroes received not the Medal of Honor, but instead were given either the Distinguished Service Cross or the Navy Cross. I have trouble with the logic that says an incredible act of courage—the same act in all cases—is worthy of the MOH if the hero dies as a result of his sacrifice but is only worthy of a lesser decoration if, by the will of providence, he survives his act. You figure that one out.

Another thing that bugs me about the awards policy today is the stingy attitude the Army has about the medals themselves. While our policy makers seem to be willing to grant awards for almost anything these days, when it comes to actually giving someone the medal they've been deemed worthy to receive, that's another story, especially if the award is the second or more of the same decoration.

An example: As most of you know, the Army has a quaint tradition of giving people awards—medals—at the end of a tour of duty. Sort of a "thank you for not screwing things up while you were here" type of arrangement. Usually, a day or two before you cram the family in the car and depart for your next assignment, you're paraded before all your co-workers, somebody reads a citation that recounts all the wonderful things you accomplished while there—that is, you did the job you were being paid to do—and then some Great or Near-Great Military Leader pins a medal on your chest, shakes your hand, and bids you Godspeed. This has happened to me a couple of times, but it's the time at West Point that I most vividly remember.

A couple of days before I was scheduled to leave the Rock for my next assignment in Alaska, my wife and I were sitting out in our front yard with some neighbors and close friends having an impromptu farewell party. I had already quit working, and we were waiting for the packers to arrive to make all our family treasures disappear. In the early afternoon, by which time most of us were pretty limber, a messenger from the Commandant of Cadets arrived to tell me that I was expected in the old man's office at 1500 that afternoon for an awards ceremony in my honor. Nothing like advance notice. The fact that standing up at that point was a real challenge caused me a little concern, as did the fact that all of my uniforms were already packed. Nevertheless, I made it to the Comm's office on time, although my wife and close friends chose to stay behind and secure the support base. After the requisite speeches were made in my behalf, the Commandant of Cadets pinned a medal on my rather wrinkled tunic—upon which I had forgotten to affix any brass other than my rank—shook my hand and bid me adieu. I got the impression he was a bit miffed at not having been invited to the party. As I was leaving his office, the adjutant approached me and said, "Excuse me, sir, we have to have the medal back."

"What are you talking about?" I asked. I figured that maybe the Comm had just remembered that last staff study I'd written the week before, and suddenly decided I wasn't worth a thank-you medal after all.

"Well, sir, you've already received one of these medals from a previous assignment," the adjutant intoned, "and since you've already been given one, this is all you're authorized." He handed me a little, brown envelope, and in it was a tiny bronze oak leaf, about the size of a wood tick. I couldn't believe it. The Army buys and authorizes these medals by the trillions, there is nothing fancy about them, surely they get a large purchase discount (although with our procurement system there is certainly no guarantee of that), but they can only afford one per customer?

When I got back to the party in our front yard, everyone was anxious to see my shiny new medal, so they were somewhat nonplussed when I pulled out my little, brown envelope and showed them the contents. They were incredulous at this miserly display of tackiness. Feeling I had been unjustly slighted, two of my comrades decided to take matters into their own hands.

The following Christmas, a delegation was dispatched to my new post in Fort Richardson, Alaska, with an appropriate award for my service at West Point. With great ceremony and lots of beer, I was presented a bronze oak leaf cluster, mounted on red velvet and enclosed in a beautiful oak frame, with an inscription plate that reads, "West Point Wood Tick." It is, far and away, the decoration of which I am most proud.

Actually, West Point is the source of quite a few ironies involving awards. Where else would you find "awards" that include punishment tours, demerits, and confinement? Puts an interesting twist on the concept of an award in my mind, but then, West Point is also the only place I know of where a guy received both an Article 15 punishment and a Legion of Merit, from the same command on the same day. I'm not making that one up, folks. I was there. It makes a good story, especially since the hero involved was my older brother.

Finally, and I'll admit this is pretty trivial stuff, I think most of our medals and ribbons are pretty ugly and unimaginative. We need to jazz them up a bit—add some precious metal and enamel and maybe some gem-stones here and there, as well, for the more important ones. I mean what the heck, if we're going to make such a big deal out of giving them to everyone, we ought to at least make them look better. Compared to most foreign decorations, a lot of ours look like they came out of a Cracker Jack box. I actually designed one once. That was back in '86, after the Department of Defense decided that all military personnel should be tested for the HIV virus annually. Seeing what was on the horizon, I sat down at my drafting table and designed an HIV Commendation Medal, to be awarded to every service member who passed the test on the first try. Alas, it has not yet been accepted by the Institute of Heraldry, but I suspect that's because I made it a bit too fancy, not because it wasn't for a worthy cause.

OK, I vented my spleen long enough. The more I think about it, the more I think I'll see if I can't get the State of Virginia to give me a license plate with a West Point Wood Tick on it. You folks take care, shine your brass, keep in step, and **BEAT NAVY.**

17. Teaching High School JROTC
September 1996

A few years back, when the editor of *Assembly* asked me if I would be willing to write this column, I confess I was surprised and more than a bit mystified, especially when he indicated he wanted it to be a humorous column. I'm not a very funny guy, and my life bears much more resemblance to a Greek tragedy than a sitcom. Since I have to draw upon my own experiences in order to write, I wasn't at all sure that I could satisfy his needs. Nevertheless, it was a challenge, and I like challenges, so I took up the gauntlet and blundered into the abyss. Since then I have done my best to carve what humor I could out of my daily observations and experiences and package that in a way that will at least make a few folks smile.

I'm not sure if that's going to work this time or not because what I'm going to pass on to you in this rendition of Freed's Foibles just might be so disturbing and frightening to you that you will fail to see any humor in it at all. And that would be understandable. I, on the other hand, have learned to laugh because that's the only way I can keep my sanity these days. You see, I'm a public high school teacher now, and what we're going to explore today is geography and history and civics, as viewed by today's youth. Lean back, pop the top on a longneck—or maybe even something stronger to get you through the rough parts—and come along for the ride. It'll take you places you have never been before, I promise you, and you can decide whether or not there's any humor in this story.

Six years ago, when the Army decided the size and contents of my stomach were far more important than the size and contents of my brain, I retired from active duty. At the time I made this decision I had not a clue what I wanted to do in the afterlife. Well, that's not really true. I knew what I wanted to do, but the reality of three young sons at home who had to be clothed, fed, housed, and possibly even educated clashed with the idea of traveling the world and fly fishing all the great trout waters on the planet. That and the fact that my wife had already made a list of what I would do with the rest of my life—one does not screw with my wife's lists—kind of put things in focus for me. Shortly after I'd told my wife I was retiring, she asked me what I had in mind for a job. "Well, gee, my little kumquat, I don't know just yet. I'm working on it," I replied. At this point she offered some input. It went something like this: "We are not going to move from here. There is a job opening for a Junior ROTC instructor at one of the local high schools. Apply for it tomorrow. Any questions?"

Well, being a high school JROTC instructor was about as high on my list of things to do as getting a root canal on a live tooth without benefit of booze or anesthesia, but I had learned the hard way many, many years ago not to question my wife's decisions, even when those decisions were about me. And, to be honest, the more I investigated the idea, the more it intrigued me. For one thing, I really like to teach, and it just so happened that at the time, I was an instructor and seminar chairman at the Armed Forces Staff College in Norfolk. Teaching high school JROTC would let me continue doing something I really liked. Also, the pay wasn't too bad—it certainly wasn't anything I was going to get rich on, but then, I had been working under that pay scale all my life. And finally, and very importantly, the hours weren't bad. What the hell, I decided, why not? How bad can it be?

Indeed! Well, I got the job, and then I got the answer to that last question. But first, since I suspect many of you may not know just what exactly Junior ROTC is all about, let me fill you in. It is NOT a pre-commissioning course, nor is it a tune up for basic training. It is also not—at least it's not supposed to be—all about boogie drill and break dancing. What it is all about is self-discipline, teamwork, leadership, and citizenship. The curriculum, which does include the obvious things you'd expect to find in an ROTC course, such as drill, map reading, leadership and marksmanship (yes, we do teach the little buggers how to shoot straight—that ought to keep you up at night), also includes such "esoteric" things as American History, the Constitution, Ethics and Morals, and Communications—both oral and written. It's open for kids in ninth through twelfth grades, boys and girls. It's supposed to turn kids into "better Americans." Well, I thought, that's certainly a noble idea; I ought to be able to do that with ease.

To say that my first year was an eye-opening experience would be the understatement of all time. For openers, you must understand that it was the first time I had been in a high school since the day I graduated from one, back when kids were expected to know how to read and write in order to achieve that milestone. Things had changed. Kids had changed. Values had changed—a lot. You would think that I would have known what to expect since I had three kids of my own, but they weren't in high school yet, so I was really caught off guard. Compound that by the fact that I came straight from a teaching assignment where I was dealing with highly motivated, professional adults who were actually interested in what they were doing, to an environment where the most important thing in life was who could wear their trousers the lowest without them falling off, and you have a powerful elixir for culture shock.

My first real shock came during the first week of school. I was talking to the kids—in this case a class of ninth-graders—about the uniforms I would be issuing them the following week. Suddenly a little girl—fourteen years old—popped off with the question, "Can I get a uniform if I'm pregnant?"

I'm proud of myself. I didn't choke, I didn't stammer or scream, I didn't even laugh. I just suggested that if that was the case, she should perhaps take another course. Well, as it turned out, she was indeed pregnant, with her second child, and nobody that I ran into—kids or faculty—thought that was particularly unusual. Yeah, things had changed.

It didn't take me long to discover that, despite the fact these kids were in high school, they didn't know very much, especially about the world they lived in. So, I came up with a bright idea: I started a "Country of the Week" program. Every couple of weeks, on Monday, I would write on the chalkboard the name of a country that was currently in the news. The kids (I still hesitate to refer to them as students, as there is a positive connotation to that word most of them have yet to demonstrate) had one week to write me a two-page essay about that particular country. They were to provide such information as where it is, what language(s) are spoken, why it is in the news, and fill in a few details about the government and culture.

I was really surprised when more than half the kids steadfastly refused to do the assignments, despite the fact that there was a hefty grade attached to them. After six years, I'm still lucky if 50% of a class ever turns a paper in. But my real problems began when I started grading their papers. Being a semi-literate geography and history buff, I naturally started grading their masterpieces not only for content, but also for basic English grammar and spelling. Big, big mistake. None of them—not one—had a prayer of getting a passing grade. I don't know what language these kids had been taught before they got to me, but it sure as hell didn't resemble the English I was weaned on. So I just graded their papers for content—did they answer the mail?—though I did correct all their grammar and spelling mistakes.

But then I took the problem one step further, and this was when I really got a shock. I made copies of the really bad papers—many of which had been turned in by juniors and seniors—and took them to the chairlady of the school English Department. I pointed out to her—very nicely, I might add—that it appeared that a number of my JROTC students were having trouble with English grammar, and perhaps a little remediation might be helpful. This was not a spiteful gesture on my part, I can assure you. Indeed, I naively thought I had actually been hired to teach, and I considered this a part of that process. Her reaction, on the other hand, was not at all what I expected. Rather than being grateful for my interest, she was incensed.

"What do you think you're doing?" she demanded. "What do you Army people know about teaching English?"

A lot of answers ran through my mind, but then I remembered that sage advice my daddy gave me when I was a little boy: never argue with a fool because if you do, a bystander can't tell which is the fool. Needless to say, I've never felt compelled to bond with the members of the English Department on an intellectual level since then.

Nor the Social Studies, History, or Geography Departments. As a result of my "Country of the Week" program, and other geography lessons and projects I have included in my curriculum over the past six years, I have learned from my charges some incredible things about this country and world we live in. I will share some of the better ones with you. Believe it—these are all actual test question answers or report statements provided by my high school students.

- There are 50 states in the country of Virginia.
- The United States of America is in Asia, right next to Australia.
- Mexico is a state.
- So is Canada. But Alaska and Hawaii aren't. Hawaii is actually one of the Japanese home islands.

- Greece is one of the Caribbean islands, right next to Cuba, which just happens to be off the coast of Italy. Got all that?
- Russia is a small country in the mid-east, wedged in between Egypt and Brazil.
- The Rocky Mountains are in Virginia. Pikes Peak is in the state of Pike.
- New Zealand is right next to Old Zealand, and they are both somewhere in eastern Europe.
- There are anywhere from 13 to 70 states, depending on whom I ask.
- The Panama Canal is in Egypt. Panama, on the other hand, is right next to China.
- New York, Ohio, and Minnesota are in the Northern Hemisphere. Virginia, Georgia, and Mississippi are in the Southern Hemisphere. The jury is still out on California.
- Saudi Arabia and the Persian Gulf are just off the coast of Florida.

As fascinating as some of the geography I've learned from these kids is, the history is even better. Some tidbits:

- The Revolutionary War was fought about 30 years ago. We were fighting against the Indians.
- On the other hand, the Civil War was a couple hundred years ago, and we were fighting the British in that one.
- The Declaration of Independence was written in 1945 by Abraham Lincoln.
- World War II ended about a hundred years ago, when we dropped an atomic bomb on Iraq.
- Robert E. Lee was a president of the United States, but Ulysses S. Grant wasn't. He was a famous wrestler. (I'm not making this up, folks.)
- The original 13 colonies belonged to France. England went to war against France in World War I to free the colonies.
- The cotton gin was a great invention because it helped make liquor out of cotton.
- George Washington was the King of England during the Revolutionary War.
- Don't even ask about the 4th of July. In six years of teaching America's teenage sons and daughters, at an average of 115 kids a year,

I have found a total of twenty-two who could tell me why we celebrate that holiday.

I could go on and on with these, but by now you're either crying or laughing too hard to keep reading. So, I'll finish with a comment about citizenship. About halfway through my first year of teaching JROTC, I was teaching a class to a group of juniors and seniors, when, right in the middle of my lecture, a girl blurted out "Colonel, what do we need to know this shit for anyway?!" The "shit" she was referring to was the Bill of Rights.

Are you laughing yet? Remember, this is the future of our country I'm telling you about.

OK, my friends, that's it for this time. It's mid-summer, and the fish are biting. My casting arm is starting to twitch. Until next time, stay in step, be nice to someone you don't know, and **BEAT NAVY.**

18. SIXTY-SEVEN ABSOLUTELY ESSENTIAL WORDS
November 1996

Author's Note: This is only one of my "Goat Poop" essays submitted to Assembly *magazine that the editor refused to publish, deeming it to be too "descriptive" and in poor taste—certainly below the standards of a West Point publication. You be the judge.*

It has been said that the English language is the richest, most powerful language on Earth. I have to assume that statement is based on the size of the language—at last count, there were more than a million accepted, defined words in English—and the fact that English is so incredibly flexible and adaptable. It is not necessarily the prettiest tongue on the planet—I happen to think that Italian has a lock on that distinction, which is probably why I love Italian wines so much. Even if they tasted only half as good as their names sound, they would be marvelous. But I digress.

If English is the richest language, then it is also the most wasted. I am disturbed by the fact that, even as we add thousands of new words to the dictionary each year, most people's vocabulary remains distressingly, boringly stagnant. Indeed, I am convinced that people today actually learn and use far fewer words than they did when I was a kid growing up, and by far and away, the most important word in the vocabulary of anyone under the age of twenty-five today is the word "like." Not as in, "I like you," but as in, "Like, you know, like, that's like really cool. You know what I be saying?"

I find myself asking the question: with all these words in the language that we don't use, why do we keep adding more? Let's start making use of what we've already got. There's some great stuff out there, just waiting to be sprinkled throughout our conversations. With that idea in mind, I decided to scour some of the better dictionaries and come up with a list of old, but really useful, words for everyday life. In my search I discovered a marvelous dictionary: *Mrs. Byrne's Dictionary of Unusual, Obscure, and Preposterous Words*. No one should be without it.

So, in my quest for more picturesque and eloquent speech, I present to you Freed's List of Sixty-Seven Absolutely Essential Words. I promise you, they're all real, and you can all find plenty of opportunities to use them every day. I'll even give you some examples.

anserine *adj.* Stupid. The possible applications for this one are practically limitless.

arfarfnarf *adj.* Very, very drunk. Been there, done that. Don't recommend it.

assification n. An asinine act. The act of making an ass of. My wife claims I'm an expert at this.

Augean *adj.* Utterly filthy. Applies to the bedrooms of most teenagers, and the dialogue of many, if not most, movies these days.

bipennis *n.* Nope, it's not what you think it is (too many *n*'s). It's a double-edged battle-ax. Of course, if it was two of those other things, it might be thought of as a double-edged battle-ax in some circles.

boobocracy *n.* Government run by boobs. This seems to be a particularly relevant and useful term these days. I'm surprised we don't hear it used more often. And I bet you thought it was a government run by women.

borborygmus *n.* The noise made by gas in the bowels; a fart. Wouldn't it sound nicer to ask "Pardon me, but are you responsible for that borborygmus?" instead of "Hey, did you just fart?" (*see* **collywobbles, crepitus,** *and* ***flatulopetic***)

brimborion *n.* Something useless or nonsensical. I need to teach my wife this word. I think I would prefer being called a brimborion to what she usually calls me.

buff-ball *n.* A party where everybody dances naked. Pretty self-explanatory. I'd love to go to one, even though I hate to dance.

cacidrosis *n.* Smelly sweat. Now doesn't this sound better than BO? "Pardon me, but you're suffering from a bad case of cacidrosis. May I recommend Right Guard?"

cacophrenic *adj.* Pertaining to an inferior intellect. As in Marine Corps.

callipygian *adj.* Having shapely buttocks. This is one of the most useful words in the language and one of my absolute favorites. *See also* **dasypygal, onolatry**, *and* **pygophilous**.

cerebropathy *n*. Hypochondria resulting from too much thinking. I suffer from this. None of my kids ever will.

cherubimical *adj*. Drunk. Would you believe there are at least 228 adjectives for this condition? What does that tell you about the importance of booze in our lives? *See also* **nimtopsical**.

clinchpoop *n*. A lout, jerk, clod, boor, slob, boob, fat-head, sap. Pretty self-explanatory.

clinomania *n*. Excessive desire to stay in bed. I suffer from this from Monday through Friday.

colluvial *adj*. Pertaining to a mass of filth, as in a teenager's room or some people's minds.

collywobbles *n*. Pain or looseness in the bowels. Frequently comes after a third bowl of chili or a Mexican dinner from a drug store lunch counter. *See also* **borborygmus, crepitus**, and **flatulopetic**.

compotation *n*. Drinking together. Much better than drinking alone. **Compotator**, a fellow drinker. You get a bunch of these together, and you're bound to end up with an afarfnarf.

crapulous *adj*. Overeating or drinking; coarse. As in "You were utterly crapulous at the wedding reception/reunion/party." This is frequently applied to me. I'll bet you thought it meant something else, though, didn't you?

crepehanger *n*. Nope, this is not a person who hangs crepe-paper. It's a gloomy person, a pessimist. You probably know a few.

crepitus *n*. A fart. "Is that crepitus I smell?" "Are you the responsible for that crepitation?" Sounds better than "Who farted?" doesn't it?

dasypygal *adj*. Having hairy buttocks. Okay in guys, but not a real popular trait in women.

deosculate *v.i*. To kiss affectionately. You know, as in when two people are trying to suck each other's faces off. You see this a lot in the movies and with teenagers.

dysania *n*. Having a hard time waking up in the morning. Most of us suffer from this on any morning we have to get up, as in Monday through Friday. On the other hand, I never suffer from it when I don't have to get up.

ebriection *n*. Mental breakdown from too much boozing. I'm not there yet, but the way things are going it's just a matter of time before I have the mother of all ebriections.

ephemeromorph *n.* Low forms of life that defy animal or vegetable classification (as in politician or Marine).

ergasiophobia *n.* A fear or aversion to work. My children all seem to suffer mightily from this malady. Wonder where they got it from.

ergophile *n.* Someone who loves work. These people need professional help.

eructation *n.* Belching or something produced by belching. Frequently accompanied by crepitation. In Arab countries, considered a compliment to the chef.

excerebrose *adj.* Having no brains. The uses are virtually limitless.

eximious *adj.* Most distinguished; excellent. I really like this word. It's classy. You can apply to people as well as things. Me, for example.

facundity *n.* Eloquence. This is another really useful word. We need more of it in our speech. That's what this little primer's all about. You should strive to be known as a very facund fellow. (This is similar to *fecund*, intellectually productive.)

firkytoodling *n.* This is a wonderful word, but if I tell you what it means, the editor probably won't print it. Use your imagination, or look it up in Mrs. Byrne's dictionary. OK, OK, it's a cool word for foreplay.

flatulopetic *adj.* Pertaining to gas production in the bowels, as in "Goodness, but aren't you a flatulopetic person!" Actually, I prefer the second usage: pretentious, pompous, inflated. We've all known a few flatulopetic folks, haven't we?

fyrdung *n.* An army prepared for battle; a military expedition. I figure that all West Pointers would want to have this word in their vocabulary. I mean, saying, "Stand to it, men, we're off on a fyrdung," sounds so much better than, "Saddle up, maggots, we're going to the field again."

galuptious *adj.* Delightful, excellent, superb, wonderful, terrific. Can be applied to most Australian beer and single malt Scotch and some women. *See also* **eximious**.

grivoiserie *n.* Lewd and lascivious behavior; a lewd act. Unknown to West Point graduates, but a common occurrence at Canoe U.

gyneolatry *n.* Worship of women. A dangerous, but common addiction. Can lead to nothing but heartache.

gynophobia *n.* Fear of women. Another dangerous, but common malady. Hard to determine which is worse, gyneolatry or gynophobia. I suspect a little of each is healthy.

hebetude *n.* Dullness, stupidity, as in, "He suffers from a serious case of hebetude." This is far more polite than saying, "He suffers from a serious case of dumb-ass."

high-pooped *adj.* Fat-assed. That's pretty self explanatory. You've got to love this word. "Yo, there goes old high-poop."

hircine *adj.* Goatlike, especially in smell; lewd. As in the hircine homilies of Goat Poop.

hircismus *n.* Having stinky armpits, usually as a result of too much cacidrosis.

hypomnesia *n.* Impaired memory. I suffer greatly from hypomnesia, especially anything my wife tells me not to forget.

immund *adj.* Filthy, dirty; filthy dirty. *See also* **Augean**.

impavid *adj.* Utterly fearless.

impeccant *adj.* Sinless. This cannot be applied to me. It can be applied to my wife. Just ask her.

infandous *adj.* Too horrible to mention; unspeakably awful. Frequently applies to my sons' behavior.

nescient *adj.* Uneducated, unaware, ignorant, stupid. Describes an awful lot of people we meet every day, doesn't it? *See also* **cacophrenic** and **hebetude**.

nimtopsical *adj.* Drunk. Another of the 228 synonyms for this condition. This isn't all bad. You can get hammered for 228 straight days and call it something different every day. *See also* **cherubimical**.

obtund *v.t.* To dull. Better yet, try **obtunded**, which means slightly more alert than stuporous. This is a great word. I have worked with several people who were in a semi-permanently obtunded state. Been there myself a few times.

ombibulous *noun* Someone who drinks everything. This normally causes one to be more than a little obtunded, not to mention cherubimical and nimtopsical.

onolatry *n.* Ass-worship. No, we're not talking about donkeys. Referring to someone as an onolatarian is a more refined term than saying someone is a tush lover. *See also* **pygophilous**.

pollaver *n.* Fawning behavior; gross flattery. A good synonym for a pusillanimous sycophant.

pornerastic *adj.* Licentious, lascivious, lewd, and horny. Know anybody whose behavior could be described this way? Got any teenage boys? *See also* **grivoiserie** and **rammish**.

proctalgia *n.* A pain in the ass. Put this at the top of your new words list. You should be able to use it at least ten times a day.

pygophilous *adj.* Buttock-loving. Another name for a tush person. *See also* **onolatry**.

quidnunc *n.* One who is curious to know everything that is going on; a gossip. Your class scribe is a quidnunc.

rammish *adj.* 1. Lustful and horny. 2. Rank-smelling or tasting. I suspect there is a logical connection between those two definitions. *See also* **pornerastic**.

rectalgia *noun* A pain in the ass. Ranks right up there with proctalgia. Considering how many pains in the ass we have to deal with every day, it makes sense to have more than one way to describe them. I suppose a real, **double doo-doo** pain in the ass could be called a rectalgic proctalgia.

spurcidical *adj.* Foul-mouthed. A growing phenomenon among young people. They need to read this list.

squabbish *adj.* Thick, fat, and heavy. Better than calling someone lard butt.

steatopygous *adj.* Fat-assed. More refined, but nearly as fun as high-pooped.

supernaculum *n.* A liquor drunk to the last drop; excellent booze. Many single malt Scotches and Irish whiskeys can be so described.

ventricumbent *adj.* Lying face down; prone. This condition usually comes from ombibuling too much supernaculum.

ventripotent *adj.* Fat-bellied; gluttonous. Nothing worse than a ventripotent, anserine, squabbish, steatopygous rectalgia. Had a boss like that once.

Okay, sports fans, there you have it—my list of the sixty-seven best words to color your vocabulary and enliven your speech. Enjoy.

Until next time, take your vitamins, eat your liver, and ***BEAT NAVY***.

Late Postscript.

It has occurred to me that two of my favorite words—words that have huge utility today—have been inadvertently omitted from this list. Here they are:

kakistocracy *n.* Government by the least suitable or competent citizens of a state. A state or society governed by its least suitable or competent citizens. Sound familiar?

Schadenfreude *n.German.* Schadenfreude is the experience of pleasure, joy, or self-satisfaction that comes from learning of or witnessing the troubles, failures, or humiliation of another. Schadenfreude is a complex emotion where, rather than feeling sympathy, one takes pleasure from watching someone's misfortune. I LOVE this word and revel in its use.

19. Army Efficiency Reports
March 1997

I was reading the *Army Times* recently—I still read that rag religiously, even though I've been retired for six and a half years, so I'll know all the latest scandal and reorganization poop when the powers that be realize they made a huge mistake in not making me a general officer and recall me to active duty—when an article caught my eye. Seems the Army is in the throes once again of redesigning that most beloved of documents, the Officer Efficiency Report. Inflation, that old nemesis of accurate fitness reporting, has reared its ugly head again, making the current report virtually meaningless.

Man, talk about *déjà vu* all over again. I remember hearing about the problem of inflated OERs even while I was cadet. In the twenty-three and a butt years I served on active duty, the Army went through no less than four different OER forms, starting with the 67-5 and ending with the 67-8, all designed and intended to slay the inflation dragon. Some were more successful than others— indeed, the current form, the 67-8, has been in use since 1979, over seventeen years, which has got to be a record. It seems a couple of the OERs that were used when I was a junior officer had a useful life span measured in months, rather than years. When you consider that this one, single piece of paper plays a greater role in determining the quality and length of your career than any other single factor, the fact that virtually no one had any faith in it did not make one's morale soar to new heights of ecstasy.

As I read through the article, which described in considerable detail the heroic efforts being made by a committee of great and near-great military leaders to reinvent the OER and restore confidence in the Army's evaluation system, I began to reflect on my own experiences over the years with efficiency reports. In a fit of nostalgic frenzy, I went to the filing cabinet and pulled out the folder containing all of my old OERs. Yes, I still keep all those old things—even my academic records from all my Army schools are in there. Drives my wife crazy, which may be why I do it.

Reading through these ancient records of my career released a torrent of memories of assignments and people and places from long ago, mostly good, some less so. As I read more and more of the reports, one question began to emerge: why wasn't I promoted to general years ago? The guy described on these pages was "intelligent, hard-working, brilliant, uncompromising, of the highest integrity, energetic, aggressive, dedicated, loyal, courageous," even "dauntless" and "exemplary." What a guy! The more I read, the more impressed I became with myself. Even my very first OER, as a new second lieutenant rifle platoon leader, described me in such glowing terms that the uninitiated would have thought I had been doing this job all my life and was the best there ever was. The next one was the same, as was the next. By the time I was a first lieutenant there was a real pattern emerging: I had no place to go but down! Hell, how could anyone be better than the guy described in these reports, despite the fact that I was all of twenty-three years old and had been involved in this profession for the grand sum of about two years ? And as I continued to read through the history of my professional life it dawned on me—not for the first time, though it's been quite a while since I took this mental voyage—that I never received a bad Officer Efficiency Report.

Or did I? I certainly never received one that *sounded* bad. And therein, my friends, lies the problem. Few OERs written in the past thirty years can be taken at face value. Indeed, there is as much a science involved in reading and interpreting an efficiency report as there is in writing one—maybe even more so. What appears to the casual observer as glowing praise for an individual can actually be the kiss of death for the officer being rated. Why? Inflation, of course. And what causes this terrible problem? Well, it's a combination of factors, I think.

First is the reluctance on the part of many, if not most, people to tell a fellow professional that they're a dud. That can get uncomfortable, so instead of being brutally honest and describing a lousy officer by saying "There's nothing wrong with this officer that a large caliber, high velocity, soft-nosed bullet fired into a vital organ from close range wouldn't take care of," the rater says something like, "Performs this duty better than most officers of his grade and experience." Now, at face value, that doesn't sound so bad. But when you consider that on every other OER he has ever written, the rater says, "This officer performs his duties better than everyone else I've ever known," well, you get the picture.

Second is the fact that in the Army there is a natural tendency to want everything to be perfect, the first time. We don't like to deal with imperfection because that somehow smacks of failure, which is, of course, totally unacceptable. At no time was this problem more perverse than back during the 1970s, when the official mantra of the United States Army was **"Zero Defects."** Man, talk about a stifling environment. This absolute lack of tolerance for anything less than total perfection created a command climate about as positive and encouraging of professional growth and creativity as a chain gang. At the same time, we were in the midst of the huge and traumatic post–Vietnam War draw down, where RIFs at the rate of one or two a year were tearing the heart and soul out of the officer corps. Not much unlike the past few years, just on a somewhat larger scale. In this climate, rated officers became really reluctant to take risks, and rating officers were loath to say anything even remotely negative on someone's OER because that could very well lead to career termination very quickly, and most folks don't want that on their conscience, even in those cases where the officer's career should be terminated.

This is the third cause of the inflation problem. Most professional Soldiers, while recognizing the requirement for maintaining the quality and integrity of the officer corps and understanding that not all folks are really cut out for the profession of arms, nevertheless are reluctant to be the direct instrument of someone's professional devastation. Indeed, the recent *Army Times* article points out the fact that the primary cause of the spiraling inflation that has doomed the current OER to death is the recent, rapid reduction in the size of the military and the fear on the part of rating officers that anything less than a perfect report would doom their subordinates to involuntary separation. The problem is, of course, if everyone's really, really great, then who actually *is* really, really great?

As I looked back through my old OERs, I began to focus on the differences in the various forms that were used throughout my career and how they evolved, beginning with the 67-5. This was a two-page form. On the front page were a couple of fairly large boxes where the rating officer and the endorser (the precursor to today's "senior rater") wrote their narrative descriptions of how they felt the officer being rated performed his or her duties. This was the most important part of the report, hence its being up front. The second page was divided into two sections. The first section, entitled "Personal Qualities," consisted of a list of character traits, such as ambition, initiative, and the like. Here, the rater and endorser gave the officer a numerical score for each of these traits, from 0 (inadequate) to 5 (exemplary). The second section consisted of a pyramid of stick figures, just like the one seen on the current OER, which represented a typical distribution of 100 officers; the rater and endorser had to indicate on this pyramid where the office being rated fell.

The 67-5 form was replaced in 1968 by the 67-6, and there were some interesting changes. First, the narrative sections of the report had been made a whole lot smaller and had been relegated to the bottom of the back page. The list of personal qualities had been expanded to twenty-four attributes and moved to the front page. These were still scored with numbers from 1 (which now was very good) to 5 (which was very bad), and 2 through 4 being somewhere in between those extremes. The little stick figures were gone on this report and were replaced with another list of fourteen qualities, called performance of duty factors, such as "displays professional knowledge of duties," "manages resources effectively," and so on, and these were also scored with a numbering system from 1 (good) to 5 (shoot this guy now). Clearly in 1968 the emphasis was on numerical scoring and not on the written word when it came to evaluating our officers. How frightfully efficient.

This is when—as a second lieutenant—I began to have some serious reservations about our system of rating officers. My real concern dealt with priorities. For example, in that list of "Personal Qualities" that had been given front page status on this form were such attributes as "appearance," "non-duty conduct," "sociability," "tact," and "integrity." This gave me some pause. I had just spent four years at an institution where the importance and value of integrity as an absolute value in our lives had been deeply ingrained in my soul, and now I'm being told that it ranks right up there with sociability on the rating scale, and there are actually varying degrees of integrity that can be acceptable. You tell me—what the hell does a 2, 3, or 4 rating in integrity mean? Does a score of 2 mean "this officer only lies occasionally, and only about small matters"? Or perhaps a 3 meant that you could be trusted three out of five times. Does a score of 1 in sociability—"never picks his nose at parties or pukes in the regimental punch or pinches the colonel's wife's butt"—cancel out a 5 in integrity? Or perhaps a 5 in tact cancels out a 1 in dependability. No one was ever able to adequately explain these mysteries, and fortunately, the only scores I ever got that were less than 1s were the occasional 2s in—can you imagine!—tact.

The form 67-6 survived until 1973, when it was replaced by the 67-7. This one ushered in some significant changes, most notable of which was the almost total abandonment of numbers on the report in favor of written narratives. While there was still a laundry list of professional attributes to be scored, these had been extensively reworded to read "Did this officer …?" or "Does this officer…?" and were scored by indicating yes, no, or needs improvement. The narrative boxes had been expanded a bit. There were still a couple places for numbers, though, the most prominent being the section where both rater and endorser had to indicate when, or if, the officer should be promoted. The highest score was 30, which meant "promote this officer immediately." This was followed by a range of points from 24 to 29, all of which meant "promote this officer ahead of contemporaries," down to a score of 1 or 0, which meant "do not promote this officer." The reality of the report was, as everyone quickly figured out, that a score of 28 or less really meant "shoot this officer immediately."

The 67-7 developed a bad reputation almost as soon as it was put into use, and within about two years, rumors were already flying about the officer corps that a new form was going to be developed that would defeat inflation once and for all. Imbued with an enlarged sense of duty and a desire to help in a very difficult situation, I and several of my colleagues—I was by this time a captain on the staff and faculty of The Infantry School—decided to submit our own proposal for a new OER. After careful study we found an old OER that had been designed by some genius years before but had never been accepted. After much spirited debate, and even more spirits, we resubmitted it up the chain of command for reconsideration. Surprisingly, it never came back down.

Performance Factors	Far Exceeds Job Requirements - 1	Exceeds Job Requirements - 2	Meets Job Requirements - 3	Needs Some Improvement - 4	Does Not Meet Minimum Requirements - 5
Quality	Leaps tall buildings with single bound	Must take running start to leap over tall buildings	Can only leap over short or medium buildings with no spires	Crashes into buildings when trying to jump over them	Cannot recognize buildings at all, much less jump them
Timeliness	Is faster than a speeding bullet	Is as fast as a speeding bullet	Not quite as fast as a speeding bullet	Would you believe a slow bullet?	Wounds self with bullet when attempting to shoot a gun
Stamina	Is stronger than a locomotive	Is stronger than a bull elephant	Is stronger than a bull	Shoots the bull a lot	Smells like a bull
Communication	Talks with God	Talks with the angels	Talks to himself	Argues with himself	Loses those arguments
Initiative	Walks on water consistently	Walks on water in emergencies	Washes with water	Drinks water	Passes water in emergencies

Well, the 67-7 actually did last until 1979, when it was replaced by the current OER, the 67-8. Again, there were marked changes in the form. Even more importance was given to narrative, versus numerical, ratings of an officer's performance and potential. The little stick men from the 67-5 were brought back. The "endorser" was replaced by the "senior rater." But perhaps the most innovative feature of all was the advent of the OER Support Form.

This is a form that each rated officer fills out when assuming a new job, wherein he or she states in part (a) precisely what they believe their significant duties and responsibilities are, and in part (b) what their major performance objectives are in the job. It's kind of like a contract between the rated officer and his or her boss—the one doing the rating. Then, when rating time rolls around, the rated officer fills out the last part of the form, listing all the great things that he or she actually did accomplish during the rating period. This is the tricky part. If you do this part right, you will make sure that you state in very convincing terms that you actually did accomplish all those objectives you said you were going to do when you filled out part (b), and that you accomplished them at a higher standard than ever dreamed possible. Your boss must believe this, of course, because in theory, he's going to use this poop to help him write your efficiency report.

Well, a few years before I retired—about the same time I realized my name had been scratched from the short list for future Great Military Leaders—I decided to have some fun with this form, while at the same time testing my boss's sense of humor. At the time I was a staff officer, one of many, many on a Major Command Staff (moment of awed silence here), and my rater was a Major General. I figured, what the heck, every now and then we need to stop taking ourselves so damn seriously, right? So this is what I turned in on my OER Support Form:

a. State your significant duties and responsibilities. "If one defines significant as 'having or likely to have impact,' then I have no significant duties. If one defines responsibility as 'the state or fact of being answerable or accountable for something within one's power to control,' then I have no responsibilities. This block is intentionally left blank because I have no significant duties or responsibilities to date."

b. Indicate your major performance objectives. "Performance implies 'the act of going through or executing in the proper or established manner.' Objective is defined as 'something that one's efforts are intended to attain or accomplish.' Major means 'requiring great attention or concern.' It seems that this block is asking me to list those things requiring great attention or concern, the act of going through or executing in the proper or established manner being something that one's efforts are intended to attain or accomplish.

I would like to remain on active duty a little longer."

c. List your significant contributions. "The opportunity for significant contributions is directly proportional to the responsibility for significant duties. Said another way:

A = All Balls B = Glass Balls
1. If A, then B.

2. If not A, then B.

I tried to keep these equations in mind at all times."
Unfortunately, my boss did not have a sense of humor. Not even a little bit. What was worse, he was so unfamiliar with what all the zillions of minions on his staff were doing, he didn't even realize that this was a very tongue-in-cheek effort at levity. Instead, he called me into his office for a briefing on the "glass balls project." And you know what: I got an absolutely glowing OER from that guy that made it very clear to me that my meteoric rise to the top of the heap had flamed out at half-colonel. I wasn't even going to get be a full one, much less a general officer.

Apparently, there was a time in our Army's history when inflation or doing someone's psyche permanent damage wasn't much of a concern. Most of you I'm sure are familiar with the officer efficiency ratings from 1813 that have been published for years in *The Officer's Guide*. There are some real gems in that report. My favorite is the one where Colonel Cass, the Regimental commander, describes one captain as "a knave despised by all," though the phrase "low, vulgar men" also has a certain ring to it. The most unequivocal statement, reserved for some hapless ensign, states that he is "the very dregs of the earth. Unfit for anything under heaven. God only knows how the poor thing got an appointment." That's telling it like it is. The closest I've heard of something that descriptive being used during my era was an officer described as "having all the qualities of a dog, except for loyalty."

Apparently our British cousins aren't quite as reluctant as we are to slam the hammer down on officer efficiency reports. The Associated Press recently ran an article that appeared in several publications and on the Internet, wherein they quoted actual extracts from British Royal Navy and Marine fitness reports. For those of you who may not have seen them, and may be getting ready to write someone's OER, here are a few of the better ones.

"I would not breed from this officer."

"His men would follow him anywhere, but only out of curiosity."

"This young lady has delusions of adequacy."

"Since my last report he has reached rock bottom and has started to dig."

"She sets low personal standards, and then consistently fails to achieve them."

"This officer should go far, and the sooner he starts, the better."

"This man is depriving a village somewhere of an idiot."

OK, sports fans, that's it for this time around. It'll be spring soon. What fun that always means. Stand up straight, suck your gut in; if you can see them, shine your shoes, and **BEAT NAVY!**

20. MY GERMAN ADVENTURE, PART II – A TRIP TO GRAFENWÖHR
May 1997

It seems there's been an awful lot of press lately about the most recent decline and fall of the U.S. Army. Sex scandals, lowering of recruitment standards, lack of training time, over-extended and over-committed units, massive force-outs of qualified Soldiers as the Army continues to try to do more with less—all in all, not a pretty picture. There have even been comparisons to the "hollow Army" of the 1970s. Now that's a scary scenario.

Well folks, take it from someone who was in that "hollow Army" and survived to tell the tale, today's Army is nowhere near that crisis point. Pop the top on a longneck, settle back in your BarcaLounger, and let me tell you a tale of that Army. It's a true story, a story of a brigade FTX to that garden spot of Germany, Grafenwöhr, in the winter of 1970. It's a tale that shows just how fouled up an army can get when the times are really bad and should help you understand just how far from being that bad our Army of today is.

In the winter of 1969–70, I was a young company commander in the 1st Airborne Brigade, stationed in Mainz, Germany. I'd just spent a year as a combat infantryman in Vietnam and was looking forward to the opportunity to relax and enjoy soldiering and my family in a somewhat more stress-free environment. Boy, was I in for a surprise. By the end of the 1960s the Army in Europe was really beginning to suffer from the effects of the Vietnam War, still raging out of control on the other side of the world, consuming all that was good and noble about our Army in its seemingly unquenchable flames. We lacked for good Soldiers, equipment, and yes, to a certain extent, sound leadership. Times were tough.

The 1st Airborne Brigade was a strange outfit, as it was actually a hybrid—some would say an oxymoron—unit, in that it was airborne *mechanized*. It was the 1st Brigade of the 8th Infantry Division. We thought we were airborne. Most other folks up the chain of command thought we were mechanized. A lot of folks didn't know just what the hell we were. Some of those folks were in the 1st Brigade.

Like all tactical units in USAREUR, we had a requirement to conduct various tactical training tests each year, down to company and battalion level. These tests involved going to one of the major field training locations in Germany for up to a month at a time. Competition for dates at these training areas was intense, as there were a lot of units in Germany back then, and there was only so much space in which to train. As luck would have it, the 1st Airborne Brigade got a month of training time scheduled at Grafenwöhr for January 1970. Luck was not good; nobody in USAREUR wanted to go to Graf in January. The weather was always horrible, training was difficult at best, and life was generally miserable. As I found out, this was an omen of things to come.

As soon as the brigade commander and staff received word from on high that we were going to the Garden of Eden for a whole month, planning for the exercise began in earnest. It was decided that we would cram the entire year's-worth of Company & Battalion Operational Training Tests (ORTTs), every squad's Mechanized Infantry Squad Proficiency Test, and a few combined arms live fire exercises for good measure, into that month. We were going to work seven days a week, every week, for the entire month. After all, we were *Airborne!* and up to the challenge, and had been honored (this was brigade command-think) by Seventh Army by being chosen to go to Grafenwöhr. It was our opportunity to shine—not to mention get a lot of majors, LTCs and the Old Man himself mentioned in dispatches. Nobody above company level seemed particularly concerned that every company was at only 50% strength, we had about one-fifth of the mechanics we were authorized, and we hadn't been to the field in about four months.

The first decision made by the brigade commander was that we would arrive at Graf in style—we would jump in, in a brigade mass tactical drop. After all, it was necessary to make the USAREUR weenies realize that we were, first and foremost, an airborne unit, despite what their own order of battle charts said. When the brigade commander was informed that there were no suitable drop zones for such an exercise anywhere near Graf, he dismissed that minor nuisance with a wave of his hand and instructions to the S-3 Air, a second lieutenant, to find one. When also told that the brigade had not conducted a large scale airborne operation during the month of January for five years because the weather in Germany in January usually precluded such an operation, he dismissed this minor nuisance with another wave and some rather vague instructions to the S-2, another second lieutenant, to make sure the weather on the day of our scheduled jump would be good. In other words, we will jump, whatever the weather. Hooo-ahhhh.

Within a week the S-3 air reported to the Old Man that he had found a suitable drop zone, although he was concerned that it was a little on the small side. What he didn't seem concerned about was the fact that it extended along the top of a ridge that was covered in very big pine trees. The brigade commander gave it his blessing. I can't remember what the official name given to this drop zone was, but within days, those of us down in the companies that had seen the map were calling it DZ Death. This was shaping up to be a very interesting FTX, and we hadn't even left the caserne yet.

The date of our arrival/jump to destiny was set at 6 January. On 2 January, we had to put all our tracked vehicles on a train for movement to Graf. This is when things really started to get exciting. As an airborne unit, we didn't use our tracks very often—only when some general told us to. About a third of the brigade's tracks broke down between the caserne and the rail head, including my own company command track, an M-114, one of the U.S. Army's greatest white elephants. This managed to tie up a lot of traffic in the little town of Mainz-Gonsenheim, which made for a lot of unhappy Germans, but by the end of the day, all the vehicles had been loaded, and the train was off. No one was real sure how the folks at the other end were going to get all those broken-down tracks off the train, but we sent a good E-8 along to figure that one out. (There's a very important lesson there.)

On 4 January, the wheeled vehicle convoy departed. For reasons that remain shrouded in mystery, someone had made the decision that this should occur in the middle of the night. The first vehicles began rolling out of the caserne at 2200 hours; at about 2300, with most of the convoy still not gone, it began to snow, but the vehicles kept rolling out of the gates. When I came back to work at 0530 the next morning, in virtual white-out weather conditions, I was surprised to see my company mess truck parked in front of the barracks; I had seen it leave with the convoy the previous night. When I summoned the driver, a young sergeant, and asked why he was still in Mainz and not on the other side of Germany where he belonged, he replied "Sir, the snow was so bad I got separated from the rest of the convoy. When I saw a road sign that said I was in Manheim, I knew I wasn't supposed to be there, and I knew I was lost. I decided the best thing to do was come home." At that moment, that young sergeant was the smartest Soldier in the brigade.

The rest of the convoy drove on through the storm and into USAREUR history. One-fourth of it, when reaching the *Autobahn* intersection near Nuremberg, turned south instead of north and ended up in Munich, where it took the better part of a week to find them all, as many of the troops in those trucks decided to enjoy some Bavarian *gemütlichkeit*. Another fourth of the convoy thundered right past Grafenwöhr and continued to the Czech border, where they were finally stopped and detained, not by the Americans or West Germans—they blew right past them—but the Czechs. It took the State Department several days to sort that one out and convince the Czechs that we really weren't invading. The rest of the convoy actually did make it to Grafenwöhr, but in the driving snow just kept driving round and round on the tank trail that goes all the way around the reservation until they all ran out of gas. I remember my motor sergeant telling me "You know, sir, after the third time around I thought it was starting to look a little familiar, but we could never find an exit." The 1st Airborne Brigade had started to arrive. So much for making an entrance.

On the 6th of January, the day of the big jump, it was still snowing like crazy. This is where the brigade commander's instructions to the S-2 ran up against an unforeseen obstacle: the U.S. Air Force. They didn't really care how tough and determined we hard-nosed mechaparatroopers were; those folks weren't about to be coaxed out of their palaces to fly through a blizzard. So, the drop was delayed for a day. Alas, the following day the weather had not improved; another day's delay, another day of training lost. On the third day, the weather was even worse. At this point, the Air Force canceled the drop altogether; they had other commitments for their planes. We would have to get to Grafenwoer on our own.

Oops. Let's see now. We sent the tracks on a train. We sent the trucks in a convoy. The troops were going to jump, but now we're not going to jump, and at this point, someone realizes that we have no way to get to Paradise. No one has planned for alternate transportation. We have 2,000 troops all dressed up and ready to party and no way to get to the ball. After another day, someone from on high announced that a German train had been found that could take us; it would simply cost the entire training budget for the next year. Try to imagine the consternation on the faces of the German citizens of Mainz that day as they watched 2,000 heavily laden Soldiers board a train in the early morning hours at the main *Bahnhof* and puff off towards the east. For many of the older ones, I'm sure it brought back stark memories of earlier scenes, as the cream of German youth played out the same scenario on their way to the Eastern Front. I'm also convinced that the damn train we were on had taken those same German soldiers on that journey. It was, old, slow, cold, and smelled bad. The only thing missing was a sign saying "40 men or 8 horses" stenciled on each car. I also remember, as we pulled out of the Mainz station, the skies clearing, the sun coming out, and the wind dying down; it was a beautiful day for a jump.

We arrived at Graf in the evening. By now, we'd lost three training days, not to mention a couple of convoys. The following day, one of the rifle companies was scheduled to conduct a live fire combined arms attack, and this event had been designated a USAREUR training highlight, which meant the USAREUR commander, all four stars worth, would be there to watch. Having lost the two days of dry fire rehearsals was a cause of some consternation, but nothing compared to the bombshell that fell at the staff meeting that night.

With all the brigade officers assembled in the briefing tent, the Old Man and his staff carefully reviewed every aspect of the next day's training plan. Despite the lost days, everyone was confident that the exercise would be a success, the honor of the brigade would be upheld, and many people would be favorably mentioned and remembered by the USAREUR Commander. Towards the end of the briefing, the Old Man asked his S-3 a seemingly innocent question: "When will you pick up the training ammunition for tomorrow's exercise?" The S-3 paused for a moment, then turned to the S-4 and asked him the same question. To which the S-4 responded, "I don't know. I thought you had arranged for the training ammunition." There was a moment of confused silence until the reality of the situation penetrated everyone's consciousness: we had an entire brigade of troops in the field for one month, scheduled to do an entire year's worth of training, and the USAREUR Commander Himself was coming to watch, and no one had ever requisitioned one round of ammunition. Not one bullet, not one blank, not one smoke grenade, not one simulator. Nada. The 1st Airborne Brigade was going to be running around the premier training area in Europe for a month saying, "bang, bang." The silence in the room was so complete, I swear I could actually hear a couple of field grade hearts stop beating. And then, pandemonium.

Alas, I don't have room to tell you the rest of the story of that month. As luck would have it, the next morning brought a new blizzard that raged for three days and shut down most training at Grafenwöhr. By the time it ended, the USAREUR Commander had other things to do and couldn't come see us play. Just goes to show that sometimes you can fall into a bucket of bat guano and come up smelling like a, well, if not a rose, at least a dandelion. Also, some enterprising NCOs in the brigade S-4 shop went on an expedition, and miraculously, ammunition started to appear. We officers didn't really know where it had come from, and most of us were smart enough not to ask, but the brigade CO, XO, and S-3 were heard complaining bitterly during that month about the heaters missing from their jeeps.

This was the month that the officers of the 1st Airborne Brigade were banned indefinitely from the Grafenwöhr officers' club, for conduct unbecoming humans. It was also the month that some enterprising young paratrooper managed to steal an entire case of fragmentation hand grenades. This was really a cause for concern since many of the Soldiers in Europe at that time had altered the chemistry of their brains with all manner of evil concoctions. Sure enough, those grenades started going off at the rate of about two a month as soon as we returned to Mainz; fortunately, no one was ever hurt, but it certainly kept the citizens of Mainz on their toes. I can proudly report that I managed to pass my company ORTT, and all my squads qualified as well. Of course, we had to do it in tracks borrowed from some "leg" (non-airborne) unit, and each Soldier only had one magazine of ammunition, but it was still fun.

There was one last fitting fiasco in this operation. A couple of days before the month was up, someone in the S-4 shop realized that another slight oversight in planning had been made. No one had bothered to requisition transportation home. Finally, someone volunteered a corps transportation battalion, and we crammed all the troops into the back of cattle cars and sent them on their merry way. No one complained.

My first act upon returning to Mainz was to put in a request for transfer back to Vietnam. I had never realized until then just what a good deal being in combat could be. So you see, sports fans, today's Army may have some problems, but it's got a long way to go before we reach the panic stage of the 1970s again.

Until next time, suck your gut in, shine your brass, trim those nose hairs, and **BEAT NAVY!**

21. The Sixth Convalescent Center, Vietnam
September 1997

Growing old is a real pain in the butt, and most other body parts, for that matter. Not that I'm old, really, but I have long since vaulted the big five-oh barrier, and my kids, who are all still teenagers (God does have a sick sense of humor), think I'm older than sin. Actually, they think I'm the original sin. What I hate about growing older is the fact that my body seems to be deteriorating at an alarmingly quicker rate than it used to. It's in a state of open rebellion. My knees are worn out, the pain in my back would make Torquemada smile, my stomach is always in an uproar, and my head usually hurts. What I really hate about all this is that most of these problems are self-inflicted, as a result of my lifestyle over the past half century. Too much of one thing, not enough of something else, waaaay too much of this or that. What makes the situation even worse is the fact that many of my medical and physical problems (but none of my mental ones) could be solved, or at least helped, by modern medical science. I've been told I can get new knees, have my back fixed, and my wife has told me countless times that the problems in my gut would disappear if I would put less of certain stuff into it. The problem is, I hate going to the doctor, and the prospect of spending time in a hospital sends shivers up and down my crooked spine.

It hasn't always been this way; after all, as a cadet I wouldn't hesitate to go on sick call if I thought there was a good chance of having a Math or Juice or Nuke writ that morning. I always considered it my lucky day indeed if the doc actually found something wrong with me and sent me home to brown boy defilade or, better yet, admitted me to the hospital for a day or two. This was especially gratifying during plebe year. But that attitude took a dramatic change after a couple of lengthy stays in hospitals as a result of choosing Vietnam for my annual vacations a couple of times. It wasn't fun, even if the last such occasion did get me sent home early from the war. For months, I was poked, prod-

21. The Sixth Convalescent Center, Vietnam

ded, injected, x-rayed, had radioactive junk injected in my veins (and other places), given foul stuff to drink, had even fouler stuff shoved up my rear end—I could write a book on the joys of barium enemas—and generally suffered more indignities at the hands of medics than the Inquisition could dream of. Then, after I was sent back to duty, the Army medical folks lost my medical records not once, not twice, but three times. Every time I got sick we would go through all that torture again. As the number of real doctors in the service began to decline precipitously in the 1970s and 1980s and the number of "contract physicians" with an English language vocabulary limited to "please turn your head and cough" increased dramatically, my faith and patience in medicine really began to suffer.

After a while, I decided that no matter what was wrong with me, it wasn't as bad as the cure would be. I did relent a couple of years ago and reported to the Army hospital at Fort Eustis, Virginia, to have a hernia repaired. Actually, it was a double hernia, and I put it off for years until I reached the point of having to stuff all my lower GI tract back inside several times a day. It was pretty gross. Nevertheless, as soon as the anesthesia wore off, I realized I had made a terrible mistake. The first time I tried to move, it felt like the surgeon, a young West Point grad from the class of '83, had sewed my knee to my chin. The real thrill came when I had to go to the bathroom. I put that chore off as long as possible, but after three days, there just wasn't any more internal storage space left.

By the end of my first week in bed, my wife was looking for a contract hit man. My kids were volunteering for the job. It will be a very long time before I surrender my body to the medical establishment again. Bad back, bad knees, bad gut, bad brain—I can live with those minor inconveniences.

What makes all the foregoing discussion so peculiar is the fact that some of my happiest memories actually come from time spent in a hospital.

It was late October 1968, and I was a young infantry lieutenant in Vietnam. My friends and I were out for a stroll through the enchanted forest one day, when we happened upon a large group of very unpleasant out-of-town visitors from the northern provinces. They were behaving in a very unpleasant way; my friends and I protested their behavior, an argument ensued that quickly became violent, and the next thing I knew, I was in a hospital having a bullet removed from my leg. This was not the happy part.

After a week at 8th Field Hospital in Nha Trang, I was transferred to the 6th Convalescent Center, located right on the beach at Cam Ranh Bay, one of the prettiest beaches on the whole planet. This was the fun part. The 6th CC was the closest thing I can imagine to a real-life version of the movie and TV show *M*A*S*H*, from the antics of the doctors and nurses, to the zany patients. They could have filmed that show at 6th CC. It was almost a happy place, if there was such a thing in Vietnam in 1968. It was a hospital where patients who could be returned to duty within 30 – 60 days were sent to recuperate, rather than evacuating them to Japan or back to the world; that was reserved for the really serious cases. Most of the patients weren't seriously ill or injured, it was on a beautiful beach, it was, we thought, safe, and life was pretty laid back. The only downside was the fact that we all knew that as soon as we were pronounced fit for duty, we would be sent back to whatever meat grinder we had come from before arriving in this paradise. No one was real anxious to get declared fit for duty.

There were several hundred patients of all ranks, including a large group of South Korean Soldiers, but they were kept together in a separate part of the hospital. We officers had our own ward—ward "P"— and when I arrived there were about thirty officers in residence. Most of us were lieutenants, though there were a few captains among us, and we were all young. In typical military fashion, there was an established chain of command on the ward, and the senior officer—at the time, a captain from the Big Red One—was responsible for maintaining good order and discipline among the troops. Right. Here we were, thirty or so young studs, on a temporary holiday from the horrors of war in what amounted to a country club on the most beautiful beach in Southeast Asia, and someone actually thought we would maintain good order and discipline.

In truth, authority, or what passed for authority on ward P, had nothing to do with one's rank. The real pecking order was established by why each individual was there. There were basically three categories of admission which were, in descending order of importance: wounded in action; injuries; and at the bottom of the heap, those folks who were simply sick. Of course, within each category there were various levels of studly-ness—some wounds carried a higher cachet than oth-

21. The Sixth Convalescent Center, Vietnam

ers, as did some diseases. Even injuries were rank ordered. There was one MI lieutenant who had broken a collar bone playing flag football at the huge Long Binh base camp. In the great scheme of things, his injury didn't count for much—certainly not as much as the infantry captain who had gotten rip-roaring drunk after coming back to base camp after thirty-five days in the bush, fell off the roof of the local officers' club, and broke his arm and leg. About half of us were WIA's, and the number of sick and injured were about equal. However, the guy with the most impressive record—and, therefore, was accorded the highest honors—didn't really fit in any of the three categories. He was a Special Forces lieutenant who, while on an ambush patrol, had to answer an urgent call of nature, caused by mixing a wee bit too much Tabasco and hot peppers in his chili LRP ration, and got bit on the ass by a snake when he squatted down in elephant grass to do his business. Gives a whole new depth of meaning to the tactical maxim to always check your rear.

Our daily routine at this early version of Club Med was pretty consistent. Breakfast was served between 0630 and 0900 in the officers' mess (since we were all more or less ambulatory, though a lot of us relied on crutches, there were no breakfasts in bed, as in most hospitals). Sometime between 0900 and noon our doctor, a great hero of medicine from Chicago named Captain Bernie Coniglio, would wander through the ward to check on our progress, but there usually weren't too many folks on the ward; we were either on the beach or in the officers' mess playing bridge, poker, or monopoly. This is the only time in my life I've seen monopoly played with real money. No problem, Bernie knew where to find us; he was a player in most of the games. The higher the stakes, the better. Bernie, God bless him, was not all that anxious to declare his charges fit for duty.

At 1300, as soon as luncheon was finished, the officers' mess hall became the officers' club; that's when the bar was opened, and that's when the healing process got serious. The 6th Convalescent Center Officers' Club had a huge supply of medicinal alcohol on hand, and there were no prescriptions required. This was medical science at its best. The club was closed between the hours of 1730 and 1830, so that supper could be served, but as soon as the last plate had been scraped into the recycle can, the club was reopened. By now we patients were joined by the staff of doctors and nurses, and the games got serious.

On Tuesday nights there was usually a floor show of some sort. There was one group of entertainers from Australia that was very popular—the girls had round eyes—but the band from Thailand was also enthusiastically received.

Alas, my second night at the 6th CC just happened to be a band night, and I got a bit carried away. Literally. After spending the entire afternoon and half the night taking advantage of the officers' club pharmacy, I was more than a little obtunded, and decided to dance—something that I ordinarily hate more than proctoscopic exams and root canals. The fact that I was on crutches and had my leg sewn together seems to have been lost on me at the time. After about five minutes of frenzied activity on the dance floor—I have no idea who or what my partner was—the day's medication caught up with me, and I passed out cold, but not before ripping all the stitches out of my leg. I was carried back to the ward on a stretcher with great ceremony by my ward mates. The following morning, I was informed by Doctor Coniglio that as punishment for my rash behavior, he would not waste any more perfectly good suturing thread on me, but instead would let my wound heal as it was, which would result in a much larger scar. It also meant it would take a lot longer for me to be declared fit for duty.

Sometimes in the mornings we would go out and watch all the Korean troops do their hour of PT. Each morning the entire Korean contingent would fall in on the beach at 0600, face towards Korea, sing their national anthem, and then punish their already wounded bodies, after which they would run laps around the hospital compound. Everyone participated, even those on crutches and hooked up to IV bottles. Very impressive. The closest the U.S. troops got to this type of activity was carrying each other back to their wards from wherever they had been getting medicated.

On some nights, to break the usual routine we would watch a movie at the open-air theater on the beach, but after you've seen the same John Wayne flick seven or eight times, that got kind of old.

One night, though, was special. We had learned from the hospital staff that there was an excellent Air Force Officers' Club at the Air Base several miles from the hospital, a place famous for its pizzas, hamburgers and round-eyed women. Of course, we weren't allowed off the hospital compound, and besides, the Air Force weenies took a dim view of a bunch of uncouth line grunts fouling their cultured digs, but those were simply challenges to be overcome. One particularly enterprising captain of engineers managed to "borrow" one of the hospital's three-quarter-ton trucks, and twenty-three of us wedged ourselves in the back for the forbidden trip. Remember, we were from the generation that invented the sport of stuffing phone booths.

Our only handicap was our uniforms—it was kind of difficult to disguise who we were, wearing blue hospital pajama bottoms, jungle fatigue shirts, and flip-flops. As soon as we arrived, the natives got hostile, and it wasn't long before the situation got a bit rowdy. MPs were summoned, and we beat a hasty retreat in our truck, taking along several war trophies captured from the Air Force bar—some large, wooden paintings of various Air Force unit insignias. Alas, in our zeal to get back to the safety of our hospital—as if nobody could figure out what unit we had escaped from—the captain of engineers ran the truck into a ditch, spilling us all helter-skelter across the terrain and resulting in a couple more broken bones.

The next several days were not pleasant. The hospital commander went a bit loony tunes, courts martial were threatened, one Air Force colonel was said to have threatened an air strike if the missing squadron insignias were not returned, and for a while our little country club resembled a POW camp more than a hospital. But within a week sanity returned and things got back to normal, and the incident was forgotten. After all, by this time it was mid-December, and Christmas was just around the corner.

On 15 December 1968, a remarkable thing happened: every officer on ward P was suddenly diagnosed with an unspecified, but highly dangerous, upper-respiratory infection. Surprisingly, no medications were prescribed, no limitations were placed on our activities, and no one died. And no one was declared fit for duty. And on Christmas Day, we all sat on the sand, in the position of honor right in front of the stage, and watched the Bob Hope show, live and in person. Bob was at his best, Ann Margaret was in her prime, and all the other young, callipygian, nubile lasses in his entourage were visions of loveliness. About halfway through the show the bottom fell out of the sky and it rained like hell, great buckets of water, but nobody cared, and nobody left. It was a far better Christmas than any of us had expected.

The day after Christmas, twenty of us were declared miraculously cured, fit for duty, and discharged back to our units. All good things come to an end.

Two weeks later, I learned that one of my fellow ward P patients, an infantry lieutenant from the 199th Brigade with whom I had shared so much fun and adventure and who had become a good friend, was killed in action on his first day back with his platoon. About a week after that, I learned that the Special Forces snakebite hero was also dead. The interlude on the beach at Cam Ranh Bay suddenly seemed never to have happened. As if to punctuate that idea, in the wee hours of one morning the following April, North Vietnamese sappers came in from the ocean and ran through the hospital, throwing satchel charges in all the wards. Thirteen Soldiers died, and 103 were wounded. Ward P was completely destroyed. I don't think the 6th Convalescent Center ever reopened after that attack.

Maybe I will go on sick call again soon. I hear there's a special on brain transplants out at that big Army hospital in Hawaii. I've got a good friend who's a doc out there, and he specializes in those things. Stay tuned………….

22. Bachelorhood, the Second Time Around
November 1997

A few months ago I decided to acknowledge defeat in my attempt to educate and motivate the teenage sons and daughters of Hampton, Virginia, as a high school JROTC instructor and seek meaningful employment in the civilized world. As luck would have it, the Association of Graduates of the Military Academy was looking for a few folks to add to their cup and flower fund, and I got myself a job back at the Womb. Talk about going from one extreme to the other—from public high school to the Hallowed Halls of Do No Evil, Speak No Evil, and so on. Whoa—culture shock in reverse! It also meant moving from the friendly, warm shores of the beautiful Chesapeake Bay of southeastern Virginia to the frequently frigid and frozen—and not so friendly—Hudson Highlands of New York. This has caused my wife considerable angst—she refused to come with me—and has thus required that I become a geographical bachelor.

I'm over fifty, been married for thirty years, and now, for the first time in my life, I get to live on my own! My own pad, my own rules, my own closet, my own refrigerator! No more smelly cat's box. Uncontested control of the TV remote! Leave the toilet seat up! God, how could it be any better than this?! Well, let's think about that for a bit.

First, you need to remember the Second Universal Law of Life—Knowledge is power. It would also help to remember the First Law—Murphy's Law—and Lowrey's corollary, which says "Murphy is an optimist," but let's reflect on that second law for a minute. Men tend to forget this rule a lot, but I'm here to tell you, sports fans, women never forget it, and they guard their knowledge jealously. This is how women maintain control. I'll give you a perfect example.

Years ago, I was the assistant G-3 of the 7th Infantry Division, and I had a secretary, whom we'll call Louise. She had been occupying the same chair in the same office since before my birth, and she knew everything about my job that could possibly be known. She knew that was the case, and she made sure that I knew it. She was also very careful never to share her knowledge unless it was necessary to prevent some disaster of my making, as a result of my not knowing something, and, therefore, stepping all over myself and inviting the wrath of many general officers. Thus, Louise was always in control.

Wives are the same way. You see, when men get married, there are certain things that they expect their wives to do as part of the marriage covenant—especially in the older, more traditional, Old School Professional Army, less politically correct type of marriages of the pre-1990s. Guys usually rely on the wife to do the shopping, the inside cleaning, the cooking, the washing, and ironing. Husbands, on the other hand, are expected to do manly things with other manly men—kill wild game, chop wood, mow grass (until the sons are old enough for this odious chore), buy and fix the cars, stock the bar, and always make sure the fishing tackle is in tip-top condition. Men tend to believe that those chores the wives traditionally perform are rather basic, mindless necessities that really don't require much skill or forethought. Women, on the other hand, know better, and since women also know the Second Law of Life, they are smart enough not to let their hubbies know what they know. Thus, in any successful marriage, it is the wife who is really in control, without the husband ever realizing it.

Well, I have been playing this bachelor role for a bit more than two months now, and I'm here to tell you, it's been quite a learning experience. So, pop the top on a longneck, and settle in for Freed's primer on bachelorhood. This is dedicated to all you new or wannabe single guys out there about to start life on your own. Pay attention.

Let's start with the most important subject: food and drink. There's a lot more to this than meets the eye—from what to buy (and not to buy) to how to store it, cook it, and dispose of it. First things first: shopping for food.

You're probably used to having your wife do this and don't give it a whole lot of thought unless she foolishly forgot to replenish the nacho cheese dip and corn nuts on her last trip to the commissary. You're used to opening the pantry and the refrigerator and seeing stacks of gaily colored cans, bags and boxes of this and that, and cute, little bottles of stuff with weird names. You don't have a clue what most of this stuff is, but most nights you get a meal put in front of you, and you automatically assume there's a connection between all this stuff on the shelves and what goes into your stomach. So, on your first trip to the commissary as a single guy, you walk down the aisles in a daze, and every time you see something you recognize—or think you recognize—you throw it in your cart. If it's something you know you like—pork and beans, for example—you throw several of them in the cart. Result: a $482.50 bill at the checkout counter and a standing ovation from the store management.

There are some important lessons here. First of all, most of the stuff you just bought has to be cooked, which means you've got to know how to do that. Well, that couldn't be too hard; after all, your wife does it, right? Well, not really in my case, not in the classic sense of gourmet cooking. My wife has a theory that if from the time she has decided what's for dinner to the time it's on the table exceeds twenty minutes, it isn't worth the effort.

But I digress. It hasn't yet occurred to you that you've got to know which ingredients to mix, what spices to use, how much of them to use, what temperatures to set (I have learned that not all things do well on the "thermonuclear" setting), and on and on. Hell, there's a whole language associated with cooking, most of which is gibberish to the average guy: blanch, glaze, pinch, brown, sauté, fold, thicken, simmer—what the hell is the difference between simmer and boil? How do you know when it's just simmering? And how do you "brown" something without blackening it? What in world do you use flour for? I've got a five-pound bag of it because my wife always had a bag of it, but I don't have a clue what to do with it. Bottom line: most of the stuff you just spent your first paycheck on is stuff you're never going to use.

Let me give you a few hints. Spices: you don't need many, and don't waste your money on anything with a name that sounds like a girl or is hard to pronounce; they're probably not even good for you. In truth, a man only needs a few condiments: salt, pepper, sugar, garlic, onion, Tabasco, A.1., Worcestershire sauce (for bloody marys), mustard, and ketchup. That's it. Double up on the garlic.

Second hint: remember, you're only buying for one, and unless you're into binging and purging, you don't need the same quantities that your wife has been buying for five, especially if it's stuff that has to be put in the refrigerator. If you look real hard, you'll see that most of that stuff comes with a little date-stamp on it. It's a good idea to check those every now and then. Take it from me, a quart of milk will *not* last two-and-a-half months, even if you don't open it. Neither will pastrami, and in case you're not sure, it's not supposed to be green.

The biggest waste of all is produce. I never dreamed what lettuce and peppers and celery and mushrooms would turn into if they were ignored for sixty days. Why in the world I bought them is still a mystery, except for the fact that I always saw them in the fridge at home, so I just figured they were supposed to be there. I figured they produced oxygen or had some other useful purpose.

The truth is, you don't need to buy much stuff that requires refrigeration, and it just wastes valuable space that could be keeping beer cold. If you're shopping smart, you won't need more than one shelf in the fridge for food; this should give you enough space for a couple cases of beer and six bottles of white wine. In fact, you could very well subsist on the Irish coffee diet, which is the only diet I know of that provides all four of the essential food groups—caffeine, alcohol, fat, and sugar—in one glass, and save a ton of money and space.

So, what do you buy? Your first purchase should be a microwave oven, and your second should be a gas grill. If it can't be cooked in one of those two places, you don't need it. Go to the frozen food section and buy anything that says "Hungry Man" on the box. You can nuke those suckers in about five minutes, and what you don't eat, you throw away. No cleanup required. Or you can get boxes of frozen hamburger patties and throw them on the grill (the patties, not the boxes).

But there are some cautions to be observed here. First, some things should not be put in the microwave. You do not want to put stuff wrapped in aluminum foil, or in steel cans, in one of those things unless you are really hard up for a sound and light show, which you will get plenty of. Trust me on that one. And some things melt in a microwave. If you can't remember whether or not you had cheese on top of whatever you just nuked, then that bubbly, gooey, yellow stuff you're looking at is probably a plastic top. Also, when cooking those frozen hamburger sliders on the grill, remember, they're about 90% fat, and once they warm up, they drip a lot. Do not get your face close to them unless you need to have your eyebrows and nose hairs trimmed.

Why not use the stove in your palace? you ask. Well, the stovetop itself can be a useful appliance, for boiling soup or frying an egg, but don't ever bother with the oven. First of all, you can't see what's happening in there. Secondly, and far more importantly, ovens must be

22. Bachelorhood, the Second Time Around

cleaned, and that is no fun. Believe me, a self-cleaning oven ... isn't. The only thing an oven is good for is storage space. You can store a whole week's worth of dirty laundry in an average-size oven.

Since I've brought up the subject of cleaning, let's spend of few moments on that topic, although I must admit, my experience level here is considerably less than in the culinary department. I guess the most startling lesson I've learned about house cleaning is that, like ovens, showers and bathtubs aren't self-cleaning. This surprised me because I use my shower at least twice a day, with lots of soap and hot water, much of which gets on the walls, so I figured it would be clean. Imagine my surprise when after the first month I discovered all kinds of black stuff growing all over the place. Guys, you've got to get on top of that stuff in a hurry because it breeds like crazy and is damn tough to kill. Brasso works, but stinks worse than the black stuff. Best solution: paint your bathroom and shower walls black.

Another thing I've discovered that breeds at an alarming rate is dust. Where the hell does all this stuff come from? I keep my castle hermetically sealed, and it is still knee-deep in the stuff. Unfortunately, it's football season, so Saturdays are not available for cleaning, and Sunday is a day of rest. I believe in keeping the Sabbath and do so religiously—on the banks of every trout stream from here to Canada. The rest of the week is work, work, work, so cleaning the house has become a real dilemma. Add to this the fact that my wife wouldn't let me bring her vacuum cleaner with me because she figured I'd break it. After the first month, you could see my footprints all over the place, and after a walk to the fridge and back for a cold one, it took hours for the dust to settle.

A couple weeks ago I decided to have a few friends over one evening and was concerned about the state of affairs in my castle, so I actually ran out and bought a vacuum cleaner. Unfortunately, it required assembly. You know, there's a real trick to getting the stupid bag hooked up right, and if it isn't, well, I'm here to tell you, the results can be pretty ugly. So, I decided I needed a cover story. I mulled several over in my mind. I could tell folks that the dust is a protective covering for my antiques and wine collection, or that I am growing mushrooms as a hobby, or that I am starting a compost pile, or that I really miss Army life and being in the field and have a need to experience outdoor living again, but I finally decided to use my wife's standby: you should have seen it yesterday—this IS clean.

Here's another problem you're probably going to face: after a long, hard day at work you come home one evening, throw open the front door, and your nostrils are suddenly assaulted with a stench that you don't recognize. First place to look is the bathroom, to see if you forgot to flush the toilet before leaving for work that morning. If that's not the problem, then check your kitchen garbage. This is especially true if your castle isn't equipped with a garbage disposal, and you've been chucking all those leftover beans and weenies and spoiled produce into your garbage can. Guys, you need to empty that thing every few weeks.

If the garbage isn't the culprit, then check the dirty clothes you've been storing in the oven. There's a good chance this might be the source of your problem, especially if you happened to slip and fall in the stream on your last fishing trip, and you just threw all those wadded up wet jeans and sweatshirts in with the rest of your dirty clothes. Finally, if you still haven't discovered the source of the smell, I would strongly suggest you change your sheets. I have learned that two months on the same set of sheets is really pushing the envelope and that a clean set will do wonders for your nose and your attitude.

This brings us to the last problem: laundry. This is by far and away the biggest challenge you will be faced with. First, there is the dizzying array of detergents to choose from—liquids, powders, with bleach, without bleach, conditioners, non-conditioners, oily, non-oily (or is that shampoo? I get them mixed up). Then there's the issue of colors. You don't do darks and whites together. Well, I can understand that, but what really gives me brain cramps is what do you do with stuff that's both light and dark? I mean, I've got shirts that are white and red and green and yellow—although that may be an old mustard stain—what pile do they go in? How about light green or yellow? Do they go in the dark or white pile? And then, there's all these choices about cold/cold, hot/cold, hot/hot, warm/hot/cold/, big load, small load, perma-press, cotton, wool, hot dry, cold dry, turbo-charge… WHOA! Back the damn train up! All I want are two buttons: one that says "wash" and one that says "dry."

There are only two solutions to the laundry dilemma, sports fans. One, go home and visit your wife and kids every weekend. But if you're like me and it's an 8-hour drive, that's not really practical. In this case, you've got to find a friend with a wife who has a strong mothering instinct, and when you've managed to get yourself invited to supper one

22. Bachelorhood, the Second Time Around

night, start whining about how much trouble you're having with your laundry. She'll take it from there. It's a good idea to have your laundry in your car when you go over to their house for dinner.

OK, it's time for me to check the Hungry Man inventory to see what's for supper tonight. I miss the good old days of pork and shrapnel LRRPS. Yum.

Stay healthy, stay sane, and **BEAT NAVY!**

23. The Sanctity of Names
May 1998

People who have known me for any length of time know that I carry a lot of emotional baggage. There are very few things I am ambivalent about; rather, I am a man of strong convictions, and there are lots—*lots*—of things I get downright excited about. Call them what you want—pet peeves, pet rocks, mental aberrations, quirks, eccentricities, whatever—I am an easy person to get stirred up, much to the chagrin of my wife and kids. However, I have mellowed a lot with age. But being the father of teenage sons in the nineties has taken its toll on my soul. Having lived through the trials of body piercing, tattoos, songs with lyrics redolent of raw sewage, clothing fashion inspired by Bozo the Clown, and green, spiked hair—and that's just the good stuff—I am not quite as quick to start foaming at the mouth about life's travails as I used to be. Actually, I think after having dealt with my kids for so long and after seven years as a high school teacher, I'm just plumb worn out.

There is, however, still one issue that I get passionate about in a hurry, and that is the issue of names. I think people's names are important. Your name defines you for the rest of humanity. Mention someone's name and your mind is flooded with images that define that person for you: how they look, how they speak, how they act, what they stand for or against, their heritage, their culture—in short, a name tells people who we *are*. Perhaps the ultimate way of dehumanizing someone is to take away their name, as in prison or the Gulag, where you're simply reduced to a number. When we're born, our name is put on our birth certificate, and when we die, it's chiseled on our headstone, for all the world to see and remember us by.

Most of us were named by our parents, who gave considerable thought to what we should be called. The names our parents gave us at birth might evoke memories of dear friends or previous family members, treasured memories in their lives, or noble ideals. Maybe they're chosen simply because they sound cool and evoke pleasant thoughts, or because our parents want our names to be as unique as we each are. Regardless of the names our parents gave us or the reasons they chose them, once ours, they mark us as individuals to the rest of the world. And because of that, I think names are important and should be treated with a bit of reverence. They should be spelled correctly. They should be pronounced properly. They should not be trivialized, for to do so is to trivialize the person they define.

Having said all that, I must now confess that I have been cursed by my name. Don't get me wrong, I don't dislike my name, though as a child, I hated it—lots of kids do—but with maturity I have come to appreciate it. Now I feel there is honor in my name—I'm named after my father, after all, as fine a gentleman and Soldier as ever lived. Nevertheless, there is a curse attached to it. The curse lies in the fact that my given name is different—that's why I hated it as a kid—and all elements of my name are destined to be forever misspelled.

My name is Willis Freed Lowrey, Jr. Yes, that's *Freed*, Fred with two *e*'s in it, and that's the name I go by. Most folks aren't prepared to accept the fact that my name isn't Fred, so that's how they spell it and pronounce it, even when I spell it and pronounce it correctly for them. They just assume I have a strange accent. I can't begin to tell you how many times I have spelled my name, slowly and distinctly, for bureaucrats who were filling out some document that was going to have a profound impact on my life, only to watch them misspell it even as I spoke.

The same is true of my family name. It's *Lowrey*; notice the last three letters—*rey*. There are lots of variants of that name—Lowery, Lowry, Lawrie, to name a few—and invariably, when people spell my name, they'll use one of those other forms, even when I spell it correctly for them and emphasize the spelling. It happens every day. I've actually had people refuse to believe that Lowrey can be spelled that way, until I explain to them that we're the Mississippi branch of the clan and that any other spelling is simply a Yankee aberration. Unfortunately, that just convinces a lot of people—Yankees in particular—that I'm the one misspelling the name.

I don't get off any easier with my first name, either. Though Willis isn't nearly as unusual as Freed, it has a tendency to become Willie, especially in the South, and I've never really wanted to be a Willie. It also has a way of morphing into William— I actually had an eighth-grade teacher who decided that William was what my name was really supposed to be, and that's what he wrote on all my report cards and school records. He then took it to the next logical step and started calling me Bill. As it turned out, this wasn't all bad, because it was in the eighth grade that I started going astray in school, and when all the nasty notes from the teacher started arriving home, complaining about Bill's conduct, my folks didn't have a clue who Bill was and assumed the notes had been mailed to the wrong parents. Alas, I finally went well beyond the boundaries of acceptable human behavior, resulting in a teacher conference with my parents, and any questions about my true identity were resolved once and for all. No matter what that particular rose was called, it still stank.

I went by Freed as a young kid because that's what my parents called me, and I didn't have any say in the matter. Besides, my father always went by Freed. However, by the time I was in the second grade, the fact that my name was so different was starting to haunt me—kids love to have fun at the expense of other kids who have anything different about them. I started getting called lots of things I didn't like—Fritos, Fredola, Furd—and was desperate for a way out of this identification nightmare, though not desperate enough to resort to Willis and the inevitable Willie.

My salvation came in the form of my first Little League Baseball coach. On the first day of practice, he lined us all up and asked what positions we wanted to play. When I boldly announced that I wanted to be a pitcher, he thought for a moment, and replied, "OK, from now on, your name will be 'Peanuts.'" It turns out there was a major league pitcher and coach of some fame that my coach thought highly of named "Peanuts" Lowrey—he even spelled his last name correctly—and he was honoring me by the association. Suddenly, I was the coolest kid on the team, and the name quickly stuck. Even though I was an Army brat and moved a lot, the name became permanent. Every time we moved to a new assignment, there was invariably someone at the new place who had known me before, and so I was always introduced as Peanuts. I loved it—it was different, but it was different in a cool way, and that meant the girls liked it, too, though they tended to modify it into things like *Peanutty*. I didn't mind that as long it was just the girls that did it.

My parents even liked it, especially my mother, though she also turned it into the feminine Peanutty. She was not particularly thrilled, however, when my high school pals reduced it to "Nuts" during my senior year because they believed that moniker to be a more accurate description of me. Ultimately, that's the version that really stuck. To this good day, thirty-five years after graduating from high school, anyone I run into from those days in Fayetteville, NC, automatically refers to me as "Nuts." Sorry, Mom.

When I went to West Point, I was a little concerned about having a cutesy handle like "Peanuts," as it didn't exactly conjure up the warrior image I was so desperate to project. As a plebe I was also scared to death some upperclassman would find out about it—I had seen the degradation suffered by some of my other classmates with names that were easy to have fun with, like the guy whose last name was Spring. I can still see and hear him after meals in the mess hall, as he had to bounce up and down all the way back to the barracks, yelling, "Sir, boing-boing-boing, I am Mister Spring." Nope, none of that for me, please. Problem was, I still wasn't ready to be called Freed, as the memories of the jokes from my childhood were still pretty vivid, and no way was I going to be a Willie.

Sometime around yearling year I decided that my eighth-grade teacher might have had a good idea, and I decided to become a Bill. But then my roommate allowed as how you couldn't really get Bill from Willis, so he called me Billis. This was obviously a no-win situation. Finally, sometime during firstie year I realized that my real name, Freed, actually had a nice ring to it, and it was my father's name, so at long last I decided that that was who I would be the rest of my life: Freed Lowrey. Except, of course, when I went back to Fayetteville, NC, where I will forever and proudly be "Nuts."

There was one small problem. By the time I made this fateful decision, I was already engaged, and my future bride was convinced that she was engaged to some guy named Bill. She wasn't at all sure she wanted to be engaged to some new guy named Freed. By the time I managed to overcome that small hurdle, it was almost graduation time, and I was confronted with the first of what would be a lifelong series of problems associated with my name: in my write up in the yearbook, *The Howitzer*, I was referred to as, yep, you guessed it, Fred.

My father has admitted to me that, as a young child he also occasionally suffered the slings and arrows of ridicule from other kids because of his name, so you might ask yourself why a loving parent would subject their own child to that angst. Well, as a matter of fact, he had nothing to do with it; my father didn't name me. Nor did my mother. In fact, I was named by a total stranger.

When I was born, just after the end of WWII, my father was off being a Soldier at a camp in Texas, where Army divisions returning from the war were being demobilized. When he got the news that my arrival was imminent, he hopped a train for home. I was impatient, though— a trait that has marked me all my life— and reported to the Nurse in the Red Sash in the Helena, Arkansas, hospital before he arrived. Now my parents, by some Machiavellian twist of logic, had assumed that since they already had one son, I would be a girl, and so had never discussed any boy names. When I arrived and it was determined beyond much reasonable doubt that I was not a girl, my mother was at a loss as to what to call me and decided to await my father's return before making that lifelong decision.

Alas, the attending nurse on the ward was not so patient. She was close to the end of her duty shift and wanted to get my birth certificate properly filled out before going off duty—a tribute to bureaucrats everywhere—so she simply inserted my father's name, stuck a "Junior" on the end of it, and that was that. By the time my father arrived the next day, my name was a fait accompli, and my lifetime of having to correct its spelling was preordained. I've never known what my parents actually would have called me had they been given a choice, nor have I ever been told what I would have been called had I been a girl. I guess it really doesn't matter. At least they never resorted to calling me "Junior," or "Bubba." As a child, I was always "Little Freed," and for the past twenty years, my wife has referred to my dad as "Big," though in fact I long, long ago surpassed him in size—but never, ever in stature.

When my wife and I started having children, we gave a great deal of thought to what they should be named and had a long list of boy and girl names selected well in advance. We wanted names that were somewhat unique, that had a nice ring to them, and which couldn't be easily bastardized into something trivial. As Catholics, who are big on covering all the bases, we wanted names that honored the saints. And finally, we wanted names that reflected our heritage, which includes a lot of Irish blood, which probably goes a long way to explaining some of mine, and my sons', aberrant behavior, as well as my fondness for good Irish whiskey. As it turned out, we named our three sons Kyle Christopher, Brendan Patrick, and Colin Kernan. These were names

23. The Sanctity of Names

we were sure they and the rest of the family would be proud of and would like and would not try to camouflage.

Our naive intentions were dashed with the firstborn, Kyle. As a baby, his maternal great-grandmother insisted on calling him Christopher, while we preferred Kyle. When asked why she refused to call him Kyle, she mumbled something about there not being any saints named Kyle, and she wouldn't call him by some pagan name. Finally, in disgust, I told my wife to tell her that Kyle was Gaelic for "Gift from God," and that did the trick. From then on you would have thought it was her idea to give him that name. Actually, in Gaelic Kyle means something like "Brave Warrior," but Nana really didn't need to know that, did she? Unfortunately, as he grew older, it became obvious that we liked the name a lot more than he did, and I still remember when his friends used to call the house and ask for "Bruce," which is what he had told folks his name was.

The middle son, Brendan, was fine until the youngest, Colin, was born. As a toddler, Colin couldn't quite pronounce Brendan—it came out as "Bruh-bruh"—and that seems to have stuck, at least in the family. Schools, on the other hand, seem to insist that his name is *Bran*don; I guess he'll go through life fighting that, as I have always fought being a Fred.

The real problem is with our youngest, Colin. The problem isn't with the spelling, though occasionally it comes out Collin. No, the problem here is one of pronunciation. We prefer the Old Country way, with a soft "o" that has the "ah" sound to it. Unfortunately, most folks in this part of the country like to use a hard "o" sound and pronounce it the same way you would pronounce the large bowel, colon. In fact, my wife even took a doctor to task once, who made that mistake. When he addressed Colin, using the hard "o" sound, my wife said, "No, the colon is the large bowel. Colin, on the other hand, is a small child." The doctor, somewhat nonplussed, admitted to having learned that fact in medical school.

Our problem in regard to Colin's name has not been made any easier by the fact that a recent chairman of the Joint Chiefs of Staff, and probable future presidential candidate, Colin Powell, insists on mispronouncing his name, and he is a rather popular guy. My wife, who takes these things very seriously, even wrote the good general a letter while both he and I were on active duty—pointing out the fact that he mispronounces his own name. For her efforts, she got an autographed photo, and I retired in grade. She made damn sure that my name wasn't misspelled in her letter.

I've been a father for over twenty years now, and if, by some horrible act of medical malpractice that should ever happen again, I would be more realistic in naming sons. I would choose names that were more likely to reflect their lifestyles and the values of the era in which they would grow up. Some names that come immediately to mind are Rancid, Algae, and Fungus, though Obtuse and Grunge also have considerable merit.

The fact that I was indeed cursed by my name really struck home in 1989, when I received a letter from the colonel at MILPERCEN, who was my personnel manager. The letter informed me that an O-6 selection board was getting ready to convene and that I was, again, in the zone of consideration for promotion, and therefore, I should make sure my file was up to date. Nice letter, except for one small problem: it was addressed to "LTC William Lowrey." Here is part of my reply to the good colonel:

"Your letter answered the nagging question that has been burning in the back of my mind ever since I was first not selected for battalion command, and then not selected for the War College, and finally, this past year, not selected for promotion to O-6. Infantry branch has obviously (and inadvertently, I'm sure) mixed up my file with some hard-core, card-carrying dud named **William** Lowrey. I don't know what this under-achiever has done, but I have to assume his flaccid conduct has been a major contributing factor in my less than meteoric rise to the top of the heap. What really scares me is the possibility the HE has already been promoted to O-6 on the strength of MY file, which must have been erroneously substituted for his. I, on the other hand, would never stoop so low. I am WILLIS, after my father, who was as fine an infantryman who ever wore the uniform. There is honor in that name, and I have been proud to have it all the 21 ½ years that Infantry branch has been controlling my destiny. It's a shame that branch never noticed."

I did not hear back from the good colonel, nor did I get promoted. But at least he knew who I was. Of course, a year later, when I retired, guess whose name was misspelled on the retirement orders.

Until next time, check your rear, make sure your range cards are accurate and you've got overlapping, interlocking grazing bands of fire all around the perimeter, and **BEAT NAVY!**

24. Trying to Beat the System as a Cadet and the Slugs That Resulted
September 1998

A few years ago I wrote one of these articles about rules and how every aspect of our lives, from the moment of conception until we're buried, is controlled by some kind of rule, or in some instances, whole books of rules. Rules are as natural a part of life as breathing and heartbeat. Most of the rules that govern our fate are natural, such as Murphy's Law, the laws of nature and physics and digestion, and the like, but a lot of the rules we must live with are self-inflicted. We make them, and because we make them, we—or at least some of us—frequently feel that we can break them. My sons, anarchists all, are particularly fond of this notion; in fact, I think the number one rule in their lives is "Rules are made to be broken."

West Point is particularly good at making rules—indeed, other than my wife and Holy Mother, the Church—West Point may be the mother lode of rules. At least that used to be true, back in my cadet days. I think cadets have a lot fewer rules today than we did, or at least the rules must be a lot easier to live with. The cadets today all seem a lot happier than we were. Maybe *they* get to make the rules now.

Don't get me wrong—I'm not complaining about rules at West Point. I actually like most of the rules at West Point—even the ones that I think are patently dumb or outright ridiculous (when I was a cadet, I thought all the rules at West Point fell into one of those two categories). You see, I think one of the reasons that West Point is such a great place and produces such outstanding leaders of character is because of those rules. More precisely, it's because cadets through the past two centuries, being highly motivated, intelligent, and high spirited, type A personalities, have made a science out of breaking the rules, within honorable bounds, hopefully without getting caught. This is as important a part of their development as leaders as anything the dean can devise, and actually complements the efforts of the commandant and his minions in honing cadets' tactical and leadership skills. Ironically, it's the commandant who makes and enforces most of the rules.

Cadets' efforts to circumvent regulations at West Point are the stuff of legends, and many a future general officer and national hero got his first serious taste of planning and executing complex, clandestine military operations while mapping out schemes to "beat the system." George Armstrong Custer, last man in the class of June 1861, was famous—or perhaps infamous—for his many and varied transgressions as a cadet. Douglas MacArthur, class of 1903, is alleged to have hoisted the reveille cannon to the top of the West Academic Building (now Pershing Barracks) clock tower late one night; it took legions of engineers and a large crane to get it back down. Apparently, no one thought of putting it on the elevator, which is probably how it got up there in the first place.

One of my favorite stories involves an overachiever in the class of 1946, Cadet Andrew Talbot. This young zealot got into a discussion with his Fluid Mechanics "P" about what would happen if every toilet and every shower in South Barracks were flushed or turned on at the same time. The "P" said nothing would happen; the cadet disagreed. Anxious to prove his point, the cadet rounded up lots of plebes, whom he stationed in every window of South Barracks facing the area and in every bathroom and the sinks, positioning himself in the center of South Area. At the appointed time he gave a signal, which was relayed by the plebes in the windows to the plebes in the bathrooms, and all the toilets were flushed and all the showers were turned on simultaneously. Well, it seems that Fluids "P" wasn't quite as smart as our cadet hero: with a roar, the water main under South Area burst from the sudden overpressure. But alas, while victory may have been sweet for Mr. Talbot, The System got the last laugh, as our hero was rewarded with a huge slug, and spent many weekend afternoons taking walking tours of West Point's scenic cadet areas of barracks.

Another one of my favorite stories involves a merry band of cadets who after taps, in the winter, when the Hudson was frozen over, would don their ice skates and cross the river to Garrison to sample the delights of the town and its drinking establishments. One night while on their return trip, they discovered that, while they were making illicitly merry, an icebreaker had come downstream and severed their lines of communication. This necessitated a breakneck dash downriver, over very rough ice, to the Bear Mountain Bridge, a distance of some four miles, crossing the bridge and skating back up to West Point. This story has a happy ending, as these intrepid wanderers arrived back in the barracks, undetected, just as the first notes of reveille were sounding. History does not record how well they performed in class that day.

There are many stories about the moles of West Point—cadets who went exploring through the steam pipe tunnels that used to run under all the buildings and cadet barracks areas. I've been told that in addition to exploring, some cadets also used to take their drags—dates to you younger grads—to the tunnels for some difficult-to-find and highly-valued privacy. During my yearling year one of the longest standing ovations during "Publication of Orders" at supper in the cadet mess was given when the slug was announced for my two classmates who, while looking for an exit from the tunnel they were in, popped open a grate and emerged into a ladies' bathroom. In the Supe's Administration Building. With a lady in residence. Among other things, they were slugged for "causing extreme consternation." Tragically, one of these true heroes was subsequently killed in action in Vietnam on 24 March 1969.

Of course, we mustn't forget the numerous times when cadets have managed to kidnap the Navy goat prior to the Big Game. The level of planning and execution involved in some of these exercises rivals some of our most spectacular combat operations, and these escapades undoubtedly proved to be fertile training exercises for future military leaders of distinction. I've always felt that, rather than punishing these heroes, they should be favorably mentioned in dispatches and decorated. Anybody that keeps a goat for a mascot deserves to have it kidnapped.

If someone with some literary skills and time to do a lot of research were so inclined, a great book could be written about the many ingenious, and not so ingenious, ways in which cadets through the centuries have tried to beat the system, and the consequences of their actions. It would be instructive if the author of that book also recorded how those cadets fared in their military careers.

As a cadet, I spent an inordinate amount of time trying to circumvent the many rules that governed our lives. Indeed, I considered the Blue Book (Regulations, USCC) as my personal challenge. As in most endeavors in life, sometimes I was successful, sometimes I wasn't. When looking back on my four years in the Womb, I realize that most, if not all, of my clandestine operations were marred by improper prior planning and faulty execution, not to mention some incredibly bad luck. It is unlikely that any of my transgressions would end up in the book of great cadet pranks.

I survived plebe year in pretty good shape, with only one major slug, a 22, 44, and 2 (for the sinless among you, that translates to 22 demerits, 44 hours walking punishment tours, and two months of confinement to the barracks)—and a few more hours on the area for minor sins and accumulating a few excess demerits. The slug resulted from me being caught, along with a couple of yearlings, trying to put one of the cannons from Trophy Point into the lobby of the library during the night of the great Penn State Rally/Riot. Since most of the corps was involved in the events of that remarkable night, the punishment was pretty lenient.

As soon as plebe year ended though, I was ready to take on the Tacs, and my troubles began in earnest. During yearling summer at Camp Buckner I got another 22, 44, and 2—for deciding to catch a few extra z's in the rack instead of accompanying the rest of my company on the daily reveille run. I was really tired that morning, as I had been out the previous night until 0500 on a clandestine mission to paint rocks. It's a long story.

This slug caused me to miss several of the football games that fall, which really distressed me, as I was, and still am, an avid, foaming-at-the-mouth fan. After missing the first three or four games I couldn't stand it any longer and developed a scheme that would at least allow me to listen to the game while walking the area. On the first cold Saturday, which necessitated the wearing of long overcoats over dress gray by cadets walking the area, I implemented my plan. First, in lieu of a dress coat, I just put on a "reveille collar," a collar cut off an old, discarded dress coat, kind of like a dickey. I taped a small transistor radio under my left armpit and ran the earphone up under the collar. Then I donned my long overcoat—it was impossible to tell I didn't have a dress coat on underneath. Once the requisite inspection of the area formation was completed and I began walking my tours, it was an easy thing to put the earphone in my ear, reach under my overcoat, turn on the radio, and, voilà! listen to the game while walking.

Alas, on this particular Saturday we were walking in North Area, and an officer—Colonel Arch Hamblen, the 2nd Regimental tactical officer—was in his office on the seventh floor of the 49th Division of Barracks. Looking out the window, he noticed the sun reflecting off my earphone. Knowing that no cadets wore hearing aids, he immediately became suspicious and decided to investigate. He approached me from the rear, so I didn't see him coming, nor did I hear him, as I was absorbed in the game. The first indication I had that my jig was up was when he reached up and yanked the earphone out of my ear. When he did that, the reveille collar came flying out of my overcoat, and most of the hair under my armpit was ripped out as he continued to tug on the earphone cord. Listening to that football game cost me another month on the area, but the price was even steeper: the officer also wrote up the guard detail supervising the area formation for lax performance of their duties. As my luck would have it, the guard detail that day was made up of cows and firsties from my company, so my name was mud for a while. It was almost like a second plebe year.

Shortly before I finished walking off that slug—I had about four hours left—some visiting foreign dignitary came to West Point and granted amnesty to all us miscreants. The next day, I got slugged again, this time for participating in a plot to get rich quick by selling ladies underwear with "Beat Navy" stenciled on them. I think this cost me another month or so. Most of my yearling year campaign against the Tactical Department was pretty much a losing effort.

By cow year, I had decided I needed more companionship than I was getting from my roommate, so I collected a couple of hamsters, which I named Napoleon and Josephine and kept in a little cage in the trunk room. One day I decided these creatures, to be proper pets of a Soldier, should be airborne qualified, so I made parachutes and harnesses for them. In the evenings I would take them to the roof of the barracks and throw them off, posting a plebe down in the area whose duty it was to retrieve them after their jumps and bring them back up to me. Things were going on quite well until one evening when the chute of one of the hamsters failed to open. He crashed and burned into Central Area, landing in a crumpled, pathetic heap at the feet of the OC (officer in charge), who had decided at just that minute to come through the sally port. He was not amused. Not only was I slugged for harboring illegal pets, but also, and far more harshly, for improperly packing a parachute, leading to the demise of said pet.

One of my more disastrous encounters with the officer in charge occurred during the winter of my cow year. Late one night I developed what I thought was a brilliant idea that would allow me to get an extra minute and a half of rack time prior to reveille formation in the morning. I took an old pair of gray trousers and cut off the legs just below the knees. I then loosely stitched these half-legs to the inside of my long overcoat. I slept with my socks on. In the morning, all I had to do was roll out of the rack, throw on my overcoat, slipping my legs through the attached pants, stick my feet in my shoes, and go to formation. I could be standing in ranks in less than a minute from the time I rolled out of bed.

The next morning I executed my plan, and it seemed to work perfectly, but again, Murphy's Law took control of my fate. The OC just happened to choose my company for his morning walk through inspection. I wasn't too concerned, though—it was still dark that early in the morning, and these reveille inspections were always cursory at best. My spirits soared as he walked past me with little more than a quick glance, but then something amiss registered in his mind. After he had gotten to the end of the squad rank, he turned around and came back, stopping right in from of me. "Spread your legs apart, mister," he ordered me. "Now, look down and tell me what's wrong with this picture." As I obeyed his instructions my heart sank as I realized that during my haste to prepare my reveille uniform, I had inadvertently sewn the trouser legs into my overcoat with the black stripes on the *inside*, rather than facing outward. Well, you win some, you lose some.

Once I got on the area, I seemed to have a hard time getting off. One fine, spring Saturday during cow year I was walking off a minor infraction in Central Area, when I was overcome by a powerful thirst. Making sure that none of the guard detail was looking my way, I dashed down into the sinks and got a Coke out of the machine. I then went upstairs into a classmate's room on the first floor that faced the area. I decided to relax for a few minutes while savoring my drink. While enjoying this interlude, the sergeant of the guard called out the command "Area squad, sound off!" This was how the guard detail kept track of their prisoners for the day; during the inspection, each cadet walking tours was assigned a number, and on the command to sound off, had to yell out his number to be accounted for. When it came to my number, I yelled it as loud as I could out the open window of the room. Imagine my surprise when the OC, who just happened to be standing on the stoops right next to that particular window, stuck his head and arm in the window and grabbed me, with a big grin on his face. Needless to say, I did not get credit for my three hours of walking that day. I did, however, get ample opportunity to atone for that mistake.

During my first class year I lived in the 23rd Division of Barracks in North Area. This division flanked a sally port, and the only cadet rooms were two rooms on the first floor. The upper floors were taken up by the Second Class Club, a large room with vaulted ceilings that had pool and Ping-Pong tables, a TV, leather chairs, and other accoutrements of a nice men's club. Since the construction of the new barracks had begun, this club also housed the North Area barbershop, which had been displaced from its former location. One of my other classmates and I had become good friends with the barbers, and we knew where they put the key to the club when they closed up shop each afternoon. We became quite fond of going up to the club and shooting pool after taps. As luck would have it, one night we got caught by the OC and were given relatively mild slaps on the wrist for being out of our rooms after taps. The next night this same officer, who was the Tac of the company next to ours in the barracks, and was a very zealous fellow, came in to inspect his company after taps. On a whim, he decided to see if my buddy and I were up to our old tricks, which of course we were. This time the quill he wrote was not so benign. The third night, he made a special trip into the barracks just to see if we were stupid enough to get caught three nights in a row. We were, and that was my first experience with the "three strikes" rule as applied to the justice system. Fortunately, that officer had a good sense of humor and enjoyed playing the game as much as I did. I was lucky enough to work for him many years later when I was a Major in the 7th Infantry Division and he was a Colonel; it was a great tour of duty. He went on to become a general officer.

I hope cadets today are still trying to devise ways to get around the system—it's an important part of their training and an invaluable part of the rich lore that makes West Point such a great place, truly a national treasure.

Until next time, sports fans, stand up straight, suck your guts in, and make damn sure you pack those parachutes right. ***BEAT NAVY!***

25. The Joy of Cars
March 1999

Author's note: this was the last "Goat Poop" essay I submitted for publication in Assembly. *Alas, my day job had become too pervasive and interfered with my personal time, especially since, as class scribe, I was still cranking out class notes for every issue. I had to make a choice: continue to crank out these literary stool specimens or go fishing. It should surprise no one which decision I made.*

Ouch! I just finished doing one of my least favorite chores—paying my monthly blood money to the auto insurance god USAA, who I'm sure disgorged a huge corporate burp after being stuffed so full of cash. You see, I have not been lucky with cars over the years, either as an owner or as a driver, and I now have teenage sons who drive, when the law allows them—which has been infrequently of late—and they are not lucky either. Nor is my wife, though she will never, ever admit to any transgressions behind the wheel of a car and routinely accuses me of being the world's worst driver. I take exception to that, considering some of the circumstances I've gotten myself into behind the wheel yet managed to escape from. To me, this would indicate my driving skills are pretty darn good.

Like most red-blooded, snake-eating, airborne/ranger, testosterone-dripping, American males, I love cars, but for some reason, they have never loved me back. It could be because, as all of my ordnance, CE, mechanics, physics, nuke, juice, thermo, fluids and other science-oriented, last section P's would attest to, I've never had any aptitude in those areas, so the concept of mechanical maintenance of complicated machinery has always been kind of fuzzy with me. If the truth must be told, I have a lifetime history of using and abusing cars. As the saying goes, I ride 'em hard and put 'em away wet. I think I actually went nine months once without checking the oil in a car, much less changing it. But then, it *was* my wife's car, and I logically assumed she would be performing her own first echelon maintenance.

25. The Joy of Cars

My first car—actually, it wasn't *my* car, but the family car that no one else drove—was a great automobile. Unfortunately, in 1961, at the age of sixteen, I didn't realize just what a treasure it was. It was a 1953 Packard Clipper, infantry blue, with a huge, straight-eight engine—the pistons were the size of garbage cans—and it was built like a tank, which was a damn good thing because I treated it like one. Thank God my daddy never knew what I did in that machine. You could comfortably get six or seven teenagers in it and, a little less comfortably, up to twelve, which isn't bad for a four-door sedan. There was only one problem—1961 was the era of big tail fins, lots of chrome, and cars built to look like rolling passion pits. The cars of that era were the very essence of cool, and a 1953 Packard was, well, dowdy seems to come to mind. Never mind that it could withstand far more abuse from me than anything built in 1961 or since, what it couldn't do was attract chicks, and everybody knows that, to a teenage boy, that is the first and most important role for any car. Having an early '50s sedan as your only set of wheels in 1961 would be the equivalent of a 1999 teenager being forced to drive the old man's '73 Pacer. It got you where you wanted to go, but there was definitely something missing in the experience.

At the time in question, I was living at Fort Bragg, NC, and there was a very popular drive-in restaurant in nearby Fayetteville called "Steve's," where all the cool kids hung out. There was a tower on top of the restaurant from which the most popular radio program in the North Carolina Piedmont was broadcast every night—a music request show called "Steve's Tower in the Sky." (That was a bit of a stretch since it was only a one story building, but all the bubbas out in the sticks who couldn't get to the big city didn't know that.) All the local kids would go there and send their requests for music up to the DJ, who would dutifully announce the requests over the air and play the songs. The requests usually took the form of "To the hot chicks in the '57 Edsel, from Hunk, in the Green Machine." All the cool guys' cars had names, and mine was no exception. My good buddy Flip Lahlem, who used to accompany me on my nightly visits to Steve's, and I decided that no way would any young, nubile, callipygian lass be enticed to respond to a song sent from "the two guys in the '53 Packard," so we named my car "The Escapade," which had a certain flair to it, reflecting the image we felt best suited us. Over a two-year period, I'll bet there were hundreds of songs played for countless girls from "Peanuts and Flip in the Escapade," alas, all without any tangible results. Once those girls found out the Escapade was a Detroit tank with neither fins nor glass packs, they were outta there. So, my first car had a very negative effect on my love life.

Unfortunately, I had to leave the Packard behind to come to West Point. Dad, bless his heart, hung on to it so I'd have some wheels to drive when I came home on leave, which, after yearling summer, I rarely did. In fact, Dad still had that car when I was a senior captain on active duty. I wish he still did; I've gotten a lot smarter with age, despite what my wife will tell you.

My next car was the one I got as a firstie—the first car I actually owned, though, of course, Dad bought it for me. It was a 1967 Pontiac GTO, a true muscle car. I thought my new GTO was pretty cool, figuratively, if not literally—I was too cheap to buy air-conditioning. Big, V-8, gas-guzzling hog of an engine, burgundy with a black vinyl roof, all black interior—and no air-conditioning. Since I had acquired the car at West Point, I hadn't given much thought to the fact that my first assignments would be in the Deep South, where it does get a trifle warm.

This car was not lucky, and because of that, USAA began to keep very close tabs on me, and I began my lifelong endowment of their new corporate headquarters building. I can't remember the exact number, but the GTO was involved in a few accidents during its first year of life. Nothing serious, mind you, just fender benders really, but it only seemed to happen when I was driving. Unfortunately, this car was not very well built, either. From the outset, it had more squeaks and rattles than a bed in a pay-by-the-hour motel room, the sources of which could never be identified or fixed.

In the summer of 1968, my Army tour director booked me on a one-year cruise to beautiful downtown Vietnam, so I decided to leave my wife in San Antonio, Texas, since her folks were stationed at Fort Sam Houston. Actually, her father was the post commander of Fort Sam Houston. She also decided that she didn't need that great big car for just her; what she really wanted was a VW Beetle. I've always believed she was suffering from latent early-1960s flower child syndrome.

Have you ever tried to sell a car that squeaks like a cheap army cot, with a black interior and no airconditioning, in the middle of the summer in south Texas? In five days? (That was all the time I had before

25. The Joy of Cars

having to leave for the war.) The slicked back, polyester leisure suit and polka-dot necktie-wearing salesman at the local Pontiac dealership knew he had me by the you-know-what and paid me not a whole lot of cash for my chariot, but it was enough to buy my wife the car of her dreams—a used 1962 VW Beetle, with a thirty-day limited (*very* limited) warranty. The next day I flew off into the sunset, and USAA breathed a huge sigh of relief, knowing it would be at least a year before they'd have to worry about my driving habits again.

As you might guess, the Beetle began to fall apart on the thirty-first day after I bought it. The brakes didn't seem to work very well, nor did the clutch. After the first three months, virtually every letter I received from my wife had some new litany of woe about her car. As I recall, it did not survive the entire year of my absence, and I'm not sure how my wife got around town for the last month I was gone. When I finally returned from the war, getting a new car was the number one priority. Well, it wasn't exactly *my* number one priority, but it was certainly hers. So, on the first full day of return to civilization, we went car shopping.

We settled, for reasons that remain a mystery to me, on a Ford Maverick. The year was 1969, and the Maverick was a new gimmick for Ford—a smallish, underpowered, ugly, family car for small, poor families. We sure fit the bill. At least the one we bought was infantry blue, which may have been its only good point.

My next assignment was in Germany, which fact, combined with my driving record, caused my insurance rates to skyrocket again. However, since I had to ship the car overseas, and it went on a very slow boat, it was safe for almost three months. Eight months later, I got orders sending me back to Vietnam—I guess I hadn't gotten it right the first time—so after a year in Germany, I put our car back on the slow boat to the States. My wife and I headed back to San Antonio, where she decided to stay again while I was gone. We didn't make it far.

It was an unseasonably and unusually miserable, cold day in October—a record breaker, as I recall—and around noon the pewter sky began to weep a noxious mixture of snow and sleet. Shockingly, this was in north Georgia! As you might imagine, since we're talking Deep South here, it was only a matter of minutes before traffic on I-85 was stopped dead in its tracks, with jack-knifed tractor trailers littering the landscape for miles. I barely managed to stop behind the endless line of carnage without hitting the guy in front of me, but as it turned out, it didn't matter. I looked into the rearview mirror just in time to see the front grill of the biggest damn 18-wheeler known to man, bearing down on us at forty miles an hour. The impact was horrendous, turning our little Maverick into an accordion. Miraculously, we were unhurt, more or less, but the car was on fire. A crowd of bystanders quickly appeared, not to rescue us, but to push our car down an embankment, away from the truck, lest our fire spread to his gas tank. The fact that my wife and I were still trapped in our car didn't seen to bother them. She finally managed to get her door open—mine was beyond hope—and I still have this lovely image of her running away, yelling over her shoulder, "Save the cats!" Nice to know where I fit into the love equation. I managed to escape out her door—with the damn cats—just moments before the Maverick turned itself into a mushroom cloud. It was all very exciting. We also lost, in addition to our car, virtually everything we owned except for our furniture, which didn't amount to much.

Despite this minor setback, we did manage to get to San Antonio the next day—how we did that is a good story in itself—and I got my date for reporting back to the war delayed a week, which gave us plenty of time to shop for a new car and pay several visits to USAA Corporate Headquarters collecting checks. Having learned my lesson about used cars, I made an inspired selection—a nifty little Fiat Spyder sports car. Great choice, I thought, except that I was not going to be around to drive it. USAA was glad of that, and as soon as I left the country, my insurance rates went down.

Upon return from my second Vietnam excursion, we obviously needed to buy a bigger, more practical car, though we were now definitely ready to be a two-car family; no way was I going to give up my sports car and cool image. Once again, I went temporarily insane and bought another Pontiac. Sometimes, I am a slow learner.

After a bit of leave, we convoyed to our next Army adventure at Fort Benning, Georgia. While the Spyder performed admirably, resulting in me starting a speeding ticket collection to rival my stamp collection, the Pontiac was a real dog—it spent more time in the shop, all under warranty, than it did on the road. On the day the twelve-month warranty expired, I traded it in for a new toy—a brand new Audi 100. No more American-made stuff for me—I had joined the growing ranks of the foreign car elitists, and the Audi was just making its entrée into the American market in earnest.

A bit too soon I'm afraid—that car broke down so often, and had so many parts replaced, that by the end of a year, little of it was original equipment. Finally, after the third air-conditioner died, I put a plastic lemon on the radio antenna—the radio didn't work either—and drove to Audi's U.S. corporate headquarters in Maryland, where I parked it in front of their building. This got me the attention of a senior official who, after listening to my tale of woe and inspecting the stack of maintenance records I had, sent me and my car to a place where he guaranteed absolutely that everything would be fixed to my satisfaction.

Alas, I'm afraid that car was beyond hope, so a couple months later, we traded it in for, would you believe, a used motor home. After all, it was time to PCS again, this time all the way across the country to Fort Ord, California, and we wanted to travel in style and comfort. Remember now, I'm not exactly mechanically inclined, and 1973 motor homes weren't the technological marvels they are today. Add to that the fact that I was going to tow the Sypder, despite having never towed anything in my life, and you have all the makings for trouble.

The first disaster befell the beloved Spyder. I didn't know what to do with the safety chain on the towing hitch, so I hooked it to something on the front undercarriage of the car. Unfortunately, that something involved the front wheels, and every time I made a turn in the motor home, the chain would draw tight. By the time we got to California, the front wheels were canted inward at about thirty-degree angles, and both sides of the car were coated in black rubber that had scuffed off the front tires. Fortunately, a good mechanic and a lot of money were able to fix the problem, sort of, but that car never ran the same again. The next problem though, was a lot messier.

When we arrived at Fort Ord, there were no quarters available, and finding a place to live was a major challenge. Fortunately, we had the motor home, and it became our home for sixty-five days. Well, it never dawned on me that toilets in motor homes don't work the same way as toilets in houses. If you don't keep a steady stream of water flowing, the solid stuff you put into the toilet doesn't go anywhere, and before long you end up with a tall pile of solidified, smelly stuff coming out of the toilet seat. There's only one way to get rid of it, and unfortunately, my arm was too big to reach into the hole. But my wife's was just the right size. Remarkably, this woman remained married to me.

Once we found a place to live, my wife, who had developed a major case of claustrophobia after sixty-five days living in a box, refused to get in the motor home ever again, so there wasn't much sense in paying insurance on it. I sold it to some guy who knew how toilets worked, and we went car shopping again.

Since the Fiat Spyder had been such a joy, before I broke its front legs, we decided to get another Fiat and settled on a sleek, new Brava 131 Sedan. This was Fiat's new flagship car, and I figured it had to be good. Never, ever, have I been more wrong about anything in my life. Think about this: when was the last time you saw a Fiat—any kind of a Fiat—on the roads of America? When was the last time you saw, or heard of, a Fiat Dealership? If you're under thirty, the answer is probably never. My friends, I am convinced the Brava was the cause of this corporate demise. It was, without doubt, the worst car ever made. Our new car went through no fewer than *six*—count 'em—alternators in the one year I owned it. I remember one day my wife came home from shopping at the PX and casually mentioned, while trying on her new dress, "Oh, yeah, before I forget, a bunch of stuff fell out of the engine down by the stoplight, but I was able to drive home anyway." That bunch of stuff was the pulley on the front of the crankshaft and the timing chain. About a month later, I was driving down the highway at seventy miles an hour, when I heard a loud **thud**. Thinking I had a flat, I pulled over; upon inspection, all the tires were OK. Then I opened the hood; something didn't seem quite right. I got down on my hands and knees and peered under the car. There, hanging by one of the belts, was the alternator—it had sheared right off the engine block. But the incident that finally put the end to the Fiat came a couple months later.

In November 1977, my wife and I flew back to West Point for my tenth reunion. In order to save $80, I had asked a friend to drive us to the San Francisco airport, rather than fly from Monterey, and to pick us up upon our return—in my car. At this point, my wife was seven and a half months large with child. On the day of our return to San Francisco, it was raining, and my friend was nowhere to be seen. After a while I got paged to the white courtesy phone; my friend was on the line with the news that my car had stopped running about halfway to the airport. It is 4 p.m. on a Friday afternoon; he had managed to get to a local Fiat dealer, who told him the car needed a new alternator. I told my friend to do it, promising repayment. He finally showed up at about 7:30 p.m., with a nice, new mega-hundred-dollar alternator installed. It's raining very hard now. I jump behind the wheel, and we begin the 100-mile journey home.

About halfway to Monterey, I notice the windshield wipers have stopped working, and the headlight beams look like pocket flashlights. We limp into a filling station, where the mechanic informs me that the alternator doesn't work, and I've been running off the battery. I make a command decision: we recharge the batter, and make a mad dash for home. The last twenty miles were done in a pouring rain, with no windshield wipers, and I would only turn the headlights on when I saw other traffic coming. It was an exciting trip. The next day, I put the Fiat up for sale.

By now, Japanese cars were starting to catch on in this country in a big way, and in January 1978 I bought us a Toyota. This was a great car; it could take mine and my wife's neglect and abuse and keep right on running—up to a point. That car survived three West Point winters, three Alaskan winters, and a few years in Virginia before giving up the ghost, but not before I had squeezed 203,000 miles out her.

Alas, her demise was painful. The floor had pretty much rusted out, and the last year or so, the brakes were iffy at best. I used to have to jump out at stop lights, race around, open the hood, poor in brake fluid, and jump back in before the traffic ran over me. My kids refused to be taken to school in it; they felt it was very undignified to be seen in that old bucket. Finally, one day I was up in the DC area, stuck in traffic at the Springfield Interchange, the greatest malfunction junction on the East Coast. When the traffic started to move, my old tub wouldn't go—I couldn't get it in to gear. I got out of the car and pushed it off the side of the road; just then, a naval officer pulled up behind me. Keep in mind, my car was festooned with many large "Beat Navy" stickers, and I was in uniform. He strode up to me, with a big smile on his face, and said, "Hi, Asshole, need a ride somewhere?" As I was in a big hurry and very definitely needed a ride, I could not make the appropriate retort.

Not long after that incident, I bought myself a new little Toyota. I had owned it about a year and a half, when I made the mistake of letting my oldest son drive it to work. Unfortunately, he decided to take kind of an alternate route, which involved a sidewalk and a streetlight. Number one son escaped injury, but the car was totaled, and Hampton,

Virginia, now has the Lowrey Memorial Streetlight, courtesy of USAA. Time to buy a new set of wheels.

After twenty-nine years of always buying my wife the good car, except for my Spyder, I decided it was *my* turn. Rewarding myself for being such an all-around great guy, I bought myself a real man's car, an Eddie Bauer edition Ford Explorer, with every option that could be crammed into it. This is one, cooooool car.

Ten days later my wife, driving number one son to work in my new car, wrecked it. Actually, some Navy guy ran into her, and the results were pretty ugly. The city of Hampton, Virginia, now has the Lowrey Memorial Stoplight at the offending intersection. USAA decides to hire more accountants to keep up with the Lowreys.

And so it's gone with me and cars. Not a pretty picture, and my wife is now making loud noises about wanting a new one of her own. Middle son has one, but the law will no longer let him drive it. However, USAA insists that I keep insuring it. Pretty soon, younger son is going to be driving; I might as well just have a direct deposit of my pay sent to USAA's account. The car gods have cursed me for all time.

That's it for this trash haul, sports fans. Stay in step, keep the faith, and remember to check your oil every now and then. **BEAT NAVY!**

26. The Recipe for a Perfect Mint Julep

Let's turn our attention to a serious topic: the evening cocktail. This story, like many in this book, is connected to West Point, but only peripherally. It involves two grads who played a prominent role in Academy and U.S. military history, and I think it's good history and just plain fun.

It is the cocktail hour here in the Hudson Valley as I write this (it's a Sunday, and it's after noon), and as I was contemplating what type of healing waters I would prescribe for myself while watching the NFL playoff games today, my memory returned to what is, in my humble opinion, one of the better letters ever written. It was written in 1937 by then-Colonel Simon Bolivar Buckner, Jr., former commandant of cadets at West Point, to Major General William D. Connor, superintendent of the Military Academy, and describes the making of a proper mint julep. Buckner went on to command the Tenth U.S. Army in the Pacific Theater during WWII and became the only U.S. Field Army commander killed in action in WWII during the battle for Okinawa. Camp Buckner at West Point, where cadets conduct their summer field training, is named for him. General Conner eventually had a street at West Point, in one of the officers' family housing areas, named for him.

My father got a copy of the letter from a dear friend of his, who was also my godfather and who was on General Conner's staff. He passed it on to me. Here it is; enjoy.

Fort George G. Meade, MD
March 30, 1937
Major General Wm. D. Connor,
West Point, N. Y.

My dear General Connor:
    Your letter requesting my formula for mixing mint juleps leaves me in the same position in which Capt. Barber found

himself when asked how he was able to carve the image of an elephant from a block of wood. He replied that it was a simple process consisting merely of whittling off the part that didn't look like an elephant.

The presentation of the quintessence of gentlemanly beverages can be described only in like terms. A mint julep is not the product of a formula. It is a ceremony and must be performed by a gentleman possessing a true sense of the artistic, a deep reverence for the ingredients and a proper appreciation of the occasion. It is a rite that must not be entrusted to a novice, a statistician or a Yankee. It is a heritage of the old South, an emblem of hospitality and a vehicle in which noble minds can travel together upon the flower-strewn paths of happy and congenial thought.

So far as the mere mechanics of the operation are concerned, the procedure, stripped of its ceremonial embellishments, can be described as follows: Go to a spring where cool, crystal-clear water bubbles from under a bank of dew-washed ferns. In a consecrated vessel, dip a little water at the source. Follow the stream through its banks of green moss and wildflowers until it broadens and trickles through beds of mint growing in aromatic profusion and waving softly in the summer breeze. Gather the sweetest and tenderest shoots and gently carry them home. Go to the sideboard and select a decanter of Kentucky Bourbon, distilled by a master hand, mellowed with age yet still vigorous and inspiring. An ancestral sugar bowl, a row of silver goblets, some spoons and some ice and you are ready to start.

In a canvas bag, pound twice as much ice as you think you will need. Make it fine as snow, keep it dry and do not allow it to disintegrate into slush.

In each goblet, put a slightly heaping teaspoonful of granulated sugar, barely cover this with spring water and slightly bruise one mint leaf into this, leaving the spoon in the goblet. Then pour elixir from the decanter until the goblets are about one-fourth full. Fill the goblets with snowy ice, sprinkling in a small amount of sugar as you fill. Wipe the outside of the goblets dry and embellish copiously with mint. Then comes the important and delicate operation of frosting. By proper manipulation of the spoon, the ingredients are circulated and blended until Nature, wishing

26. The Recipe for a Perfect Mint Julep

to take a further hand and add another of its beautiful phenomena, encrusts the whole in a glistening coat of white frost. Thus harmoniously blended by the deft touches of a skilled hand, you have a beverage eminently appropriate for honorable man and beautiful woman.

When all is ready, assemble your guests on the porch or in the garden, where the aroma of the julep will rise Heavenward and make the birds sing. Propose a worthy toast, raise the goblet to your lips, bury your nose in the mint, inhale a few breaths of its fragrance and sip the nectar of the gods.

Being overcome by thirst, I can write no further.

Simon B. Buckner
Colonel, United States Army

27. Thoughts on Veterans Day, 2017
Posted on Facebook 10 November 2017

Tomorrow is Veterans Day, 2017. In some respects, it is the most restrictive of our national holidays, as it belongs to those of us who are military veterans in the service of our nation. It is our Special Day. Sadly, today we are a huge minority in this country, certainly in the general population as a whole, but especially in the Congress of the United States and in the White House—the two entities that send our nation's treasure to war. The majority of the occupants of both of these institutions have no real firsthand experience of what it means to serve and sacrifice at that level. That's a subject for another diatribe.

Yes, the nation certainly does honor its veterans on their Special Day, but in a criminally pathetic way. You can get great deals on furniture and appliances and new pick-um-up trucks. Some places offer free coffee or a slice of pizza. Where I live, the local garbage company will even pick up my garbage on Veterans Day. Of course, they don't do that on REAL holidays, those that are important to them, including Columbus Day, Martin Luther King Day and Presidents' Day, but what the hell—Veterans Day and Memorial Day, sure we'll pick up the trash. For much of America, these holidays are no big deal; they've lost their meaning, other than the chance to turn a profit. That saddens me tremendously.

I suspect most folks in this country don't even know the origins of Veterans Day. It started life via executive order by President Wilson on 11 November 1919 as Armistice Day, to be celebrated on the 11th of November to mark the end of fighting in World War I, the "War to End All Wars," one year earlier. Well, we all know how that turned out, don't we? It was renamed Veterans Day by Congress in 1954. The bitter truth is that what it has mostly been in the seventy-two years of my life is an opportunity for big sales by retailers, large and small.

In honor of Veterans Day this year I am posting two photographs. The first is of my father, LTC Wills Freed Lowrey, while he was commanding the 3rd Battalion of the 31st Infantry Regiment, 7th Infantry

Division, on Heartbreak Ridge in North Korea in the fall of 1951. Dad, a career infantry officer, served with great distinction and valor as an infantry company commander in both theaters in WWII (Aleutian Campaign in the Pacific and Rhineland Campaign in Germany), as an infantry battalion commander in Korea for eighteen months during some of the most bitter fighting of that war, and in the Cold War. We lost Dad at the ripe old age of 93 in 2004.

LTC Wills Freed Lowrey, Heartbreak Ridge, North Korea, 1951.

Brothers Mark and Freed Lowrey, Lai Khe, Vietnam, spring 1969.

The second photo is of my older brother Mark, USMA '60, and me, standing in front of the 1st Infantry Division Tactical Operations Center at Lai Khe, Vietnam, in the spring of 1969. Mark was on his second Vietnam tour, and I was wrapping up my first. He also served with great distinction and valor as an infantry company commander and battalion operations officer and received the Silver Star, six Bronze Stars, and three Purple Hearts for his service. He died suddenly and unexpectedly on 30 August 2017. We buried Mark at West Point on 4 October of this year. Dad and Mark were hands down the two finest Soldiers I have ever known, Period.

In addition to my father and brother, I also especially honor my thirty West Point classmates—29 of whom graduated, one who did not graduate but picked up the gauntlet of service and sacrifice—who were killed in action in Vietnam. An incredible and immensely sad legacy of service, these were the finest men I have ever known. My class of 1967 only graduated 583, but received at least 157 Purple Hearts that I have been able to account for. Duty. Honor. Country. Service. Sacrifice.

Since it's Veterans Day, I got a free car wash today. That also happened to me several years ago. On that occasion I decided to report my thoughts in my West Point class news magazine. I've decided to dredge them up again today and repost them. In honor of all of us who have served and sacrificed.

It is 11 November, Veterans Day, as I write this. This is a holiday that has always been special for me in a quiet, subdued way. I don't normally dwell on it or spend any time celebrating it, other than wishing my fellow Veterans good wishes and thanks on this, our special day. But today, for the oddest of reasons, it took on the character of a poignantly evocative event.

This morning I took my car to the car wash. As I pulled up to the start of the line the young man who was collecting money—he couldn't have been more than twenty—asked me what kind of wash I wanted. When I replied that I just wanted the basic no frills car wash, he asked me if I was a Veteran. When I replied that I was, he stuck his hand in the window to shake mine and said "Thank you for your service, sir. Today your car wash is free, and it's the diamond deluxe."

This really took me by surprise. I thanked him, rolled up my window and started the slow roll down the car wash tunnel. For some reason, this simple act of kindness and respect triggered an unexpected emotional response in me; I was suddenly overwhelmed with a mixture of sadness, pride, nostalgia, and lost youth. My mind was flooded with those memories and emotions that many years ago I folded up and stored away in that footlocker I keep in the attic of my mind. Mostly, I started thinking of lost comrades and the bittersweet price of service. The young man's act of kindness rekindled an ember that every so often needs to be fanned.

There are many of us—perhaps all—upon whose mind's eye there remains indelibly imprinted a vivid and moving tapestry of battlefield images. At any moment of reflection, we can recall with precise clarity the gaunt, strained faces of men under fire, the opaque visages of the wounded, the gray pallor of the dead. We can taste fear, hear cries of anguish and pain, feel the bone numbing fatigue, and smell the livid stench of mortified flesh, vomit, and offal. We all know too well the meaning of that kind of sacrifice. That our sacrifice, in the case of Vietnam, was for naught doesn't lessen its meaning. Anyone who ever had to send home to grieving parents the remains of their young son or daughter who died on some alien soil for a cause whose meaning he or she could hardly fathom should have the opportunity to be refreshed by such a simple act of kindness and respect as that young man showed me.

I drove away from that car wash feeling a huge sense of pride. Proud to have been a Soldier, proud of all the Soldiers I've ever been fortunate to have served with, proud to have known them, to have served with them, to have suffered and bled with them, proud of what we shared. And of course, I am especially proud of my class, of all of you.

So, my brothers, on this our Special Day, thank you from the bottom of my heart for your selfless service, which continues unabated, for your countless sacrifices, for your comradeship, your counsel, your passion, your friendship, your leadership, and your love of this great nation and of each other. You are truly **Unsurpassed.**

28. Thoughts on Veterans Day, 2020
Three American Heroes
Posted on Facebook 11 November 2020

A couple days ago I posted a series of Veterans Day 2020 tributes honoring my classmates from the West Point class of 1967. Today I want to post a few more tributes—I want to honor three great American Soldiers who I think don't get nearly the recognition nor understanding of how outstanding they were and the incredible roles they played in defending the nation. I will be the first to admit that I'm not a casual historical observer here, as all three of these giants were close friends of my family. I grew up listening to their stories while surrounded by their museum-quality military memorabilia collections in their dens, what today we'd call their Man Caves. My admiration for them is based on many years of close, personal contact, as well as what the history books have to say about them, so I do have a bit of personal bias. All three of these fine Soldiers are West Point graduates who played extraordinary roles in World War II.

My first subject is General William Hood Simpson, West Point class of 1909. The number nine features prominently in this story, as you will see.

Pictured here is a U.S. 9th Infantry Regiment belt buckle. The 9th Infantry Regiment—the "Manchus," so named because of their service in China during the Boxer Rebellion, 1898–1900—traces its current lineage to 1855, although there were earlier 9th Infantry Regiments dating to the War of 1812 and the War with Mexico. It is one of the most decorated units in the U.S. Army and has covered itself in great glory in every U.S.

The Manchu belt buckle owned and worn by GEN William Hood Simson.

28. Thoughts on Veterans Day, 2020

conflict since it was first activated. It is also the only unit in the U.S. Army authorized to wear its distinctive unit insignia as a belt buckle.

GEN Simpson

This authorization was first issued by the adjutant general of the Army on 2 December 1923, but it took a couple more years for the design to be approved. This was back in the good old days when U.S. Army dress uniforms actually looked like military uniforms. Officers wore tunics with Sam Browne belts, and NCOs and enlisted Soldiers wore large, leather belts with their tunic. The approved design—a replica of the unit distinctive insignia—was worn as the belt buckle on both the officer and enlisted uniforms. The buckle shown below is the original design, and they are now extremely rare. It measures two and one-half–inches high and two and one-quarter–inches wide. This particular buckle dates to the mid-1930s.

So, what is the connection to Veterans Day? you ask. This belt buckle was owned and worn by then-Colonel William Hood Simpson, USMA class of 1909 (Patton's classmate), when he was regimental commander of the 9th Infantry Regiment at Fort Sam Houston, Texas, 1938 – 1940. By 1944 he was commander of the U.S. Ninth Army, the largest field army we had in the European Theater of Operations. The Ninth Army had three corps, the VIII, XIX, and XXI, and at one point had as many as ten Infantry and five Armored Divisions assigned or attached. It would probably have been the Army tasked with capturing Berlin, had Ike not given the honor of that hell-on-earth effort to the Soviets.

The Simpsons and my family were lifelong friends, which is why I have his Manchu buckle; he gave it to me when I volunteered to serve as the class aide for his class—1909—for their seventieth reunion at West Point. There were—you guessed it—nine attendees: three grads, three wives, and three widows. By the end of the reunion I was exhausted, but I had a lifetime supply of "Georgie" Patton stories. I took a photo of Simpson and his two classmates sitting on the base of the statue of their classmate George Patton; that photo was used as the cover photo for the Fall 1979 issue of *Assembly* magazine, shown below. Also shown below is the cover from the March 25, 1945, issue of *LIFE* magazine featuring "Simpson of the Ninth."

General Simpson died 15 August 1980 and is buried in Arlington National cemetery. His widow asked me to write his obituary for *Assembly*, which I did; it appeared in the March 1982 issue. She also asked me to check with the West Point Museum to see if they would like General Simpson's 1909 class ring. Their response was, "No, we don't need it. We already have a ring from '09." Keep in mind, this was one of the finest Soldiers of the twentieth century, a U.S. Field Army commander during the greatest conflict in human history. *Sic transit gloria mundi.*

Here is General Simpson's obituary that I wrote for *Assembly*:

> On the afternoon of 20 August 1980, the stillness that lay over the gently rolling hills of Arlington National Cemetery was shattered by the thundering reports of seventeen cannon shots and the crackling of three volleys of rifle fire. Then, in the haunting melody of a lone bugle playing taps, the stillness returned. William Hood Simpson, USMA Class of 1909, General, United States Army, was laid to rest among many of the great military leaders

of this country. As the smoke drifted away and the last notes of taps echoed through the hills, a great chapter in the history of the Army, and of the nation, came to a close. "Texas Bill"—the "Doughboy General"—stood his last muster.

General Simpson was born in Weatherford, Texas, on 19 May 1888, the son of Edward J. and Elizabeth Hood Simpson. The military tradition ran deep in his family. His father had served in the famous Tennessee Cavalry under Nathan Bedford Forrest during the Civil War, and his Uncle John was on General Forrest's staff. It was a tradition that young Bill Simpson quickly adopted as his own calling, and for forty-one years he was to add to it with a devotion rarely matched and never exceeded.

Bill grew up on his grandfather's farm in Weatherford. He passed the entrance exam for the United States Military Academy the year before he was to graduate from high school. At the age of seventeen, he reported to West Point to begin his military career in June of 1905, the youngest man in his class. Almost immediately, the special nature of this man became evident to all those around him—classmates and upperclassmen alike. Tall, quiet, and unassuming, Bill had the marvelous knack of gaining the instant admiration and friendship of anyone he came in contact with. Academics at West Point proved to be his first great battle in the Army and his first significant victory. To be sure, the margin of victory was slim—graduating third from the bottom of his class—and it was only gained with the help of many others, cadets who realized that in Bill Simpson, the Army had a resource too precious to lose before its time. But graduate he did, in June of 1909, along with some pretty good company—George Patton, Jacob Devers, and Robert Eichelberger were all his classmates.

While he may not have blazed any trails of glory in the academic sphere, he certainly left his mark on the fields of friendly strife, excelling in football, polo, and wrestling. As history was to show, Bill Simpson was a man of action!

His assignments over the next thirty-seven years read like an almanac of the great events in American history during this century. Commissioned in the Infantry, Second Lieutenant Simpson's first assignment was with the 6th Infantry Regiment, stationed at Fort Lincoln, North Dakota. Reporting for duty in September 1909, he soon found himself overseas, as the 6th Infantry was posted to the island of Mindanao, in the Philippines, in January of 1910. There for the next two and one-half years he served under the command of General Pershing in the campaigns against the Moros. Returning to the United States with his regiment in 1912, he spent the next few years performing normal company duties with the 6th Infantry at the Presidio of San Francisco and Fort Bliss, Texas.

In 1916, he again found himself in action under the command of General Pershing. As a new first lieutenant, he entered Mexico in command of the lead company, in search of the Mexican outlaw Pancho Villa. In February 1917, he became aide-de-camp to Major General George Bell Jr., Commander of the El Paso Military District. Promoted to captain in May of 1917, Bill moved with Major General Bell to Camp Logan, Texas, to activate the 33rd Infantry Division for action in Europe in World War I. The division deployed overseas in April 1918, and went into action on the Western Front shortly thereafter. By the end of the war in November, Bill Simpson had become a lieutenant colonel and was serving as the Division Chief of Staff, at the ripe old age of thirty. For his actions with the 33rd Division in World War I, he was awarded the Distinguished Service Medal, the Silver Star for Gallantry during the Meuse Argonne Offensive, the French Legion of Honor, Degree of Chevalier, and the French Croix de Guerre with Bronze Star.

With the war in Europe over, Bill returned to the United States with the 33rd Division in June 1919. During the next few years, he served in a variety of billets throughout the United States, including duties as Chief of Staff of the 6th Infantry Division at Camp Grant, Illinois; duty in the Office of the Chief of Infantry, the War Department; as a student at the Infantry Advanced Course and the Command and General Staff School; Executive Officer of the 3rd Battalion, 12th Infantry at Fort Meade, Maryland; Professor of Military Science and Tactics at Pomona College in California; and student, and then instructor at the Army War College.

Bill's most significant accomplishment during these post-war years was to take Ruth Krakauer as his bride. They were married on Christmas Eve 1921 in El Paso, Texas.

In September 1938, Bill was promoted to Colonel, and soon found himself commanding the 9th Infantry Regiment located at Fort Sam

Houston, Texas. By October 1940 he was a brigadier general, and in April of 1941 was commanding the Infantry Replacement Training Center at Camp Wolters, Texas. It was in this assignment that his genius as a trainer of Soldiers was brought to the fore. In the fall of 1941 he was promoted to major general and commanded in succession the 35th and 30th Infantry Divisions and the XII Army Corps, preparing, in turn, each of these units for overseas deployment and combat. By September of 1943, Bill was a lieutenant general and commander of the Fourth United States Army, spread throughout the South and Southwest.

In April of 1944, the Fourth Army was renamed the Eighth and ordered to Europe. Upon arrival in England it was again renamed, now becoming the Ninth. This time the name stuck, and Bill Simpson was about to make the world take notice.

General Simpson's Ninth Army landed on the Continent of Europe on 30 August 1944 and set up its first command post in the field of St. Sauvier, France. On 5 September, the Army took over the Siege of Brest from his classmate George Patton's Third Army. After the capture of Brest in September, General Simpson moved his Ninth Army into Holland into line between General Hodge's First Army and the British Army. The Ninth Army, under General Simpson's command, was the first Army to reach the Rhine River. After crossing the Rhine in March 1945, the Fighting Ninth advanced 219 miles in 19 days and was the first Army to cross the Elbe, only 85 miles from Berlin, where further advance towards Berlin was stopped by General Eisenhower. On 30 April 1945, troops from the Ninth Army made the first contact with the Russian Army near Zerbst. During their dash across the German heartland, the Ninth Army participated in the encirclement of the German Ruhr and the capture of over 300,000 German troops.

After the German surrender in Europe, General Simpson was preparing to take the Ninth Army to China when the war with Japan ended in August 1945. For his service during the war, General Simpson was awarded his second Distinguished Service Medal; the Legion of Merit; the Bronze Star; the Order of the British Empire (KBE); the French Legion of Honor, degree of Commander; the Russian Order of Kutuzov; the Grand Commander of the Order of Orange-Nassau (Netherlands); and, from the Belgians, the Grand Officer of the Order of Leopold with Palm and the Croix de Guerre. But perhaps a far greater honor and indication of the nature of the man was the statement made by his boss, General of the Army Eisenhower, when he said, "If General Simpson ever made a mistake as an Army commander, it never came to my attention. Alert, intelligent, and professionally capable, he was the type of leader that American Soldiers deserve."

General Simpson returned to the States and commanded the Second Army until his retirement for medical reasons on 30 November 1946. He was promoted to full General by an Act of Congress in 1954.

Following his retirement, the Simpsons took up residence in San Antonio, Texas, and quickly became prominent in the local civic and social communities. General Simpson was not about to slow down. He became chairman of the extremely successful drive to raise funds for the Santa Rosa Children's Hospital, raising vast sums, and served as a member of the Board of Directors of the Alamo National Bank and the Government Personnel Mutual Insurance Company. He also served as Director of the Greater San Antonio Chamber of Commerce and Chairman of the Board of the Alamo Chapter, Association of the United States Army.

In 1971 Ruth Simpson passed away in the fiftieth year of a most happy marriage. The next several years were ones of increasing hardship, as the General first battled phlebitis and then increasingly severe attacks of neuritis. As he himself said, "It's one of the worst battles I've ever had to fight." Having never been a loser, he was not about to change that habit at the age of eighty-nine. General Simpson found the perfect solution; on 9 April 1978, he married the lovely Catherine (Kay) Berman. The next two and one-half years were among his happiest. Perhaps the high point came during June Week of 1979, when the Simpsons traveled to West Point to join other classmates for their seventieth Reunion. It was at that time and place, perhaps more than anywhere else, that the greatest tribute was paid to the Doughboy General. For four days, everywhere he went, Bill Simpson was besieged by Old Grads—many of whom were famous in their own right, who had served under him in the past. They were all openly moved to see him again. There were tears; there was awe. Bill Simpson remembered them all and had a warm reminiscence to share with each one.

That was the true measure of William Hood Simpson. He was a "people" person. He loved Soldiers. His oft stated philosophy was "Never send an infantryman where you can send an artillery shell";

and because of this, his Soldiers—from the lowest to the highest—loved him.

General Simpson passed away quietly and peacefully on 15 August 1980 at the age of 92. He is survived by his wife, Kay; a daughter, Mrs. Jean Vincent of Fairbanks, Alaska; three grandchildren; and a sister, Mrs. Frank M. Long. His passing has left a void that will not soon be filled.

"Grip hands—though it be from the shadows—
While we swear as you did of yore,
Or living, or dying, to honor —
The Corps, and the Corps, and the Corps!"
—W. F. L.

My second tribute is for a great American Soldier I'm sure few, if any of you, have ever heard about: Major General Roscoe B. Woodruff, West Point class of 1915.

Roscoe Woodruff wasn't just a member of the class of 1915—the "class the stars fell on," the class of Dwight D. Eisenhower, Omar Bradley, Joe Swing, James Van Fleet—he was the cadet First Captain of the class of 1915.

I first met Roscoe Woodruff when I was a baby in Kyoto, Japan, in 1946. He was the commanding general of I Corps, and my father was one of his staff officers. In 1949 he was rotated back to the United States and given command of First Army, headquartered on Governor's Island in the shadow of the Statue of Liberty in New York harbor; he brought my father along as his aide-de-camp. I'm here to tell you, growing up on Governor's Island in 1950–51 was a magical experience, but that's another story.

General Woodruff had covered himself in glory in both WWI and WWII. In WWII he commanded the famed 24th Infantry Division during the Philippine campaign, but that's not how he thought things were going to work out.

With the United States at war, Woodruff was promoted to brigadier general, and in March 1942, became the assistant division commander of the 77th Infantry Division, a unit in the Organized Reserves which had been recently called up for active duty. The division was composed almost entirely of conscripts (or "draftees"). From June 1942 to May 1943, Woodruff, recently promoted to the two-star rank of major general, took full command of the division during its pre-deployment training in Fort Jackson, South Carolina, prior to its assignment to the Pacific Theater in the spring of 1944.

In May 1943, he relinquished command of the 77th Division to Major General A. D. Bruce and took command of VII Corps, then stationed in England. Eisenhower, now the supreme Allied Commander in Europe, **initially selected Woodruff as one of three corps commanders, along with Major General Leonard T. Gerow, commanding V Corps, and Major General Willis D. Crittenberger, commanding XIX Corps, for the Allied invasion of Normandy**. All three were well-known and trusted by the supreme Allied Commander.

When Woodruff's West Point classmate and fellow infantryman Lieutenant General Omar Bradley, who had just arrived in England from serving in the Mediterranean Theater of Operations, was selected to command the U.S. First Army for the upcoming Normandy invasion in October 1943, Bradley's concern was that his three corps commanders all lacked experience in amphibious operations and combat command. Neither Woodruff nor Gerow had fought in World War II, and Crittenberger did not fight in either of the World Wars. Gerow, who was close to Eisenhower and a protégé of General George C. Marshall, Jr., the U.S. Army chief of staff, was retained, but Crittenberger moved to command of IV Corps on the Italian Front, and Woodruff was shuffled off to command of XIX Corps, Crittenberger's former command, for several weeks before returning to the United States, when he handed over command of XIX Corps to Major General Charles H. Corlett. Upon his return to the United States, Woodruff assumed command of the 84th Infantry Division, then in training at Camp Claiborne, Louisiana, from March to June 1944. Taking over the command of VII Corps was Major General J. Lawton Collins, who had commanded the 25th Infantry Division with distinction in the Pacific. Roscoe Woodruff was extremely bitter about this experience, and for the rest of his life refused to forgive his classmates Eisenhower and Bradley for this affront. He took it very personally.

In November 1944, Woodruff's chance at large-scale combat command finally came as commanding general of the 24th Infantry Division in the southwest Pacific. His welcoming reception in the theater was celebrated at the paratroop headquarters, fueled with five gallons of torpedo alcohol, furnished by U.S. Navy patrol boat sailors, as the key ingredient for liquid refreshments. He led his command in the five-month Battle of Mindanao to liberate that island of Philippine archipelago from Japanese occupation in the closing phases of the Leyte campaign.

He never gave up his quest to command a corps in combat. When the Korean War started in June 1950, he asked to be relieved of command of First Army and given command of XV Corps, which was being reactivated for combat in Korea. His wish was granted—a demotion from Army to corps command—but alas, the XV Corps was never deployed to Korea.

Here is Roscoe Woodruff's obituary that appeared in the March 1977 issue of *Assembly* magazine:

> Roscoe Barnett Woodruff, known affectionately by his comrades and friends by the nickname of either "Woody" or "Spike," was born in Oskaloosa, Iowa, on 9 February 1891, the only child of Rhoda Barnett Woodruff and Calvin Woodruff. He attended the public schools in Oskaloosa and subsequently was enrolled at the State University at Ames for his freshman year of college training. He applied and qualified for entrance into the United States Military Academy in 1911 as a member of what later was to be adjudged the distinguished class of 1915. The choice of a military career was largely influenced by his father, "Cap" Woodruff, who had conspicuously served as a captain in the Infantry in the Federal Iowa Militia from Oskaloosa during the Civil War. He also gained from his father the various skills of craftsmanship, the satisfaction of outdoor activities in nature's realm, competitive sportsmanship, marksmanship and a thorough indoctrination in the arts of fishing, hunting, canoeing and backpacking. All of these skills he retained and practiced throughout his lifetime.
>
> With this background it is understandable that as a cadet he excelled in physical fitness challenges. He established a new record for the hammer throw and had the distinction of kicking the winning field goal in the Colgate-Army football game of 1913. He earned his coveted "A" in both football and the hammer throw. However, the capstone of his cadet career was selection as First Captain of the Corps in his first class year. Based on his own de-

sires, upon graduation he was commissioned a second lieutenant in the Infantry together with his fellow classmates Omar Bradley and "Ike" Eisenhower and many more of the class of 1915 destined to achieve distinction in their later years of military and public service.

After graduation Woody was posted along with several classmates to the Infantry, then positioned on the Texas-Mexican border, to counter the Mexican threats of the Pancho Villa regime. It was there that he met Alice Wallace Gray, daughter of Colonel Alonzo Gray, United States Military Academy class of 1887, a hearty cavalryman of the 14th Cavalry. Woody and Alice were married at Fort McIntosh, Laredo, Texas, on 17 May 1917. Of this union there were two children, Roscoe B. Woodruff Jr., (United States Military Academy class of 1941) and Dorothy Woodruff Daniels, with nine grandchildren and several great-grandchildren. Woody would often quip that in 58 years of married life with a "cavalry girl" there were never any family arguments about the relative merits of the cavalry and Infantry; although he was never completely comfortable in his required Academy equitation classes!

After the Mexican border difficulties, Woody as a young captain in the Infantry in command of Company H, 9th Infantry Regiment, 2nd Infantry Division, was among the first of his classmates to enter combat in World War I in the fall of 1917. This combat experience during 1917-18 served him in good stead in his later command and staff assignments during the final stages of the war and in the post-war operations.

During the fallow times between World War I and II, Woody's assignments followed the normal course of events of a Regular Army officer of the combat arms: staff, command, schooling, instructorships and overseas stationing in Panama in 1921-24. He was designated an honor graduate at the Command and General Staff College in 1927. As a result, following graduation he was detailed as an instructor at the College during 1927-1931. Other significant highlights in his career included duty as a tactical officer at the United States Military Academy during 1932-1936. It was during this tour he earned the nickname "Spike," awarded to him secretively by the cadets since Woody had been assigned the

28. Thoughts on Veterans Day, 2020

additional impossible duty as the official censor of the contents of the *Pointer*!

After attendance at the War College in 1931 and duty with the War Department General Staff during 1936-1940, the days immediately prior to World War II found Woody as a battalion commander and later the regimental commander of the distinguished 23rd Infantry Regiment of the 2nd Infantry Division; the same organization he had served in World War I. Subsequently, he was designated as the assistant division commander of the newly activated 77th Infantry Division in early 1942 and later became the division commander. Other wartime assignments included command of VII Corps, the 84th Infantry Division, Army Garrison Force 248 in the Pacific area, and later commander of the 24th Infantry Division during the campaigns on Leyte, Luzon and Mindanao in the Philippines. In the occupation of Japan from 1945 to 1948 he commanded I Corps of the Eighth United States Army. Upon return to the United States in 1948 he served as the deputy commander, First United States Army at Governors Island, New York, and briefly as the Army commander. His last duty assignment was the Commanding General, XV Corps at Fort Polk, Louisiana.

Alice and Woody retired from the service in 1953 at Fort Polk after a total of 42 years in uniform and faithful service to his country. Actually, Alice topped Woody's record by several years with a rightful claim to "service" as an Army "brat" with her cavalry father including an overseas tour in the Philippines as early as 1903.

As might be expected, Alice and Woody retired in San Antonio close by Fort Sam Houston, Texas, in the area where so much of their respective lifetimes in the service had been spent. In retirement Woody continued to pursue his hobbies of craftsmanship, active participation in physical fitness activities such as tennis, and without exception always maintaining his avid interest in the out-of-doors—hunting, fishing and marksmanship.

After retirement, within the family circle, when quizzed on the question of what he thought were his significant accomplishments in a lifetime of military service, he would reticently suggest the honor accorded him as selection as First Captain of

Here are photos of MG Roscoe Woodruff as CG, I Corps in Japan in 1948 and CG, XV Corps, 1951:

the Corps; the recognition accorded him to command infantry troops in every grade from second lieutenant to major general; the deep appreciation of being afforded the opportunity of serving as a tactical officer at the United States Military Academy for four years from 1932-1936 where he felt deeply his responsibility in contributing to molding the character and development of literally hundreds of "his cadets" during their impressionable and formative years.

Woody has left us now... further depleting the thinning ranks of the distinguished class of 1915. He will be remembered by literally thousands of service men and women whom he touched in his 42 years in uniform in his command assignments and staff associations...a stern but fair commander and let's not forget his ever sparkling sense of humor and imperturbability to adverse conditions when the going was rough. He was ever proud to be a commander and above all, an infantryman!"

My third and final 2020 Veterans Day tribute is for another great, unsung hero of WWII, Major General Charles D. W. Canham, West Point class of 1926.

I first met Chuck "Skull" Canham in the summer of 1961. I was a rising junior in high school, attending Fayetteville Senior High School

28. Thoughts on Veterans Day, 2020

in Fayetteville, NC. My dad had just retired from active duty as the deputy G3 of the XVIII Airborne Corps at Fort Bragg. My brand-new girlfriend was a fetching young lass named Sally Canham. Her father was also a colonel of Infantry stationed at Fort Bragg. They lived in the then brand-new section of town know as Cottonade Estates. Anyone of you who has ever been stationed at Fort Bragg knows the Cottonade development well. I remember it when it consisted of three old homes on a farm surrounded by dense woods. In 1959, I used to go deer hunting in the area with a high-powered rifle. But I digress.

Sally's grandfather lived right across the street from her, and for reasons obscure to me then and now, he took a real liking to me. Possibly it was because he knew I aspired to attend West Point. I spent many a pleasant and fascinating afternoon after school in his man cave, surrounded by some of the most incredible WWII military artifacts imaginable, listening to his riveting stories.

Chuck Canham became famous for his exploits on Omaha Beach on D-Day. Commanding the 116th Infantry Regiment, the lead assault regiment of the 29th Infantry Division on the right flank of Omaha Beach, he heroically exhorted his men to get off the beach and on the high ground, despite being badly wounded by a German machine-gun. He is famous for this quote that day: "We're getting slaughtered down here; let's go up there [pointing to the heights] and get slaughtered."

Later in the Normandy campaign he was promoted to brigadier general and became assistant division commander of the 8th Infantry Division. It was Chuck Canham, along with a squad of riflemen, who accepted the surrender of the German commander in Brest. When the German demanded to see Canham's credentials, he pointed at his Soldiers and said, "These are my credentials." That quote quickly reverberated around the world.

Here is Major General Canham's obituary that appeared in the Summer 1964 issue of *Assembly* magazine:

> Charles D. W. Canham was truly "born" on 23 May 1919 when he first entered the Army, for he was born to be a Soldier. No single event before that date had been of greater moment for him. There had already been instilled in him, though, a love for the country where an individual might rise to the heights and the initiative and drive necessary to reach those heights.

From his enlisted service he acquired a love and a respect for the rank-and-file Soldier which was to stand him and the country in good stead during World War II. From these early days, too, he learned the meaning of an age-old leadership maxim, "Take care of your men, and they will take care of you." He interpreted this to mean that a Soldier-leader never rests until he has done everything within his power to ensure the survival of his men in battle. To him it also meant the application of timely pressures to produce the hardened, well-disciplined Soldier. This early-acquired empathy with the common Soldier accounts in large measure for the fierce, lifelong loyalty he held for the men of every unit he ever served with. He understood well that this was the only way a leader could expect the loyalty of his troops. It was no accident, then, that the units he commanded showed a consistently high state of morale.

From USMA came the foundation for those early lessons which were to come from commands of infantry platoons and companies. From these early commands also came a reluctance to bend or compromise his own personal standards.

During the years before WWII he sought and acquired a reputation as a strict disciplinarian and troop leader. It was this reputation that won for him that which he desired more than anything else—a World War II tactical command.

The 116th Infantry Regiment, 29th Infantry Division was training in England when he took command of it. Under his direction this regiment spent every training day as if it were going into battle the next. As a result, this superbly trained outfit, although untested in battle, was chosen to go ashore on Omaha Beach as the sister assault unit of the much-bloodied 16th Infantry Regiment, 1st Infantry Division.

When the colonel landed with the third assault wave, his beloved regiment was being decimated by a well-dug-in, heavily-armed, determined enemy. A correspondent for the *New York Times*, seeing him at this time wrote of him: "Although he was wounded, he walked upright, up and down the beach, brandishing his .45 like a 105 howitzer."

From there he pushed his regiment inland, and out of this action came his Distinguished Service Cross, the first of his many awards for personal valor.

28. Thoughts on Veterans Day, 2020

It was this same action which was to generate the volume of letters that was to become General Canham's most prized possession. These letters, written by the men of the 116th who survived the war, all expressed, in a variety of ways, the sentiment of the one who wrote simply and bluntly, "When you were training us so hard in England, when other units appeared to be sitting on their butts, I used to think you were an SOB, but I know now that I owe my life to your efforts."

After the Battle of St. Lo came a promotion and, as assistant division commander of the 8th Division, he was now Brigadier General Canham. It was in this capacity that he took, in the name of his 8th Division troopers, the surrender of Brest. When he entered General Ramcke's bunker, accompanied by a squad of infantrymen, this commander of the German 2d Parachute Division asked, "If I am to surrender to you, where are your credentials?" Without hesitation General Canham pointed to his men nervously fingering their M-l's and said, "These are my credentials." The account of this event which appeared in the *New York Times* saw in this spontaneous statement of a combat leader the greatest tribute ever paid to the real power of the American Army." **Freed Lowrey note**: *ever since then, in honor of that incident, the motto of the 8th Infantry Division has been "These are my credentials."*

The stories of the general's exploits while fighting with the 8th Division are legion. It is enough to say of him that he followed closely his two guiding principles: an army must be capable of fighting at all times, and its soldiers and leaders must be prepared to die. He devoted his every effort to the former. Of the latter he was prone to say, "Let the devil take the hindmost."

General Canham felt that it was every officer's duty to leave his unit better than he found it. During his several postwar assignments—the 82nd Airborne Division, the 3rd Infantry Division, Bremerhaven Port, Director of Posts, Europe, and the XI Corps—he clearly demonstrated the application of this self-imposed mandate.

He appreciated the fact that the lasting way to accomplish his goals was through the training of Soldiers and junior leaders, not by stressing menial, housekeeping details. The natural outgrowth of this attitude was the establishment of a leadership academy in the 82nd Airborne. Begun in 1946, this special training facility, known as "Canham's College," became the prototype of the many that were to follow and set the standard for thousands of non-coms and junior officers.

The emphysema which he contracted several years before his retirement, and the coughing spells that accompanied it, caused him to withdraw from the people and the social functions he always enjoyed so much. It was this same malady which eventually succeeded where enemy shellfire and the rigors of Hurtgen Forest had failed, and his gallant heart succumbed to it on 21 August 1963.

> "The tumult and the shouting dies;
> The captains and the kings depart:
> Still stands thine ancient sacrifice,
> An humble and a contrite heart.
> Lord God of Hosts, be with us yet,
> Lest we forget—lest we forget."
> —Rudyard Kipling

I'm happy to report that Chuck Canham lived long enough to see me enter West Point. Shortly before his death he sent me a marvelous, heart-felt letter of congratulations, which also urged me to never stop caring for my Soldiers. Mission accomplished, sir.

Here is a photo of Major General Charles D. W. Canham and an artist's rendering of him accepting the German forces at Brest, along with his "credentials."

29. Thoughts on Memorial Day, 2021
Honoring a Fine Regiment and Its Soldiers
Posted on Facebook 31 May 2021

As has become my habit the past several years, I have some thoughts I want to share on Memorial Day in honor of our fallen heroes of all ranks and in all services who secured and protected our liberty over the past 245 years. I did not write this year's entry and can take no credit for it other than bringing it to the attention of others, but the ideas it espouses resonate very strongly with me, and I feel it is certainly appropriate for the day.

My post on this Memorial Day was written by my older brother, Mark Perrin Lowrey, West Point class of 1960. Like me and our father and every generation of Lowreys dating to the Revolutionary War, Mark was an infantryman. He served two tours in Vietnam. In the spring of 1967, with the war in Vietnam in full tilt, he was assigned to his first combat tour, initially as a rifle company commander of Company D, 1st Battalion, 2nd Infantry ("Dracula," the "Black Scarves"), 1st Infantry Division (the "Big Red One"), and then as the Battalion operations officer. During this tour of duty, he fought and excelled in some of the most vicious battles that had occurred in the war to date, including the Battle of the Ong Thanh Stream, which decimated a sister battalion and was made famous by David Maraniss's Pulitzer Prize–winning book, *They Marched into Sunlight*. Mark's first combat tour was cut short when he was seriously wounded in the hip on 19 March 1968 and was medevaced home. During that first tour he was awarded the Silver Star for exceptional heroism in combat, three Bronze Star Medals (one for valor), three Purple Hearts for wounds received in combat, six Air Medals (one for valor), two Commendation Medals (one for valor), and the Combat Infantry Badge.

Mark returned to Vietnam in early 1969 and was initially assigned as assistant division operations officer, working in the Division Tactical Operations Center (TOC) at the forward command post at Lai Khe. After several months on the Division Operations staff, Mark became the battalion operations officer for the 1st Battalion, 18th Infantry, and again more than proved his worth as a warrior. He returned from his second Vietnam tour in early 1970 with four more Bronze Star Medals (one for valor) and another Air Medal for valor.

Mark was especially proud of his service in command of American Soldiers in the 2nd Infantry. He proudly wore his combat-worn black scarf at all formal occasions; it now has a place of honor in my home (we lost Mark on 30 August 2017 at the age of 80). On one very special occasion in the 1990s, Mark was asked to give a speech honoring the fallen of the 2nd Infantry Regiment in Vietnam. The occasion was the dedication of a memorial honoring the Soldiers of the 2nd Infantry killed in Vietnam. That speech is my offering on this Memorial Day. I could not express my love for Soldiers better than Mark. Here are his words:

We are assembled here today to honor the fallen of this fine old regiment. We will dedicate this simple stone memorial to the memory of our colleagues, and I am greatly honored to be able to participate in this ceremony. I hope that you will understand if I avoid the use of words like glory and fame. I will leave them to those who have never had to add up the ledger of misery and death. The names of 554 Soldiers of the 2nd Infantry are inscribed on the Big Red One Monument beside the White House and Vietnam Memorial on the Mall. Let us do these men, and all others who fell throughout our regiment's history, the simple honor of honesty. War itself is the ultimate atrocity—a frightening abomination—whose objective is to impose our government's will by the killing of our fellow man. Those whom we come to honor fought with courage, fortitude, and the hope of better days. What they did cannot and will not be forgotten by their families and by those of us who marched, stood, and fought alongside them. But their memory is forsaken by the rest of their countrymen and most of all by the very government that sent them to achieve whatever was the "Great National Objective" of the moment. Politicians on the stump like to say that war is cruel. But no one knows how deeply, monstrously cruel it is unless he himself has walked through the fire and been seared by its heat. The men we honor today and all of you have done that. Many who fell died horribly, and more than a few died needlessly.

29. Thoughts on Memorial Day, 2021

When I stand mutely before the black granite wall of the Vietnam Memorial and trace with my fingers the names of those who fell under my own command, I am sickened by the towering unfairness that my own name is not there in their stead.

A.E. Houseman, an English writer of the early twentieth century summed up this matter as well as I have ever seen when he wrote:

"Here dead we lie because we did not choose to
live and shame the land from which we sprung.
Life, to be sure, is nothing much to lose;
but young men think it is, and we were young."

All of the men who fell under the 2nd Infantry's banner in all our nation's wars were young. A country's treasure is in its youth, and their loss is terrible beyond measure because it is irreparable. More often than not, it is the good man who dies—the large act—the spendthrift heart: the medic who goes out to bring in the wounded man, the rifleman who covers his patrol's withdrawal, the Soldier who throws himself on a grenade to shield his comrades, the NCO who deliberately exposes himself to deadly fire in order to move his unit forward.

To a man our regiment's dead were singularly trusting. They followed their leaders willingly—asking no collateral for the probable surrender of their lives. They demanded no special privileges, no distinctions, no enhanced power or influence as they walked steadily into that fatal valley. Their fate was in our hands and—in part—in the skill of their enemies. Their destiny was to be robbed of their youth. They would never sit and dream as old men on a sunlit riverbank while all around them their grandchildren played without fear.

Our task is to ensure that their sacrifice is not forgotten, that their lives had meaning, that their deeds will be remembered, that their achievements will be honored.

This single, simple stone is not enough. We must ensure that the young men who follow today in their footsteps know the value of their inheritance. We must tell the story of the 2nd Infantry to the men in Kosovo, Germany, and at Fort Reilly; to their families and friends and descendants. The great tradition, the priceless legacy, the matchless heritage of the 2nd Infantry from 1808 until far beyond our own time must be burnished and spread. This is our task. The men who lie buried here all around us will expect no less.

"Give me your hand, my brother and search my face;
Look in these eyes lest I should think of shame;
For we have made an end of all things base.
We are returning by the road we came.
Your lot is with ghosts of soldiers dead,
And I am in the field where men must fight.
But in the gloom I see your laurelled head
And through your victory I shall win the light."
—Siegfried Sassoon, 1918

30. My Retirement from Active Duty Speech

Author's Note: I retired from active duty as an Army officer on 31 July 1990. At the time, I was stationed at the Armed Forces Staff College as a seminar chairman and course director. This is the speech I gave on that occasion. It was published in the September 1990 issue of Assembly *magazine.*

Twenty-nine years ago, almost to the day, I stood on the parade ground at Fort Bragg and watched the finest man and most professional Soldier I've ever known retire from the Army. Of course, as a young boy, I really didn't understand or appreciate the significance or solemnity of the occasion. Having been born and raised in the Army, I'd seen countless parades, and this wasn't the first time I'd seen a medal pinned on my father's tunic. In retrospect, I realize I was a bit bored with the whole affair, just as I'm sure my three young sons here today are bored with these proceedings. It was, after all, a pretty summer day, and I had better things to do. Armed now with the advantages of age and the experience that comes with twenty-seven years in uniform, I have a new and much more poignant sense of appreciation for the emotion that my father must have felt on that day. It is a curious mixture of pride and pain, satisfaction and anxiety.

I fell in love with soldiering and the Army as a very young boy, and fortunately my dad did nothing to dampen my enthusiasm. Watching him jump out of airplanes, going to the field with him—surely against every regulation in the book—and watching his Soldiers do soldier things filled me with a spirit of adventure and awe that has never waned. Going to West Point was the fulfillment of my most cherished childhood dream; graduating was the beginning of the greatest continuous adventure of my life. The day my father administered the commissioning oath to me, I swore that I would stay in the Army as long as I was in love with the idea of being a Soldier. Well, experience has taught me that the day I stop feeling that way will *never* come. Nevertheless, the time has come to hoist the rucksack on these shoulders and cross the Line of Departure for the last time. There is a family to think about, and since I'm probably not in the running to be the next chief of staff, I'd better start looking for a new adventure to pay the bills.

It's altogether fitting and appropriate that my last assignment be here at the Armed Forces Staff College, where the commitment to teaching and learning is so strong. It's appropriate because the whole of the past twenty-seven years has been spent in a teaching and learning environment. While it doesn't advertise itself as such, the Army is the greatest school on Earth, and it provides as rich and varied a curriculum as you can find anywhere. The teachers are the very best, for they are the people, big and small, important and not so important, that ARE the Army. The curriculum is about life and what really counts. I can't think of too many days in the last twenty-seven years that I haven't learned something worth storing in my duffel bag of knowledge. Some of the lessons, and the teachers from whom I learned them, remain indelibly imprinted in my mind. The learning started the day I reported to West Point, and a guy named Ferguson, my first squad leader, taught me that it is possible to take a scared, young kid and motivate, mold, guide, and lead him where you want him to go, without being abusive or degrading or vulgar. He taught me more than I had ever known about the dignity in all of us and how important it is to respect that. He was the first of many to teach me the real meaning of Leadership.

Over the next four years, we were taught a great deal about the credo of West Point: "Duty, Honor, Country," but it wasn't until after I graduated that I really learned what those words meant. A young nineteen-year-old kid named Jackson taught me more about Duty than you'll ever find in a library full of textbooks. He had the unenviable job of being my radio operator for six months in Vietnam, and he saved my life more than once. Three weeks before he was to go home, we were trudging up yet one more nameless, jungle-covered mountain, looking for the ever faceless enemy. When the shooting started, I turned for my radio, which was always right there waiting for me, but this time it wasn't there. Jackson was on the ground, two bullets through his chest. His last words were, "I'm sorry, sir." It was the only time he had ever called me Sir, having always preferred the less formal and more popular "L.T.," and I've always wondered, why then. But in my heart, I know. Jackson was teaching me a lesson about Duty, and I've never forgotten it.

30. My Retirement from Active Duty Speech

A lot of people have taught me a lot of things about Honor, but probably none so eloquently as a grizzled, old, company first sergeant I had when I was commanding in Germany. His name was Bizzelli, and he used to get furious at the all too pervasive practice of inflating unit readiness reports. "Damn it, Captain," he would say, "it ain't right. You tell somebody a unit is ready for combat when it's not, and someday those Soldiers are going to get sent to a fight they're not ready for, and most of them won't come home." And, of course, he was right. He taught me about a lot more than just Honor; he taught me the most precious resource we have is our Soldiers, and we owe them the full measure of our devotion.

Everyone I've ever served with has taught me the meaning of Country. All those weeks and months and years away from home, sharing mud-filled and freezing foxholes and bunkers in godforsaken places with other people just as miserable and scared and lonely as I was, guys like Lt. Clark and Sgt. Niten and Pfc. Sutten, and countless others; all the rest of you who, like me, frequently answered the phone at 2 a.m. to rush to the barracks to get on an airplane to go someplace you didn't know a damn thing about for a reason too obscure to remember. All of you who have spent long, lonely days filthy beyond belief, eating your meals out of an OD can in the pouring rain; who have crammed your family into the car to move from one set of cramped quarters across the country to a smaller set of quarters, and through it all, you've laughed, and walked with your heads held high, full of pride and a sense of worth. You didn't do it for the pay, or the prestige. You did it, we did it, all of us, you and me and Mom and the kids, because of the chill that runs up our spine when we see the Stars and Stripes flying high over a parapet, or draped around the shoulders of a jubilant hockey player at Lake Placid, or covering the coffin of a Soldier sent home to his family for the last time. We do it for Country and for that great feeling you get in the pit of your stomach, having realized what you are a part of. It's called Service, and it's linked inexorably with Duty and Honor. Service IS an honor. Honorable service, on the other hand, is a Duty. So many of our unit mottoes try to capture the spirit of that idea. The 1st Infantry Division's may be the most eloquent: "No Mission Too Difficult, No Sacrifice Too Great, Duty First." But my favorite motto is that of the 23rd Infantry Regiment, one of the units I was honored to serve in, which says, quite simply, "We Serve." I know of no prouder boast.

I said the Army's a great school; it's also a wonderful, loving family. Never was that point more vividly illustrated than during two terrifying weeks in Alaska a few years ago, when our youngest son lay near death in the hospital. My wife and I were inundated with love and support and caring shoulders to cry on. I was *ordered* not to go to work; we were overwhelmed with food and people to clean the house and watch the kids and do all the other mundane chores of day-to-day survival, so that all we had to concentrate on was prayer and our vigil. And when Colin came home from the hospital a healthy little boy, our friends' joy and celebration in his life was as genuine and heartfelt as was ours.

I have loved wearing this uniform and being a part of what it stands for, and I shall hate to take it off and hang it up for the last time. It will be like putting part of my soul on ice. God knows, I will even be a little bit envious of those of you who still get called at two in the morning to go to places you've never been before—even if it's only to your own motor pool to get ready for the damn IG inspection. It has been the greatest thrill of my life to have walked among you and to have been able to say I was one of you. While there is certainly pride in the fact that I have shared in the profession and experiences of men like Patton and Grant and the other great captains, the real boast lies in being able to say I was a Soldier with the likes of Jackson and Bizzelli and Niten and so many others I shared a poncho and a bunker with. It's nice knowing that when my time comes to report to that orderly room in the sky to sign in, when The Man asks me what I did to deserve my place in line, I'll be able to look him square in the eye and, with a smile on my lips, say **I am an American Soldier**.

31. Glossary

I've used quite a few military and cadet slang terms in many of these essays. Since the meaning of most of these terms is probably not familiar to the non-military, non-West-Point-acquainted reader, here are my attempts to translate them into the Queen's English. They are listed in alphabetical order.

AIT: Advanced Individual Training, the training course new recruits go through after completing basic training. It is during AIT that new Soldiers learn how to do the jobs/tasks associated with their Military Occupational Specialty (MOS).

APC: Armored Personnel Carrier. Lightly armored vehicle designed to carry Soldiers and weapons into combat. Assigned primarily to Mechanized Infantry and Armored Cavalry units. During the 1960s through the 1980s the principal APC in the US Army was the M113. It could carry a squad of infantry, or if reconfigured it could carry an 81mm mortar or a 4.2 inch mortar and crew. There were quite a few variants.

Area, or the Area: At West Point cadet barracks are arranged around large courtyards; these are referred to as Areas. In the 1960s each area was named based on the barracks that surrounded it. Thus, there was New South Area, South Area, Central Area, and North Area.

Art: Cadet slang for the senior year academic course History of the Military Art. During this year-long course, we studied the history of warfare of the ancient Greeks and Romans, the campaigns of Napoleon Bonaparte, the American Revolution, the Civil and Spanish – American Wars, World Wars I and II, and the Korean war.

BOQ: Batchelor Officers Quarters. Military quarters assigned to batchelor officers who wished to live on post rather than in civilian housing off post.

B-robe: A cadet bathrobe. Upperclassmen had different B-robes than the thin, cotton robes issued to plebes. The upperclassman B-robes were heavy, gray wool with black and gold stripes on the arms and around the bottom; they were made of the same material as the gray blankets issued cadets. Upperclassman B-robes were one of a cadet's most prized possessions, as they represented a rite of passage from being a plebe to being a human. In one of the few departures from strict uniformity, cadets were allowed to decorate/adorn their B-robes almost any way they wished. B-robes were also used as currency. During the Army-Navy football game each year, cadets would bet a B-robe on the outcome of the game against a midshipman's B-robe. In the Air Force game, the bets were a cadet B-robe against a Zoomie parka, and in the Army-RMC (Royal Military College of Canada) hockey game, the bet would be a B-robe for an RMC cadet lamb's wool dress hat. I still have my cadet B-robe, along with a Navy B-robe and an RMC hat.

BP: Barracks Police. At West Point, the BP were the janitors and maintenance men who maintained the cadet barracks. They also removed snow from the cadet areas.

Brown Boy: The 1960s name for the thick, light-brown comforter issued to all cadets. The brown boy may have been a cadet's most prized possession. During times of stress, the approved solution was to spend as much time as possible in "brown boy defilade," curled up on your bunk swaddled in your brown boy.

Butt (as in two-and-a-butt years): West Point cadet slang for a fraction of time – years, months, weeks, days, hours, minutes. For example, two-and-a-butt days meant somewhere between two and three days.

Classmate (used as a verb): Everyone recognizes the definition of classmate as someone in the same academic year as you in school. However, at West Point, classmate is also used as a verb. It means to do something negative to a member of your class: report him for some rule violation, volunteer him for some odious chore, give a miserable assignment to him—in other words, to shaft your classmates. Thus the term, "I got classmated."

Corps Squad; Corps Squad Athletes: The West Point term for varsity intercollegiate sports as opposed to club sports or company intramurals. A cadet on a varsity sports team is called a corps squad athlete. His team represents the entire Corps of Cadets in intercollegiate competition.

Cow: A member of the junior class at West Point. Why are juniors called cows? you ask. The tradition dates to the period before WWII when cadets were not given leave away from West Point until after the end of their second year. On the night prior to reporting back to the Academy from leave, many cadets would gather in New York City for one last celebratory dinner. The next day they would report en-masse back to school. This event became known as "the cows returning to pasture." Thus, juniors became known as cows.

Division of Barracks: In the older barracks at West Point in the 1960s—Central Barracks built in the 1850s, North Barracks in the 1880s, South Barracks and New North Barracks in the 1930s and early 1940s—the buildings were built with vertical stairwells. There were four cadet rooms on each floor. These stairwells were called Divisions of Barracks and were numbered. The 1st through 18th Divisions were in Central Barracks, 19th through 30th in North Barracks, 31st through 39th in South Barracks, and 40th through 55th (the 50th through 55th are called the Lost Fifties) in New North Barracks. In the mid-1960s, Central and North Barracks were torn down to make space for new barracks—Eisenhower, Bradley and MacArthur Barracks, built in the hotel or apartment style, with long horizontal floors rather than stairwells of cadet rooms.

Dress Coat: One of the most time-honored and iconic cadet uniform items for semiformal wear. It consists of a heavy wool, gray, form-fitting waistcoat with a black choker collar and a black vertical stripe running down the front that covers the zipper. Thin black stripes on the lower sleeves indicate a cadet's class year (1st, 2nd, 3rd, or 4th class), and black chevrons on the sleeves indicate cadet rank. In the 1960s, the Dress Coat was worn far more often than it is now. It was mandatory for supper and any activities (lectures, movies, athletic events, etc.) after retreat (when the flag is lowered in the afternoon) and on weekends, and for any travel away from West Point. In the fall and winter it is worn over gray, wool trousers. The uniform is called Dress Gray. In the spring it is worn over white, cotton trousers starched so heavily they require opening the legs with a bayonet prior to putting them on. This uniform is officially called Dress Gray over White, but in cadet parlance it is known as 50-50.

Ejection Seat: In the 1960s a cadet who ranked last in his class in any academic course was said to occupy the "Ejection Seat," implying that dismissal from the Academy for failing the course was a distinct possibility.

ES & GS: Earth, Space, and Graphic Sciences. An academic department at West Point in the 1960s. It still exists, but its name is now the Department of Geography and Environmental Engineering. In my day it taught a number of plebe (freshman) courses from Draftsmanship to Vector Calculus, Geography, Introduction to the Computer and writing code (in 1963!), and several other obscure engineering courses. It was referred to as "Squint and Print." It is one of the oldest academic departments at West Point, which was established as the nation's first engineering school in 1802. Being able to draw—both to make maps and record discoveries—was a critical part of an Army officer's job. When I was a plebe in 1963–64, these classes were always after lunch and on the fifth floor of Washington Hall, which was not air conditioned. Hot air rises, and in the early fall and spring, the sound of snoring frequently drowned out the sound of the professor.

Firstie: A cadet in the senior class. At West Point, cadet classes are referred to as 4th class (plebes, or freshmen), 3rd class (yearlings, or sophomores), 2nd class (cows, or juniors) and 1st class (firsties, or seniors).

Fluids: Mechanics of Fluids. An academic course, part of the required core curriculum in the 1960s, this was a one-semester course taken during cow (junior) year.

FTX: A military field training exercise; war games.

Full Dress Coat/Uniform (FD): The most iconic of all West Point cadet uniforms, this is the uniform worn for all formal occasions. The Full Dress Coat, known to cadets as an FD Coat, is a form-fitting, gray, wool waistcoat with tails and a choke collar, with three vertical rows of oval brass buttons on the front of the coat, a brass button on each side of the collar, and three brass buttons aligned vertically on the bottom of each sleeve. Diagonal gold stripes on the bottom of each sleeve indicate cadet class, and gold and black chevrons on the sleeves indicate rank. Worn over either gray wool or white cotton trousers, depending on the season.

Galloping Greek: The cadet nickname for Captain Bill Giallourakis, West Point class of 1958, an instructor of Electrical Engineering (Juice) when I was a cadet. Famous for his classroom antics and frenetic activity.

Gama Goat: A six-wheeled articulated off-road vehicle designed for the US Army during the Vietnam War to replace the Jeep and light trucks. Official designation was the M561. Soldiers had lots of names for it, none of them complementary. It was, to put it nicely, a piece of crap.

Goat: A stinky and exceptionally stubborn animal of foul disposition; the mascot of the United States Naval Academy (aka Canoe U.). In West Point cadet parlance, a cadet who graduates at the bottom of a class academically is called the Class Goat; the class academic dunce (frequently destined to become a Great Military Leader). Cadets who rank academically in the bottom quarter of a class are collectively referred to as "goats."

G1, G2, G3, G4, G5, etc.: Military staff positions. Staff jobs are identified by a combination of a letter and a number. The former indicates the level of command: S for Battalion and Brigade, G for Division

through Department of the Army level, and J for Joint Commands—commands made up of multiple services. The number describes the function of the office. The offices referred to in this book are:
G1—Personnel and Administration
G2—Intelligence
G3—Operations, Planning, and Training (the G3 Air is responsible for planning airlift support)
G4—Logistics

Hellcats: The West Point Band's field music group is comprised of bugles, piccolos, and drums and serves as a showpiece for the United States Army and the United States Military Academy. The Corps of Cadets gave the Hellcats their name as a friendly jibe in response to the group's early morning playing of the wake-up call reveille every day at West Point. As the Army's first and only remaining field music group, the Hellcats trace their heritage back to the American Revolution, when General George Washington established the garrison of West Point and appointed a fifer and drummer for signaling in camp.

IG: The Inspector General

Juice: The cadet term for the year-long academic course in Electrical Engineering. This was part of the required core curriculum in the 1960s and was taken during cow (junior) year.

LRP Rations: Pronounced "lerp," this is the military acronym that stands for "Long Range Patrol Rations." These were dehydrated meals that in the late 1960s replaced the decades-old C rations as field rations for Soldiers. They came in vinyl bags and had to be reconstituted with boiling water. While they had advantages over the old C rations—they were much lighter and easier to carry—there were also drawbacks, not the least of which was the need for plenty of water and a means to heat it. There were eight different menus: beef hash; beef and rice; beef stew; chicken and rice; chicken stew; chili con carne; spaghetti with meat sauce; and pork and scalloped potatoes, usually referred to as "pork and shrapnel." The chicken and rice wasn't bad; the rest had a tendency to sit in your stomach like depleted uranium.

31. Glossary

MILPERCEN: Military Personnel Center. The Army command that is in control of the assignments and destiny of all Soldiers. Headquartered in Alexandria, Virginia.

Nuke: Nuclear Engineering. An academic course, part of the required core curriculum in the 1960s, this was a one-semester course taken during cow (junior) year.

O1, O2, O3 etc.: The pay grades for U.S. military officer ranks. In the Army an O1 is a second lieutenant; an O2 a first lieutenant; an O3 a captain; all the way to O10, a four-star general. While it is common for military folks to refer to Soldiers by their pay grades rather than their ranks, it's really very poor form and lousy etiquette and shouldn't be done.

P: Cadet slang for an instructor, short for professor. The individual teaching a class is referred to as the "P." If one is assigned to West Point as an academic instructor, he/she will say "I'm a P" (or a Juice/Nuke/Math P, for example).

PCS: Permanent Change of Station. Military talk for a permanent move. Read essay # 2, March 1993.

Plebe: A freshman at West Point and the Naval Academy. Almost the lowest form of life. When I was a cadet (1963 – 1967), all plebes were required to memorize this response when asked, "Who do plebes rank?": "Sir, the superintendent's dog, the commandant's cat, the waiters in the mess hall, the Hellcats, the generals in the Air Force, and all the admirals in the whole damned Navy."

Poop: In military usage, poop is information, usually vital information, the basis of critically important decisions.

Punishment tours, also called Walking the Area: A form of punishment for cadets who have violated regulations. Walking the area consists of walking back and forth for hours on end with a rifle on your shoulder. These walkabouts take place during the little free time cadets have and are conducted in one of the cadet areas of barracks.

Punji stick: A sharpened stick, usually made of bamboo, partially buried in the ground in high grass and protruding upward at an angle, designed to cause severe wounds to the feet and lower legs. These were common booby traps employed by the Viet Cong (VC) during the Vietnam War.

PX: Post Exchange. The military equivalent of a department store, similar to a Target or a Walmart, located on military installations.

Sally Port: A gate or passage in a fortified place for use by troops making a sortie. Most of the cadet barracks at West Point have at least one sally port bisecting the building, through which cadet formations march when on parade.

Section: At West Point, a small classroom of cadets. One of the hallmarks of a West Point education is small classrooms; the student-to-instructor ratio is very low. Even today, no individual class can have more than seventeen cadets in it without the approval of the dean of the Academic Board. The system of education at West Point is referred to as the Thayer System, and dates to the period 1817 – 1833, when Colonel Sylvanus Thayer was superintendent of the Military Academy. Among the many academic policies and traditions he introduced was a standard four-year curriculum, small classrooms (called sections), and the fact that every cadet was graded in every subject every day. Most of those policies are still in effect, although daily recitations and grades in every subject had started to disappear when I was a cadet, except in plebe and yearling math courses. Up until the late 1970s, cadets were grouped in sections based on their grade point average in that subject. If a course had 600 cadets taking it at one time, the top fifteen or so cadets would be in the 1st section, the next fifteen or so in the 2nd section, on down the line to the cadets at the bottom of the class academically, who were in the last numbered section in that course. To make it even more interesting, everyone changed sections and instructors (Ps) every month. If I had a good month and managed to pull my grade up a few tenths, then I might get to move up a section next month. Of course, that worked both ways; I could also drop a section or two in the next monthly re-sectioning.

The fun didn't stop there. Every cadet within a section room was actually assigned a seat based on his grade point average. The cadet with the highest GPA (in that course) in the section was called the section marcher (a throwback to the days up until the 1950s when cadets marched to class every day). His job was to take the roll and, when the "P" entered the section room, render his report: "Sir, Section 15 is all present or accounted for," or "Sir, cadet Dumbjohn is absent." If there was an absent cadet, it was the section marcher's job to find out why, and if there was not a legitimate reason, to report the miscreant to his chain of command.

This brings us to the earlier discussed concept of the ejection seat. The cadet who occupied the last seat in the last section of an academic course was the cadet in the ejection seat in that course. During my cow year my roommate and I would alternate, almost monthly, being in the ejection seat in Juice. We also tutored each other. And we both graduated.

Sinks: The basements of cadet barracks. In the older barracks this is where the communal toilets and showers were located, along with gym lockers and company trunk rooms, where cadets stored what little civilian clothing and gear they had since that was not allowed in their barracks room.

Slug: A serious punishment for cadets, involving a combination of demerits, punishment tours (hours "walking the area") and even confinement to the barracks during non-duty hours. A slug for a minor infraction could be as small as a 5 and 2—five demerits and two hours of walking. On the other end of the scale, a serious infraction of the rules would result in a disciplinary board by a group of officers, and the punishment would start at 22 - 44 - 2 (twenty-two demerits, forty-four hours of walking and two months' confinement to the area of barracks). The worst slug meted out while I was a cadet was for a fellow in the class of 1965 who got drunk while on summer training in Germany and pretty much destroyed a *Gasthaus*. He received a 50 - 100 - 6, and a five-minute standing ovation from the Corps of Cadets when his "award" was announced during the dinner meal. He also went on to have a stellar Army career, retiring as a major general. He was a damn fine Soldier.

Solids: Mechanics of Solids. An academic course, part of the required core curriculum in the 1960s, this was a one-semester course taken during cow (junior) year. It was the companion course to Fluids.

South Aud: South Auditorium, a large auditorium in the south end of Thayer Hall, one of the primary academic buildings at West Point. In the 1960s it was the largest auditorium at West Point, with a seating capacity of about 2,800. It was the location for most major lectures and important indoor events. It has since been renamed Roscoe Robinson Auditorium in honor of General Roscoe Robinson, class of 1947, and the first African-American four-star general in the United States Army.

Speck; speckoid: Learning by rote memorization. Cadets frequently speck a subject before a test. The Galloping Greek hated cadets to learn by speck; his worst insult, frequently hurled at me was, "Mr. Lowrey, you're a speckoid!"

TDY: Temporary Duty Travel, also known as temporary additional duty (TAD), is a designation reflecting an United States Armed Forces Service member's travel or other assignment at a location other than the traveler's permanent duty station.

Tenths: This one is complicated. Until the late 1970s, the Thayer System of education referred to earlier used a different grading scale than other schools in the United States. Instead of the standard 4.0 system, with accompanying letter grades of A, B, C, D, and F, the grading system was based on a 3.0 scale, with no letter grades. If a cadet had a grade point average of 3.0, it was the maximum; it was very good, like having an A-plus average. The minimum passing grade was 2.0. Having a 2.0 GPA was called being "tangent"; it was like having a C-minus GPA. So, if a cadet's grade point average in a course was anywhere between 2.0 and 3.0, he was proficient, or "pro" in cadet terms, in that course. If his grade point average was below 2.0, he was deficient in that course, or "D." The question was, just how "pro" or "D" could one be? That was where tenths came into play.

Let's say a cadet had a grade point average in a course of 2.5 and had been graded ten times during the semester. Calling the tenths portion

(.5) five, multiply by ten, and he had 50 tenths to the good, or a cadet would say, he was "50 tenths pro" in that course. If his grade point average was 1.8, that was 2 tenths below the 2.0 average required for proficiency, so he was "D" in that course. To find out how badly "D," multiply those 2 tenths by the number of times he had been graded—let's say ten again—and he is 20 tenths "D" in a course.

Thermo: Thermodynamics. An academic course, part of the required core curriculum in the 1960s, this was a one-semester course taken during cow (junior) year. Usually referred to as thermo-goddamnics.

Trou: Cadet slang for trousers. Gentlemen wear trousers. Only women and midshipmen wear pants.

USARV: U.S. Army Vietnam, the major command in Vietnam responsible for all the U.S. conventional Army units fighting in the war. Commanded by a four-star general, it was subordinate to MACV, Military Assistance Command Vietnam.

Wherry housing (also known as Capehart housing): Low-cost family housing build on military posts from 1949-1962 primarily for married junior officers and senior non-commissioned officers. Let's just say they were adequate. They certainly weren't plush.

Writs: Cadet slang for an academic test or exam. Daily writs were worth 3.0. More comprehensive exams that covered whole blocks of instruction—like mid-terms but administered far more frequently—were called **WPRs**, or Written Partial Reviews, and were worth 6.0 (so you had to score at least 4.0 to pass the test, or be "pro"). Term-end exams at the end of the semester were called **WGRs**, or Written General Reviews. They were each worth 9.0, which meant a passing grade was 6.0. However, many courses, especially plebe and yealing Math, gave multiple WGRs at the end of a semester, not just one. It was no damn fun.

Yearling: A sophomore cadet. Remember why juniors are called cows? Well, it only makes sense that sophomores be called yearlings—young calves.

About the Author

Freed Lowrey graduated from West Point in 1967 and was commissioned in the Infantry. He spent the next twenty-three years on active duty, with combat assignments in Vietnam and troop and staff assignments at various posts in the Continental United States, as well as Alaska and Germany, and exchange assignments in Australia and Finland. After retiring from active duty, he spent seven years teaching Junior ROTC in Hampton, Virginia.

Freed hung up his military uniform for good in the summer of 1997 and returned to West Point to work for the West Point Association of Graduates, the Academy's alumni organization, as a major gift fund raiser in the Development Office. He retired from that career on 31 December 2014. He is still trying to figure out what to do with the rest of his life.

Freed has served as the class of 1967 scribe and historian since 1979. In that capacity he authored 207 sets of "Class Notes," reports on the activities of the class of 1967 for publication in the Association of Graduates magazine *Assembly*, until the magazine ceased publication in 2011. In 2019 he published all those articles, along with the accompanying photographs, in a single volume titled *USMA Class of 1967 Assembly Class Notes—The Complete Collection*. He also publishes *The Pooper Scooper*, a quarterly news magazine for the class of 1967. In preparation for the 50th reunion of the class, he put together the official reunion book, 744 pages of classmate biographies, photos, and class history. In 2021 he published a photographic history of the class of 1967 titled *Faces of Service, Faces of Sacrifice, Faces of Valor: A Photographic History of the Service to the Nation by the West Point Class of 1967*.

Freed lives with his wife, Victoria (Vicki), in Fishkill, NY. He has two living sons—Kyle, who lives in Spokane, WA; and Brendan, in Hampton, VA. His third son, Colin, passed away in 2020, ten days shy of his 38th birthday.

He loves fly-fishing, travel, good friends, good books, good food and good drink, and beating Navy in everything.

MAIN ENTRANCE AND BALCONY

**GIFT OF THE CLASS OF 1967
IN MEMORY OF CLASSMATES WHO DIED
IN THE SERVICE OF THEIR COUNTRY**

James Robert Adams
Richard Oliver Bickford
James Kenneth Brierly
Hugh Bernard Brown, III
John Patrick Brown
Gary William Carlson
John Thomas Corley, Jr.
Donald William Dietz
Donald Homer Dwiggins, Jr.
Tom Emerson
Raymond James Enners
Hampton Allen Etheridge, III
Ronald Lloyd Frazer
Roger Allen Fulkerson
Douglas Taylor Gray, III

Ellis David Greene
Frank Allen Hill 3d
John Edward Kelly, Jr.
Terry Lee Ketter
Karl William Mills
Michael Leo Nathe
Norman Louis Nesterak
Daniel Leo Neuburger
Michael Gramling Parr
Jose Manuel Pena
Leonard Lee Preston, Jr.
Gus Blakely Robinson
Warren Michael Sands
Wayne Keith Shaltenbrand
Thomas David Thompson, Jr.

West Point Class of 1967 Memorial Window memorializing classmates killed in action during the Vietnam War, located in Herbert Hall, the Alumni Center at West Point. Photo by Freed Lowrey.